THE REFERENCE SHELF   VOLUME 44 NUMBER 3

AMERICAN YOUTH
IN A
CHANGING CULTURE

EDITED BY
GRANT S. McCLELLAN
Editor, Current Magazine

THE H. W. WILSON COMPANY
NEW YORK   1972

THE REFERENCE SHELF

The books in this series contain reprints of articles, excerpts from books, and addresses on current issues and social trends in the United States and other countries. There are six separately bound numbers in each volume, all of which are generally published in the same calendar year. One number is a collection of recent speeches; each of the others is devoted to a single subject and gives background information and discussion from various points of view, concluding with a comprehensive bibliography. Books in the series may be purchased individually or on subscription.

Library of Congress Cataloging in Publication Data

McClellan, Grant S   comp.
    American youth in a changing culture.

    (The Reference shelf, v. 44, no. 3)
    SUMMARY: A collection of articles concerning the cultural, educational, political, and economic aspects of youth in our changing society.
    Bibliography: p.
    1. Youth--United States--Political activity.
2. Youth--United States. 3. United States--Social conditions--1960-   [1. Youth--United States.
2. United States--Social conditions--1960-   ]
I. Title. II. Series.
HQ799.2.P6M3   301.43'15'0973   72-5196
ISBN 0-8242-0466-2

PREFACE

The "youth revolt" has been debated hotly and seemingly without end over the past half-decade. It is perhaps irrelevant whether the word *revolt* accurately defines the phenomenon sometimes referred to as the generation gap, the rise of a new consciousness, or the youthful opposition. Most observers are aware, however, that what we have witnessed is an extended and diverse social development encompassing hippies, the so-called Woodstock nation, university student protest, and erratic youthful political organizations, as well as communal groups and the later "Jesus followers" and Eastern mystic cultists.

Probably no such diverse social change could have simple roots. And, in fact, it is generally agreed that youth not only reflects but has caused some of the changes of the larger society in which the fast pace of social change is today an outstanding characteristic. This compilation attempts, then, to set the changing youth picture in the larger frame of general social change.

The first section, "The Youth Revolt in Perspective," brings together several articles which take a penetrating look at the subject, indicating how pervasively and deeply our social milieu is involved. Section II, "Youth and Cultural Change," delineates the broader changes that have taken place and how they have involved challenges to our value systems and the outcropping of religious enthusiasm. In the third section, "Youth and Our Changing Education," the student protest movement of college-age youth is dealt with at some length, since this movement has in many ways been central to the whole youth revolt. Changes wrought in university life since the middle sixties, also dealt with in this section, again testify to the centrality of our educational institutions and intellectual life in today's society. Various facets of the political activity youth has undertaken in recent

3

years are covered in Section IV, "What Political Role for Youth?" And in the fifth section, "Youth and the Future Economy," the impact on our practical work-world is reviewed, mainly in terms of those young people opposed to the present economic system and in terms of actual population changes which can now be forecast. Last, in Section VI, "Youth's Future Role," the apparent waning of the youth revolution is surveyed and wider-ranging assessments are given to the cultural changes that appear likely ahead, including those which youth has precipitated.

The editor wishes to thank the authors and the publishers of the selections which follow for permission to reprint them in this compilation.

GRANT S. McCLELLAN

June 1972

CONTENTS

IV. WHAT POLITICAL ROLE FOR YOUTH?

V. YOUTH AND THE FUTURE ECONOMY

I. THE YOUTH REVOLT IN PERSPECTIVE

EDITOR'S INTRODUCTION

Many analysts as well as youth protesters point to the fact that the latter have recently reevaluated and rejected some of our society's deepest beliefs and mores. This rejection, labeled Consciousness III by Charles A. Reich in his much-discussed study *The Greening of America,* is youth's reaction against the traditionally liberal socioeconomic view, which Reich calls Consciousness II (Consciousness II was a reaction against the original American ethic of economic individualism, Consciousness I). Other observers, however, believe that the youth rebellion is a religious phenomenon, in part a religious revival. This aspect is dealt with more fully in Section II.

Needless to say at this point, the general public has been greatly puzzled by the "youth revolt" or rise of the "youthful opposition" in the decade just ending. The first article in this section indicates that our social analysts have likewise been puzzled. In the article from the *Chronicle of Higher Education,* one of its special contributors, Malcolm G. Scully, briefly refers to the various theories of recent years expounded by social analysts for the phenomenon of youthful revolt. He touches on many points which are later more fully developed throughout this compilation.

Some of the popular myths about youth today are surveyed in the next selection, a *Wall Street Journal* article by Landrum Bolling, president of Earlham College, Richmond, Indiana. President Bolling urges that we develop "ways of bringing younger and older people into creative, productive teamwork for the common good."

In the third and last selection in this section a man who has been most concerned and articulate in his analysis of what he prefers to call the "youthful opposition" surveys that opposition in a full-length review. Kenneth Keniston, professor of psychology and director of the Behavioral Sciences Center at Yale University School of Medicine, discusses here the two most widely held theories of the youth revolt: the one which claims the revolt to be a counterrevolutionary force, and the other which believes it is a revolutionary force. Professor Keniston contends that further analysis is needed and outlines some factors regarding our entire culture which he believes must be considered in viewing the youth revolt in perspective.

WHO ARE/WERE THE YOUTH IN REVOLT? [1]

In December 1964, sociologist Nathan Glazer wrote of the Free Speech Movement at the University of California at Berkeley:

> I and many other faculty members are filled with foreboding. We see neither a clear nor a near end to the crisis. And I am afraid it will not be easy for our friends in other places to understand what is going on here; it is hardly possible for those of us closest to it to agree on an interpretation.

Eight years and countless analyses later, the American student movement, which began with those events in the fall of 1964 at Berkeley, still eludes a fully coherent explanation.

By the end of 1971 there had been more than one hundred empirical studies of student activists. Out of that vast research has emerged a relatively consistent picture of their numbers and their background. Beyond that, however, much of the data can be and has been interpreted in a variety of ways.

And the apparently dwindling intensity of the movement after the nationwide protests against the US incursions into Cambodia in the spring of 1970 has posed new questions for the theorists of student revolt.

[1] Article entitled "Who Are/Were Those Kids and Why Do/Did They Do Those Awful/Wonderful Things?" by Malcolm G. Scully, a special contributor to the *Chronicle of Higher Education*. *Chronicle of Higher Education*. 3:8. Mr. 13, '72. Reprinted by permission.

What we do know is that the percentage of students who called themselves "radical" rose during the late 1960s, but has begun to decline again since the Cambodian incursions.

Louis Harris reported that 4 percent of the students surveyed during the spring of 1968 called themselves radical. In later surveys, 8 percent said they were radical in the spring of 1969, 11 percent in the spring of 1970, and 7 percent in the fall of 1970.

We know too from many studies, as cited by Seymour Martin Lipset of Harvard University in *Passion and Politics: Student Activism in America,* that leftist, activist students are the children of leftist or liberal parents.

In addition to those findings, Kenneth Keniston of Yale University has reported that activists differ from other students in having a high level of moral development.

Beyond such generalizations, however, researchers find themselves on less firm ground.

Mr. Keniston illustrated the problems in *Youth and Dissent: The Rise of a New Opposition* in a discussion of the environmental factors, such as religion, on the rise of activism:

> . . . the issue cannot be settled with only the evidence at hand. In all probability, several interacting factors are involved. On the one hand it seems clear that *if* children are brought up in upper-middle-class professional families with humanitarian, expressive, and intellectual values, and *if* the techniques of discipline emphasize independence and reasoning, and *if* the parents are themselves politically liberal and politically active, then the chances of the child's being an activist are greatly increased, regardless of factors like religion. [See articles by Professor Keniston, "Reconsidering the Youthful Opposition" in this section, and "The Agony of the Counter-Culture" in Section VI.—Ed.]

Some of the early truisms about left-wing activists—that they were the best and, psychologically, the most healthy students, and that they held more democratic values than their peers—have been challenged in recent research.

Mr. Lipset reports that the research indicates that active students, regardless of their political views, seem to be academically more qualified than their passive counterparts.

Similarly, both Mr. Lipset and Mr. Keniston cite a study at Yale showing that students who actively supported, or actively opposed, the war in Vietnam were more like each other in some important ways than either group was like students who opposed the war passively.

What this may come down to is simply that action is viewed as healthier than inaction and that in the late 1960s most of the action was on the Left.

Despite the problems of identifying independent causes for radical behavior, there is some general agreement on who the radicals are, or were. Interpretations vary widely of why they did what they did and may still be doing.

At one end of the spectrum are purely psychological theories, and at the other are purely political or historical theories. In between are psychohistorical theories that may or may not be compatible with the psychological and political.

The chief psychological theory—that the activists are Oedipal rebels—has been advanced in detail by Lewis S. Feuer, professor of sociology at the University of Toronto in his book *The Conflict of Generations.*

Mr. Feuer argues that the "conflict of generations is a universal theme in history" and that it becomes "bitter, unyielding, angry, and violent" when the older generation loses its authority in the eyes of the younger.

Such a "deauthorization" has taken place in the United States, he says, because the younger generation perceives the older as having failed in its efforts to solve pressing social and political problems.

The younger generation rebels against the deauthorized, symbolic fathers, but suffers terrible feelings of guilt in the process, Mr. Feuer adds.

In effect, he sees each student rebel as a "would-be parricide" who seeks to merge himself with peasant, proletarian, the Negro, the poor, the alien race. He can conquer his guilt only "with the demonstration that he is selfless and by winning the comforting maternal love of the oppressed: they bring him the assurance of his needed place in the universe."

Because of the psychological nature of the movement, Mr. Feuer believes that activists, when choosing among tactics, will "usually tend to choose the one which involves a higher measure of violence or humiliation directed against the older generation."

While Mr. Feuer's theory has been the most widely reported, other purely psychological theories have been advanced as well. Bruno Bettelheim, an orthopsychiatrist at the University of Chicago, has argued that "Spockian permissiveness," among other things, accounts for the lack of restraint on the part of radicals, and John R. Searle, professor of philosophy at the University of California at Berkeley, believes that the student movement is essentially a religious search for the sacred that permits gross distortions of reality.

On the opposite end of the spectrum are theories that find solely external causes for the activism and deny that any kind of pathology is involved in the activists.

Some Marxists have argued, for instance, that students are an oppressed working class, apprenticed in the universities to learn the skills needed to run the capitalist state. They rebel as they become aware of their oppression.

George Wald, professor of biology at Harvard, has argued that students are reacting to the pervasive militarism in American society which has made them unsure of their future.

In some form or another, most of the liberals and sympathizers with the movement view some form of external cause as central to the protests. Mr. Lipset, who is by no means a supporter of the radicals and has in fact been the target of radical criticism, concludes:

> The larger explanation for the rise of activism during the past half decade or so must lie primarily in political events: the emergence of the civil rights and Vietnam issues in a particular post-Stalinist political epoch. These gave to the more radically disposed students the issues; their social situation gave them the stimulus; and the campus situation furnished them with the means to build a movement.

Beyond such approaches, which consider the psychological state of the protester less relevant than the issues that generated the protests, are psychohistorical theories, especially those advanced by Mr. Keniston.

He believes that the emergence of the "youth opposition" cannot be explained by traditional theories of society and the individual. Instead, he says, "youth" represents an entirely new stage of development that has been created by the unprecedented prolongation of education needed to prepare people for the postindustrial society:

> I believe that the emergence of a youthful counterculture is an event that can be understood only psychohistorically. It involves the interaction of individual personalities in all of their complexity, depth, and changeability with new social, cutural, and educational conditions. . . .

Such theories as Mr. Keniston's do not contradict another group of theories that present opposing views of the future of the movement. Essentially, one group of theorists argues that the movement is counterrevolutionary, another that it is revolutionary.

The chief spokesman for the counterrevolutionary theory has been Zbigniew Brzezinski of Columbia University, who argued in the *New Republic* (reprinted in *The University Crisis Reader*) that dissenting youth are displaced humanists who see themselves as homeless in the postindustrial, technetronic era.

The reaction of many of the leaders of campus disruptions "reflects both a conscious and, even more important, an unconscious realization that they are themselves becoming historically obsolete," he writes.

"Rather than representing a true revolution, some recent outbursts are in fact a counterrevolution. Its violence and revolutionary slogans are merely—and sadly—the death rattle of the historically irrelevant."

Charles A. Reich, in *The Greening of America*, has argued the reverse of Mr. Brzezinski's thesis. Mr. Reich believes that the counterculture is a revolutionary vanguard that will humanize the currently dehumanized society. Therefore, he, and Theodore Roszak in the earlier *The Making of a Counter Culture*, welcome the youthful opposition and expect it to reinvigorate the nation.

So we have a plethora of theories: Student protesters are sensitive, idealistic politicians, or they are unwitting performers in a psychological melodrama; they are a psychologically new type of man, or they are acting out age-old conflicts in modern dress.

In the meantime, the decrease in overt confrontations over the past two years poses some interesting problems for the theorists. While it may not be true, as Herman Kahn asserts, that if the 1960s were the "Reformation," it is at least true that the violence and overt confrontations have declined on the nation's campuses.

If Mr. Keniston is correct, why did the psychologically new group of people react as it did in the late 1960s and not now? What changes have taken place in the historical climate? The war in Vietnam continues, if at a lesser intensity; the racial crisis seems far from solution; and the universities remain much as they were.

Or, if Mr. Feuer is correct, why have the immediate successors to the guilt-ridden would-be parricides of the late 1960s refrained from acting out their aggressions thus far in the 1970s? Is some new generational equilibrium being reached? Has the older generation been "reauthorized?"

In one sense, all of the speculation and theorizing about the activists seems a little dated. Something new apparently

is occurring on the campuses just when people are beginning
to try to make sense of the previous crises.

Clearly, the issues that motivated students in the late
1960s have not vanished. With all the studies that have been
done on them, we still do not know exactly why they reacted
to the issues then, but are not reacting to them in the same,
aggressive way now.

SOME MYTHS ON YOUTH [2]

Everybody over forty is an expert on the youth problem,
and much of what everybody knows about that problem just
isn't so. Consider these widely held viewpoints:

1. That youth discontent is the result of Communist influence.

The truth is that the Communists are as puzzled by today's youth as are the capitalists. In Communist countries
the Establishment is resentful toward most young people
and, far from knowing how to direct the forces of youth discontent in capitalist countries, the Communists don't know
how to cope with their own young people at home. Long
hair, beards and rock music distress Communist bureaucrats
in Moscow, Prague or Warsaw no less than bankers in El-
mira, Keokuk or Cheyenne. Student agitation against the
established order, though less demonstrative in Communist
countries than in America and France, is widespread in the
Soviet Union and its satellite countries.

2. That America's youth discontent is caused by the Vietnam war and will fade away when the war and the draft are
ended.

A lot of us would like to believe this, but the problem is
not that simple. Youthful discontent is powerful in countries
not involved in the Indochina war, and American youth are
unhappy about many other things besides Vietnam and the
draft—and will remain so long after the war is finished. End-

[2] Article entitled "Some Popular Myths on Youth," by Landrum Bolling,
president of Earlham College, Richmond, Indiana. *Wall Street Journal*. p 10.
Je. 28, '71. Reprinted by permission.

ing the war will surely improve the state of mind of the young—and of their elders. However, protest against the war, though serious, is but one of many symptoms of a deep-seated disaffection of the young—and of the disaffection of a lot of the rest of us.

3. That more money spent on education, housing and the care of the poor will eliminate discontent among the young.

Young people do indeed attack their elders for what they consider niggardly handling of social problems. A few of the more perceptive complain with equal reason about the unimaginative and inefficient way the Establishment uses the money it already spends on these aspects of our troubled life. While the young undoubtedly favor a higher rate of spending on education and social welfare—and are thoroughly turned off by talk of the need to "hold down inflationary pressures"—they are so convinced of the wrongness of vast national spending on war, the space program and the SST that merely moderate and "reasonable" increases in appropriations for education and welfare will fail to impress them very much. Moreover, the current young do not have the innocent belief that their New Deal parents have, or once had, that increased Federal financing will solve all problems.

4. That a new all-out program of liberal reform will win back the young.

The truth is that few of the young show any sustained interest in working to correct the defects in current national policies and programs. The assassinations of the Kennedy brothers and of Martin Luther King, the disappearance of Lyndon Johnson's domestic reformism in the swamps of Vietnam, disillusion with their one-spring hero Eugene McCarthy, and boredom with most of the political choices of recent memory—these are the factors, at least in their minds, that cause the young to be skeptical and hesitant about responding to some new liberal battle-cry. Though a mini-minority loudly, and at times violently, proclaim their intention to bring down the system, most disaffected youth have little faith in either drastic revolution or the plodding ways of reform. Among them there is widespread apathy and a sense of impotence and hopelessness toward all proposed solutions to the situations they deplore. They just don't see any answers to the problems of pollution, urban decay, racial conflict and war—and they don't think their elders do either.

5. That this generation's rebellion is essentially the same as all earlier manifestations of youthful revolt against the elders—and will soon pass.

Not so, say the most thoughtful historians, psychologists and social anthropologists—and a lot of commonsense parents and grandparents. The discontent is deeper, more widespread, and more far-ranging in its effects than any "normal youth revolt" ever known heretofore. Even among the "straight kids" who shun both violence and the hippie culture there is great uncertainty about values, attitudes, life styles and goals of family and community. Few American parents can be sure of what their teen-age children really believe about fundamental purposes and values. The elder generation can surely not believe any longer that, "after sowing a few wild oats," today's young will comfortably settle down into the same proper, well-established life pattern of their parents.

6. That the trouble with today's youth is that they have lost interest in religion and must be won back to the old-time faith.

The fact is that this is probably the most open and seeking generation of young people with respect to spiritual matters we have known in this century. Their searches are taking some of them down some pretty bizarre byways: Zen Buddhism, Hindu mysticism, witchcraft, astrology. Yet many are caught up in a rediscovery of simple old-fashioned emotional religious orthodoxy now largely abandoned by the mainline churches. Pentecostalism is the fastest growing wing of American Protestantism, and many young people, including college students, are part of that growth. Resistance to the traditional services of traditional churches is, to be sure, great among many young people today. However, many sophisticated, highly intelligent young people are turning their backs on the materialistic, scientific objectivism of their largely secularized parents, grandparents and teachers and affirming the reality of the spiritual, the esoteric, the supernatural, the transcendent. In part, they are revolting against what they consider the too aridly intellectual, against the perverse misuses of reason. But also, in a variety of ways, they are carrying on man's eternal quest to find the divine element in life and to relate themselves to it.

7. That the youth have lost all sense of ethics and morality and need basic training in how to distinguish right from wrong.

Some have, and do. This is also true of too many people in all age groups. Yet to be certain about the real standards of ethics and morality of a given group of people at a particular time is difficult. Whatever you say will produce an argument. Some claim that this is the most truly moral generation in this century, the most idealistic young people who ever lived. Others are convinced that they have been corrupted into every imaginable form of wickedness. What is probably true is that today's youth are, like all human beings through history, a mixture of good and evil, idealism and selfishness, morality and immorality.

In some aspects of ethics and morality this is one of the most austere and puritanical generations in the memory of living man. Their standards of honesty, integrity and social responsibility are often severely demanding. Their most common criticism of the older generation has to do with charges that their elders are dishonest, hypocritical and irresponsible. In this there is much humorless, morally arrogant self-righteousness. Too often they are blind to their own hypocrisy. Too many of them have not learned about the inherent weakness and finitude of all human beings, including themselves. Still, for all their confusion and occasional self-deception, it must be said that this generation of young people is profoundly concerned about ethical and moral issues. The established structures of church, school and family are not working very well in transmitting the accumulated wisdom from the past on basic value questions. Perhaps the greatest challenge facing home, school and church is to find ways to engage all age groups in a shared and honest exploration of the eternal questions of purpose, meaning, ultimate value—of religion, morality and ethics. The old simple methods of Sunday school indoctrination are widely rejected. The most famous last words must surely be those that begin, "Now, when I was young—." The better substitutes are yet to be found.

These assorted popular myths about the young can give the older generation little guidance for dealing with the problems of the generations. But if we examine those myths seriously, we are compelled to search for new strategies for trying to cope with our fundamental social problems of which youth discontent and the conflicts between the generations are but symptoms. Those strategies, I believe, must involve us in developing ways of bringing younger and older people into creative, productive teamwork for the common good, and in making some significant changes in the pattern and quality of education.

RECONSIDERING THE YOUTHFUL OPPOSITION [3]

No issue today divides the public or intellectual community so deeply as does the "counterculture," the "new culture," "Consciousness III" [See Editor's Introduction, above.—Ed.]—what I will call the new youthful opposition. . . .

The emergence of a youthful opposition is an instance of an historical event that was predicted by no one twenty years ago. Marxist theorists either continued to cherish hopes of a working-class revolt in the capitalist nations, or else devoted their theoretical energies to explaining how monopoly

    [3] From *Youth and Dissent: The Rise of a New Opposition*, by Kenneth Keniston, professor of psychology and director of the Behavioral Sciences Center, Yale University School of Medicine. Harcourt. '71. p 370-400. © 1971 by Kenneth Keniston. Abridged by permission of Harcourt Brace Jovanovich, Inc.

capitalism had successfully coopted the potentially revolutionary spirit of the working class. Even the most sophisticated neo-Marxists did not predict that those who apparently
benefited most from capitalist societies would help lead a
new attack upon them. In a comparable way, what I will
group together as "liberal theories" not only failed to anticipate the emergence of the youthful revolt, but predicted
that such a revolt would become progressively *less* likely as
affluence and higher education spread. To understand the
theoretical importance of the current debate over the meaning of the youthful opposition therefore requires us to examine in broad outline the widely shared theoretical assumptions of liberal thinkers in the 1950s and early 1960s.

The "Liberal" Analysis

Liberal theories of man have usually started from the
malleability or plasticity of human nature. . . . Malleable
man was said to be related to stable society through a series
of special socializing institutions like the family and the
education system, whose primary function was to "integrate"
the individual into society. Specifically, families' and schools'
chief job was to teach children the social roles and cultural
values necessary for adult life in that society. Key societal
norms, symbolic systems, values, and role models were said
to be "internalized" during the socialization process, and
their internalization resulted in adults who were "adjusted"
—who "functioned" with the symbols, values, and roles expected by their society. . . .

Liberal social theorists did not naively confuse stability
with stasis. A society in a state of basic equilibrium might
still be a society that was changing rapidly: the equilibrium
could be "dynamic." Social change created social strains and
psychological stresses; but if all went well, it did not finally
upset the basic social equilibrium. . . .

Nor were liberal social theorists ignorant of the fact that
revolutions, social convulsions, and dramatic upheavals
abound in history. But compulsive social upheavals were

almost always seen as symptoms of a breakdown of the system of social control, and as regressive or destructive in their consequences. "Meaningful social change" was thought most likely to occur through "gradualism" and piecemeal social reform." . . .

In looking to the future, liberal theorists naturally enough foresaw more of what their theories led them to view as normal, desirable, and inevitable: more industrial productivity, more technologization, more piecemeal reform, higher education, more stability, and more effective management. Admittedly, problems were anticipated—for example, the problem of avoiding political apathy when most major social and ideological problems had been solved. Most liberal writers urged that new ways must be found to involve the young in the political future of their nation, and most deplored the "privatism" of the "silent generation" of the 1950s. Other problems were also foreseen: the problems of mass culture, of the lonely crowd, of the use of leisure time, of the organization man, of rapid job obsolescence, and so on. But compared with the old problems of scarcity, economic depression, class warfare, and ideological conflict, these new problems seemed minor. . . .

Theories like these attempted to explain—indeed they *did* explain—the relative domestic stability of the Western democracies in the 1950s, along with the general acceptance, acquiescence, or apathy of educated youth. But in retrospect, they were too airtight and too historically parochial. We can now see that they took a particular historical moment—one that today seems abnormal in its tranquillity—and constructed theories that elevated this particular moment into the natural state of affairs. And among other things, this liberal system of ideas—it would be fair to call it an ideology —effectively prevented us from anticipating, much less understanding, what was increasingly to happen among a growing minority of the young during the 1960s. . . .

Yet in its treatment of the relationship of youth to society, liberal social thought, like Marxism, predicted precisely the opposite of what has actually happened. And that fact alone should impel us to question and redefine the basic assumptions from which liberalism began. The emergence of a youthful opposition, then, demands new theories not only of youthfulness, but of human nature, of society, and of their relationship. Theoretically, this is perhaps the prime significance of the youthful revolt.

Two Current Theories

. . . Two new analyses of the youthful opposition are emerging that have theoretical depth, scope, and profundity: they properly attempt to understand the new opposition in terms of a broader theory of man and society. The first theory, which is an adaptation of liberal theories, asserts in essence that the youth movement in the industrialized nations is historically a counterrevolutionary movement, a reaction against the more basic forces involved in the growth of a new technological society. The second theory counters by claiming that the dissenting young are true revolutionaries, an historical vanguard that is defining a new and better society. . . .

Youth as a counterrevolutionary force. Consider first the "counterrevolutionary" theory of youth. The most thoughtful proponents of this view are men like Zbigniew Brzezinski, Lewis Feuer, and, in very different ways, Raymond Aron, Daniel Bell, Alvin Toffler, Bruno Bettelheim, and Herman Kahn. These thinkers differ on a great many key issues, and it does each an injustice to group them together without also underlining their differences. But they are usually in essential agreement on several major points.

First, they agree that we are in the midst of a major social transformation that is taking us out of an industrial society into the postindustrial, technological, postmodern, superindustrial, or, in Brzezinski's terms, "technetronic" society of the future. The new society will be highly rationalized. It will be characterized by high productivity, automation, increased leisure time, more individual choices, better social planning, greater opportunities for the expression of individual interests, rapid rates of social change, more rational administration, and the demand for enormously high levels of education among those who occupy positions of leadership. It will be a society of complex large-scale organizations, global communications, and a basically technical approach to the solution of human problems. In this society, power will lie increasingly not with those who possess economic capital, but with those who possess educational "capital." In the technetronic society, the "knowledge industry," centered above all in the professoriate and in the universities, will be the central industry of society and the central motor of historical change.

The second assumption common to the counterrevolutionary theory of youth is that periods of basic historical transition are inevitably marked by social disturbances. The introduction of factories in Europe and America in the nineteenth century was marked by growing class conflict and the Luddite Movement, which led displaced agricultural workers to try to destroy the factories that were depriving them of work. Today, the transition into the technetronic age is marked by an equally violent revulsion by those whose skills and values are made obsolete by the new social revolution.

Specifically, a postindustrial society imposes what Daniel Bell terms a heavy "organizational harness" upon the young: it requires them to study for many years, to acquire highly specialized technical skills, to stay in school, and to postpone gratification well into biological adulthood. Equally important, this new society renders obsolete a large number of traditional values, skills, and outlooks. A technetronic society above all needs skilled executives, systems analysts, computer programmers, trained administrators, and high-level scientists. Those who possess these skills are in the forefront of historical change: their talents are needed; their outlooks are valued. But those identified with "traditional" fields like the humanities and the social sciences find that their values and skills are becoming increasingly unnecessary, irrelevant, and obsolete; they are today's neo-Luddites. The ideals of romanticism, expressiveness, and traditional humanism may dominate the contemporary youth culture, but they do not dominate the social structure—the specific institutions that are changing our lives. One consequence, then, is what Bell terms the disjuncture between the culture—specifically the adversary culture of intellectuals and many students—and the dominant social structure of large-scale organization, technology, mass communications, and electronics.

The conclusion that the revolt of the young is essentially counterrevolutionary follows from the first two points. According to this theory, the humanistic young are rebelling because of their latent awareness of their own obsolescence. The "organizational harness" around their necks is too tight and heavy for them to endure. An ever-larger group of young men and women feel that they have no place in the modern world, for they lack salable skills, basic character styles, and value orientations that are adaptable to the emergent post-industrial society. They are, as Bruno Bettelheim puts it, "obsolete youth." They rebel in a blind, mindless, and generally destructive way against rationalism, intellect, technology, organization, discipline, hierarchy, and all of the requisites of a postindustrial society. . . .

Although theorists differ as to precisely *which* unconscious forces are expressed in student dissent, the logic of the counterrevolutionary argument makes a recourse to psychologism almost mandatory. For if the manifest issues of student unrest are seen as pseudoissues, disguises, and rationalizations, then we are forced into the realm of the not-conscious in our search to locate the "real" motives behind the youthful opposition. And in today's post-Freudian age, such explanations are likely to involve recourse to concepts like unconscious Oedipal feelings, adolescent rebellion, castration anxiety, and the "acting out" of feelings that originate in the early family. . . . Whatever the precise irrational forces behind the youthful revolt are said to be, the counterrevolutionary theory, by denying the validity of the youth movement's own explanations of its acts, is forced to hypothesize unconscious motivations as the "real" motives behind the revolt.

A final conclusion follows from this argument: no matter how destructive the revolt of the young may be in the short run, that revolt is historically foredoomed to failure in the long run. The technetronic society, the postindustrial world, the superindustrial state—these forces are unstoppable. The liberal democratic state is being basically transformed, but the rantings and rampagings of the young, devoted to obsolescent ideas of self-expression, anarchism, romanticism, direct democracy, liberation, and the expansion of consciousness, cannot stop this transformation. The revolt of the young may indeed be, in Daniel Bell's phrase, the emergent "class conflict" of postindustrial society. But from Bell's analysis, it follows that students are a neo-Luddite, counterrevolutionary class, and that their counterrevolution will fail. Increasingly, power will be held by those who have more successfully acquired the capital dispensed by the knowledge industry. The counterculture is, in Brzezinski's words, the "death rattle" of the historically obsolete.

The counterrevolutionary theory of the youth revolt is a reformulation of liberal theory, modified to make room for the convulsions of the last decade. Within any social equilibrium theory, there must be room for the possibility that the system will temporarily get "out of balance." The assumption of thinkers like Brzezinski is that we have entered a period of imbalance that accompanies the transition from an industrial to a technetronic society. In this transitional period, traditional mechanisms of social control, older forms of integration between social structure and culture, and previous forms of socialization have ceased to function adequately. But in the future, it is assumed, equilibrium can once again be regained. Upon arrival in the technetronic society, the postindustrial society, or the world of the year 2000, the temporary storm squalls on the weatherfront between industrial and postindustrial society will have dissipated, and we will once again be in a state of relative social equilibrium. If we can only wait out the transition, maintaining and repairing our basic institutions, we can build a new equilibrium—one that will grind under the youthful opposition just as triumphant industrialism destroyed the Luddites. In the meanwhile we must fight to preserve decency, civilization, rationality, and higher education from the depredations of the mindless young.

Youth as a revolutionary force. The second major theory holds that the dissenting young are historically a revolutionary force. This theory views the counterculture as a regenerative culture, and interprets those forces that oppose it as ultimately counterrevolutionary. This view is expressed in different forms in the works of Theodore Roszak and Charles Reich, in the writings of members of the counterculture like Tom Hayden and Abbie Hoffman, and, most convincingly of all, by Philip Slater. [See "Whither the Two Cultures" in Section VI, below.—Ed.] Let us consider the basic assumptions of the revolutionary view of the youth culture.

First, this theory also accepts the notion that industrialized societies are in a period of major cultural, institutional, and historical transition. But it alleges that the thrust of the liberal democratic state has exhausted itself. What is variously termed "corporate liberalism," the "establishment," or the "welfare-warfare state" is seen as fundamentally bankrupt. Admittedly, industrial states have produced unprecedented wealth. But they have not been able to distribute it equitably, nor have they found ways to include large minorities in the mainstream of society. Furthermore, their basic assumptions have led directly to disastrous "neoimperialistic" wars like the American involvement in Southeast Asia. Corporate liberalism has produced a highly manipulated society, in which "real" human needs and interests are neglected in the pursuit of political power, the merchandising of products, or the extension of overseas markets. Large-scale organizations have dehumanized their members, depriving men of participation in the decisions that affect their lives. The electronic revolution merely provides the rulers of the corporate state with more effective means of manipulating the populace. Corporate liberalism has today revealed its bankruptcy.

The second assumption of this theory is that the economic successes and moral failures of liberal industrial societies today make possible and necessary a new kind of consciousness, new values, new aspirations, and new life styles—in short, a new culture. . . .

It follows from this analysis that the new oppositional culture is not an atavistic and irrational reaction against the old culture but a logical outgrowth of it—an expression of its latent possibilities, a rational effort to remedy its failings, in some sense its logical fulfillment. If the central goal of the old culture was to overcome want and if that goal has been largely achieved, then the counterculture stands on the shoulders of the old culture, fulfilling, renewing, and expressing that culture's latent hopes. Far from being historical reactionaries, the counterculturists are the historical vanguard. Their alleged anarchism and anti-intellectualism are but efforts to express the desire for human liberation whose roots lie in the postponed dreams of the old culture. As the British philosopher Stuart Hampshire has recently suggested, the dissenting young are not against reason, but only against a constricted definition of reason as a quantitative calculus that ignores human values and needs.

The revolutionary theory of youth also entails a definite view of the psychology of young rebels and revolutionaries. It asks that we take them completely at their word when they state the reasons for their protests, disruptions, dropouts, or rejections. The dissenting young are seen as miraculously healthy products of the irrational, dangerous, and unjust world they inherited. Their motives are noble, idealistic, and pure, while their statements of their goals are to be taken at face value. They are not animated by their childhood pasts, but by a vision (which they may, however, find it difficult to articulate) of a freer, more peaceful, more liberated, and more just society. As for the Oedipus complex, to discuss the psychological motives of the members of the youthful opposition at all is seen as a typically "liberal" way of distracting attention from the real issues. Thus, even if the dissenting young behave in an undemocratic, dogmatic or violent way, one "understands" their behavior by discussing the undemocratic, dogmatic, and violent society to which they are objecting.

This view of the psychology of the youthful opposition follows logically from the assumption that the young are in the historical vanguard. For in general, historical vanguards must be endowed with ordinary wisdom and prescience, and with a special freedom from that gnawingly irrational attachment to the personal or historic past that plagues most nonvanguard groups. In the views of one theorist, "radical man" is the highest possible form of human development. . . . Finally, as is by definition true of any historical vanguard, the triumph of this vanguard is seen as ultimately inevitable. With rising abundance, new recruits to the counterculture are being created daily. It is the old, then, who are obsolete, not the young. . . .

In many respects the theory of the youth movement as revolutionary is embryonic and incomplete. The counter-revolutionary theory builds upon the highly developed resources of liberal social thought. But the "revolutionary" view, rejecting both liberalism and Marxism, presents us more with a vision of what the counterculture might be at its best than with a complex or thorough social analysis. . . .

The Limits of Both Theories

No matter how oversimplified this account of the revolutionary and the counterrevolutionary theories, if either interpretation of youthful dissent were fundamentally adequate, this discussion could end. It therefore behooves us to examine each of these theories critically.

We should first acknowledge that each of these views has its highly persuasive points. Those who view the new opposition as historically counterrevolutionary are correct in underlining the increasing importance of technology, complex social organizations, and education in the most industrialized nations. They have pointed accurately to the new role of a highly educated and technologically trained elite. And they seem to help us explain why youthful dissenters are virtually absent among potential engineers, computer specialists, and business administrators, but disproportionately drawn from the ranks of social scientists and humanists.

Above all, however, the opponents of the youthful opposition are accurate in their criticism of that opposition. They rightly argue that the counterculture almost completely neglects the institutional side of modern life. Thus the call for liberation, for the expansion of consciousness, and for the expression of impulse has not been matched by the creation or even by the definition of institutions whereby these purposes could be achieved and sustained. Furthermore, in its cultural wing, the new opposition has often been callous to continuing injustice, oppression, and poverty in America and abroad. In its political wing, the counterculture has been vulnerable to despair, to apocalyptic but transient fantasies of instant revolution, to superficial Marxism, and to a romance with violence. Finally, the youthful opposition as a whole has never adequately confronted or understood its own derivative relationship to the dominant society. Perhaps as a result, it has too often been a caricature rather than a critique of the consumption-oriented, manipulative, technocratic, violent, electronic society that it nominally opposes. In pointing to the weakness of the counterculture, its critics seem to me largely correct.

Yet there is a deep plausibility, as well, in the theory that the youthful opposition is in historical terms a revolutionary movement. In particular, the "revolutionary" theorists accurately capture the growing feeling of frustration and the increasing sense of the exhaustion of the old order that obsess growing numbers of the educated young in industrialized nations. Furthermore, they correctly recognize the irony in the fact that the most prosperous and educated societies in world history have generated the most massive youthful opposition in world history. And in seeking to explain this unexpected opposition, the revolutionary theory understands well its relationship to the "systemic" failings of corporate liberalism—its failure to include large minorities in the general prosperity, its exploitative or destructive relationship to the developing nations, its use of advanced technology to manipulate the citizens in whose interest it allegedly governs, its neglect of basic human needs, values, and aspirations in a social calculus that sees men and women as merely "inputs" or "outputs" in complex organizations.

The strengths of each theory, however, are largely negative: in essence, each is at its best in pointing to the flaws of the culture or the social system defended by the other. But judged for its positive contribution, each theory tends to have parallel weaknesses: each disregards the facts at odds with its own central thesis. In order to do this, each operates at a different level of analysis: the counterrevolutionary theory at the level of social institutions, the revolutionary theory at the level of culture. As a consequence, each theory neglects precisely what the other theory correctly stresses.

The counterrevolutionary theory of the new opposition starts from an analysis of social institutions, modes of production, and the formal organization of human roles and relationships. Despite its emphasis upon the psychopathology of the new rebels, it is fundamentally a sociological theory of institutional changes and technological transformations. It stresses the importance of applied science, the growth of new educational institutions, and the power of the new elite that dominates the "knowledge industry." In defining the future, it emphasizes the further development of rational-bureaucratic institutions and the revolutionary impact of new electronic technology upon social organization, communication, and knowledge. But it tends to forget consciousness and culture, treating ideas, symbols, values, ideologies, aspirations, fantasies, and dreams largely as reflections of technological, economic, and social forces.

Theorists who argue that the new opposition is historically revolutionary operate at a quite different level of analysis. For them, the two key concepts are culture and consciousness. What matters most is feelings, aspirations, outlooks, ideologies, and world views. Charles Reich's recent analysis of three kinds of consciousness [See Editor's Introduction, above.—Ed.] is explicit in asserting that institutions are secondary and in the last analysis unimportant. Most other revolutionary theorists also start from an analysis of a "new consciousness" to argue that the decisive revolution is a cultural revolution. How men view the world, how they organize their experience symbolically, what their values are —these are seen as historically determining. Institutional changes are said to follow changes in human aspirations and consciousness.

Daniel Bell has written of the disjuncture of social structure and culture in modern society. We need not accept his entire analysis to agree that this disjuncture is reflected in theories about youthful dissent. For on closer examination, they turn out to be talking about either social structure *or* culture, but rarely about both. The key weakness of the counterrevolutionary theory is its neglect of consciousness and culture, its assumption that social-structural, technological, and material factors will be decisive in determining the future. The parallel weakness of the revolutionary view of youthful dissent is its disregard of the way organized systems of production, technology, education, communication, and "social control" influence, shape, and may yet coopt or destroy the youthful opposition. In fact, then, these two theories are not as contradictory as they seem: in many ways, they are simply talking about two different aspects of the modern world.

A second limitation of both theories is their assumption that the trends they define are historically inevitable. In this respect, both theories are eschatological as well as explanatory. The postindustrial, or technetronic, view assumes the future inevitability of a postindustrial, technetronic, technocratic society. Given this assumption, it follows logically that anyone who opposes the technetronic society is historically counterrevolutionary. . . .

But this claim that the future is in fact predetermined by blind historical forces is open to major question. In retrospect, most previous claims about the historical inevitability of this or that trend have turned out to have been mere expressions of the wishes of those who made these claims. It makes equal or better sense to believe that "history" is on the side neither of the technetronic revolution nor of the counterculture. In fact, we may deny that history is on anyone's side, arguing that history is simply made by human beings, acting individually and in concert, influenced by the institutions in which they live *and* by the consciousness and culture.

If we reject the assumption of historical inevitability, both the counterrevolutionary and the revolutionary theories must be understood in part as efforts to justify a set of special interests by attributing historical inevitability to them, and perhaps ultimately as exercises in the use of prophecy to convince others of the truth of the prophecy and thereby to make the prophecy self-fulfilling. . . .

What both theories fail to comprehend is the extent to which the emergence of a new youthful opposition requires us to embark upon a critical reexamination of concepts of man, society, and their interrelationship that we have heretofore taken largely for granted. This inability to come to grips with the theoretical challenge posed by the new opposition is seen clearly in each theory's attitude toward education. Neoliberals who view student dissent as largely counterrevolutionary are committed to a view of education as socialization. Given this view, it follows that a postindustrial society characterized by prolonged higher education should be a society where youthful dissent is rare. The eruption of wide-scale disaffection among the most educated products of the most industrialized societies thus requires neoliberal theories to posit wide-scale "deviant socialization," or else to argue that higher education is failing to "do its job." In fact, however, the extensive evidence concerning the backgrounds of young dissenters provides little support for the "deviant socialization" interpretation of the new opposition. And paradoxically, those institutions of higher education that liberals have traditionally seen as doing the "best job" seem to be the breeding grounds for the greatest disaffection.

Those who view youthful disaffection as a revolutionary phenomenon are faced with the same dilemma. They tend to see higher education as a way of "integrating" or "coopting" youth into the existing society. It therefore comes as a surprise that higher education seems to promote disaffection and to be closely related to the emergence of a youthful counterculture. But those who view the youth movement as revolutionary have so far failed to offer any adequate explanation of why many young men and women in so many nations have escaped the net of socialization.

The fact that theorists of neither persuasion can explain the contemporary correlation between higher education and dissent indicates the need for a critical analysis of our prevailing assumptions concerning human malleability, social equilibrium, and socialization. . . . In brief, the work I believe needs to be done falls into three broad categories. First, there must be a critical reanalysis and reformulation of the theoretical assumptions with which we attempt to understand man and society. Second, we must begin to come to terms with the characteristics of modern society and modern man in their own right, and not in terms of strained analogies to the past. Third, a revised theoretical framework and a better understanding of contemporary man in society should help define a new political agenda.

Plasticity, Equilibrium, and Socialization

The first assumption to be reanalyzed critically is the assumption of virtually limitless human malleability and influenceability. Without denying that men can adapt to most surroundings, that they often conform to the pressures of their peers, or that they internalize social norms and cultural concepts, we need to rediscover and emphasize those elements in "human nature" that make men less than totally plastic. . . . Here it should suffice to note that a developmental approach clearly contradicts the almost exclusively environmental view of psychological change that has dominated liberal thought. Critically interpreted, the work of Freud and Piaget may help us understand man not merely as an adjusting and adapting animal, but as a creature whose growth has both important societal prerequisites and a dynamic of its own. We can then think of man as possessing a "human nature" that can be "violated" by social expectations; we may then be better able to see man as possessing innate potentials for autonomy and integration that may at times lead him into conflict with his society.

We will also need to explore in detail the ways in which these developmental potentials may be actualized or frustrated by any given social or historical context. . . . In other words, we need to examine not only the beliefs men hold, but the *way* they hold them—the complexity, richness, and structure of their views of the world. Politically and socially, it may be more important that members of a given subculture possess a relativistic view of truth than that they are conservatives or liberals.

Finally, the role of conflict in human development needs to be reexamined. Liberal psychology has tended to minimize the catalytic importance of conflict in growth: conflict was seen as neurotic, undesirable, and productive of regression. But there is much current evidence that individuals who attain high levels of complexity in feeling, thinking, and judging do so *as a result of* conflict, not in its absence. Students of cognitive development, like observers of personality development, find that disequilibrium, tension, and imbalance tend to produce growth. If this is true, then the absence of psychological conflict or tension may be as pathological as the overabundance of conflict, and the liberal view of the ideal man as smoothly socialized and conflict-free may need to be discarded. . . .

Turning to broader theories of society, a comparable critical reexamination of basic assumptions seems in order. Above all, the utility of the equilibrium model of society must be examined. Increasingly, critical sociologists have begun to suggest that a "conflict" model of society and of social change may be more suited to the facts of contemporary history than a theory of societal balance. Just as we should appreciate the catalytic role of conflict in human development, so the critical importance of conflict in social change must be acknowledged. Both human and social development, I believe, are best viewed as dialectic processes, involving force, counterforce, and potential resolution; thesis, antithesis, and potential synthesis. At a societal level, such a view would require us to start from change, struggle, revolution, and transformation as the basic and "natural" state of affairs rather than viewing them as unfortunate exceptions that require special explanation.

This view of society would put social change in the first chapter, not in the last chapter as one of the unexplained problems of our theory. It would see conflict between individuals, groups, and historical forces as a necessary and vital component of historical change, not as a result of a "failure" of the "mechanisms of social control." It would also entail that any given "resolution" of conflicting historical forces should in turn generate new antithetical forces which will oppose that resolution, thus continuing the dialectic of change. A sociology based on the theory of conflict would especially attempt to understand the processes by which new conflicts are generated out of apparent equilibrium, rather than focusing solely upon how equilibrium is maintained. . . .

If we abandon the notion of society as a stable and homogeneous entity, then the process whereby individuals and their societies interrelate becomes vastly more complex. For if every society contains within it important internal conflicts, then growing children are exposed not to a stable, self-consistent set of social expectations and cultural values, but to social and cultural contradictions. Intrapsychic conflicts and social contradictions will thus be mutually related, although never in a simple one-to-one fashion. Furthermore, in times of rapid historical change, the societal conflicts to which one generation is exposed will differ from those of the previous generation; partly for this reason, individuals of different historical generations will typically differ from each other in basic personality. . . .

Contradictions Within the Knowledge Sector

The second, related theoretical task is to understand in detail the special characteristics of modern personality and modern society. Even if a critical analysis of the basic assumptions of liberal thought were completed, the substance of a more adequate account of what is unique about our own era would still be lacking. . . . If we start from a dialectical view of historical change, but admit that Marx's juxtaposition of a revolutionary proletariat and a reactionary bourgeoisie did not necessarily mark the last stage in the dialectic, then we must entertain seriously the possibility that the conflicts about which Marx wrote have been largely resolved and that new conflicts have today begun to emerge. . . .

In the period before and after the Second World War, then, the dominant class conflicts of the nineteenth and early twentieth centuries were increasingly resolved, reconciled, or synthesized in the liberal-democratic-capitalist or socialist states in Western Europe, America, and after the war, Japan. . . . First in America, and then increasingly in Western Europe and Japan, the middle class grew to be the largest class, the working class became increasingly prosperous, and both classes became more and more committed to the preservation of the existing society. Especially during the years of the cold war, a domestic equilibrium was reached in the liberal democracies, and this equilibrium provided the empirical ground upon which liberal thought grew and by which it seemed confirmed. To be sure, like all historical syntheses, this one was far from complete: large minorities were excluded from the general prosperity; problems of poverty amidst affluence continued; subtle forms of imperialism replaced the earlier forms, and so on. . . . [Meanwhile] there arose a new generation that took for granted the accomplishments of corporate liberalism, expressing neither gratitude nor admiration for these achievements. To this new generation, what were instead important were first of all the inabilities of a liberal society to fulfill its own promises; and second, the surfacing of a set of cultural and psychological goals that had previously been deferred in the liberal society. These newly surfaced aspirations had to do above all with the quality of life, the possibilities for self-expression, full human development, self-actualization, the expansion of consciousness, and the pursuit of empathy, sentience, and experience. . . .

To understand the new conflicts in corporate liberal society, I believe we must above all examine the role of the "knowledge sector." For the liberal-democratic and industrialized nations are increasingly dominated neither by capitalists nor by workers, but by a vast new "intelligentsia" of educated professionals who exert unprecedented influence on both public policy and private practice. In some ways their contemporary role is analogous to the traditional role of intellectuals, artists, and bohemians in earlier historical eras. But because of their increasing numbers and influence, they occupy an altogether different place in technological societies. What they share is that the enterprises in which they are engaged depend upon extensions, manipulations, or applications of knowledge and ideas. The knowledge sector thus includes not only universities, scientific laboratories, research institutes, and the world of creative artists, but a much broader set of enterprises including corporate research and development, the communications industry, data analysis and data processing, the major higher professions, advertising, merchandising, administrative science, personnel management, entertainment, systems analysis, and so on. So defined, the knowledge sector is clearly that sector of contemporary industrialized societies that has grown most rapidly in size and power. . . . Often exploited yet more often manipulating, immensely influential yet vastly vulnerable, an interest group but one that possesses unprecedented power, the role of the knowledge sector in modern society must be defined as unprecedented, new, and *sui generis*. . . .

In the last decade, it has become clear that the "value-free" self-definition of the knowledge sector masks an important ideology, an ideology increasingly recognized and challenged by the new opposition. This ideology can be termed "technism," that is, a set of pseudoscientific assumptions about the nature and resolution of human and social problems. Most highly articulated in various forms of systems analysis, technism insists that the highest rationality involves measurement and consigns the incommensurable (feelings, values, "intangibles") to a lesser order of rationality and reality. . . .

Paradoxically, however, it is from within the knowledge sector that today there also emerges the most astringent critique of technism. Institutions of higher education, once predicted to become the central institutions of postindustrial society, have indeed become the prime exemplars of a technist approach to problems of government, business, and social planning; but they have also become the prime generators of the antitechnist, romantic, expressive, moralistic, anarchic humanism of the new opposition. Rejecting technism, this opposition stresses all those factors in human life and social experience that do not fit the technist equations. If "value-free," objective technism is the dominant voice of the dominant knowledge sector, then expressive subjective anarchism is the subversive voice. . . .

The intimate relationship between the knowledge sector and the new opposition is also apparent when we examine the social origins of the members of the opposition. For the core of the counterculture consists not of the children of the working class or of the lower middle class, but of the children of the knowledge sector. I have elsewhere insisted that the new opposition is not monolithic, and that we must distinguish its "political" from its "cultural" wing. Available evidence suggests that members of the political wing tend to be recruited disproportionately from among the children of professors, social workers, ministers, scientists, lawyers, and artists. These young men and women are the most concerned with institutional, social, and political change, and are also most likely to express solidarity with the basic values of their parents. Recruits to the cultural, expressive, esthetic, or "hippie" wing of the counterculture, in contrast, tend to be drawn to a much greater degree from the families of media executives, entertainers, advertising men, merchandisers, scientific administrators, and personnel managers. These young men and women are more concerned with the expansion of consciousness, the development of alternative life styles, and the pursuit of communal ways of living. As a rule, they reject not only the conventional values and institutions of American society, but the values and life styles of their parents. The parents of the "politicals" are thus the more established members of the knowledge sector, while the parents of the "culturals" are the "newly arrived," whose membership in the knowledge sector is more tenuous and ambivalent. . . .

A variety of factors within the knowledge sector clearly cooperate to generate its own opposition. Among these, for example, are the ambivalences of the parents of youthful dissenters toward the very knowledge sector in which they are employed. But no factor is of greater importance than the impact of higher education upon its recruits. Higher education bears a paradoxical relationship to the knowledge sector. On the one hand, higher education is essential for the maintenance and growth of the knowledge sector; but on the other hand, higher education provides many of the catalysts that push students to develop a critical consciousness which leads them to become part of the youthful opposition, and thus to oppose the dominant ideology of the knowledge sector. . . .

Precisely because a technological society cannot rely exclusively upon a narrowly technical system of higher education, it must foster a high degree of critical consciousness among its most educated products, and this critical consciousness is readily turned against the dominant assumptions and practices of the technological society. In a way not often acknowledged by educators but increasingly sensed by the general public, higher education today is "subversive" in that it is helping to create youths who challenge many of the basic assumptions of their society. . . .

These notes on contemporary society are obviously incomplete, sketchy, and doubtless often wrong. They should indicate, however, my conviction that in analyzing contemporary technological societies, we do well to start from one of the central points emphasized by the "counterrevolutionary" theorists, namely the ascendancy of the knowledge sector. But an analysis of the meaning of this sector, I believe, leads not to the conclusion that it will inevitably triumph, but rather to the realization that the knowledge sector is riven through with basic contradictions, and that it is generating its own critics on a mass scale.

A New Politics

The connection between social theory and political action is exceedingly complex. No matter how refined, precise, and detailed a theory, it does not necessarily or automatically lead to a political agenda. Yet on the other hand, political action in the absence of social theory tends to be random, haphazard, trial-and-error, and empirical in the worst sense. Such is the case with much of what today passes as "radical politics": lacking any grounding in critical social theory, it tends to consist in *ad hoc* reactions of moral indignation, to lack any long-range direction, to fritter away the best energies of its members in internecine battles, or to adopt programs inspired by a pop-Marxist analysis of guerrilla warfare in some far-off ex-colonial nation. . . .

Several general political implications follow from this line of reasoning. For one, it follows that visions of immediate social or political revolution are based on a flawed social and historical analysis. The processes of sociohistorical change in which we are living are long-term, secular processes, which will take at least a generation to work themselves out. Those who have a serious interest in effecting meaningful social change must therefore be prepared to devote decades, and even a lifetime, to this enterprise; those whose energies flag after a week a month, or a year will be of little help.

If we view this youthful opposition as reflecting emerging contradictions within the dominant knowledge sector of technological societies, then we would be wrong to ally ourselves politically with either the "value-free" technism that I have defined as thesis in this conflict, or with the subjective anarchism that I have defined as the antithesis. In the long run, what will be called for will be a synthesis of technism with anarchism, of "scientific objectivity" with the romantic expressiveness of the counterculture. It would therefore be a political mistake to embrace unreservedly the future of either the systems analyst or of the tribal communard. Instead we should work toward a future that could bring together the enormous power placed in man's hands by his technology and the vision of human liberation proclaimed by the counterculture. A politics that aligns itself with either the thesis or the antithesis will be a politics that settles for too little.

Another corollary of the views outlined here concerns the need to support a particular kind of higher education. Those who bitterly oppose the new opposition are already eager to limit higher education to technical education, eliminating or deemphasizing its critical component. This strategy, if successful, could well reduce the numbers of those who possess that critical consciousness which seems vital for membership in the new opposition. It is therefore important for all who sympathize with the opposition to seek to extend higher education that is truly critical. The current radical attack upon higher education is, I think, misguided when it fails to discriminate between technical and critical education. Higher education in the broad sense not only has been but should continue to be the nursery for the new opposition. . . .

The proposition that social forces that begin as progressive generally end as reactionary obviously applies to the youthful opposition itself. As the youthful opposition ceases to be youthful, it must constantly guard against further evolution into a reactionary force. Already we can envision how this could occur: the collectivism of the counterculture could readily become an insistence upon the abrogation of individual rights; the tribalism of Consciousness III could well portend a society of coercive group membership; the counterculture's opposition to technism could degenerate into a mindless hatred of reason, science, intellect, reflection, and accuracy. Today the youthful opposition is so weak politically that none of these dangers seems socially or politically important. But should the opposition gain in strength, its own reactionary potentials might well unfold.

In essence, then, a politics consistent with this agenda must be one that rejects both the "value-free" technism of corporate liberalism and the subjective anarchism of the counterculture, attempting instead the painful and slow work of creating a synthesis of the institutions of technological society with the culture of oppositional youth. That synthesis must ultimately entail the creation of a culture where the concept of liberation is not merely a facile slogan, but a commitment to the hard work of creating institutions within which genuine human relatedness may be attained. That synthesis must attempt to combine new-culture participation with old-culture competence, Consciousness III enthusiasm with Consciousness II professionalism—and all of this in ways that have hardly begun to be imagined, much less tried. It must involve an effort to turn modern technology around so that it facilitates man's liberation instead of encouraging his manipulation, so that it makes wars less possible rather than more likely, so that it helps men understand each other rather than oppose one another.

It is easy to call for a synthesis in general terms; it will be difficult to achieve it in practice. Nor do I believe that such a political synthesis is inevitable or even highly probable. We are indeed at an historical juncture, a turning point, a cultural and institutional crisis. And the youth revolt, the counterculture, the new opposition—these define one pole, one catalyst, one ingredient in that crisis. But history is not necessarily on the side of progress, synthesis, or the good. What happens in the next decades will depend not upon blind institutional and cultural forces, but upon the intelligence, good will, and hard work of countless individual men and women. It is possible today to begin to imagine a society far better than any society we have known—a society where technology serves man, where abundance makes possible higher levels of human development, where men and women attain new freedom not only from hunger, injustice, and tyranny, but from the inner coercions of greed, power-lust, and envy.

II. YOUTH AND CULTURAL CHANGE

EDITOR'S INTRODUCTION

Just how deeply cultural factors have been involved in the contemporary youth revolt is discussed at some length in this section; the following sections extend the discussion to specific cultural areas and institutions—educational, political, and economic.

In the first article, Paul Goodman, educator, social critic, and author of *Growing Up Absurd,* compares the present youth revolt to the Reformation period of the early sixteenth century. This is followed by two other selections on the religious fervor associated in part with the youth revolt or youthful return to religion, both Christian and Eastern.

Changes in life-style and morals have most often been noted by the general public in connection with the present youthful rebellion. In this connection the topic of communes as an alternative life-style is covered by Herbert A. Otto, chairman of the National Center for the Exploration of Human Potential, La Jolla, California.

The final selection offers a broad analysis of the cultural changes underway in the United States and the part our youth is playing in them. It suggests that a full-scale cultural revolution, if not more, is at hand. The author is a Frenchman, Jean-François Revel, writer and columnist for *L'Express;* his article consists of excerpts from his book *Without Marx or Jesus.*

THE NEW REFORMATION [1]

For a long time modern societies have been operating as if religion were a minor and moribund part of the scheme of

[1] From article by Paul Goodman, social critic and author of *Growing Up Absurd.* New York *Times Magazine.* p 32-3+. S. 14, '69. © 1969 by The New York Times Company. Reprinted by permission.

things. But this is unlikely. Men do not do without a system of "meanings" that everybody believes and puts his hope in even if, or especially if, he doesn't know anything about it; what Freud called a "shared psychosis," meaningful because shared, and with the power that resides in deep fantasy and longing. In advanced countries, indeed, it is science and technology themselves that have gradually, and finally triumphantly, become the system of mass faith, not disputed by various political ideologies and nationalisms that have also had religious uses.

Now this basic faith is threatened. Dissident young people are saying that science is antilife, it is a Calvinist obsession, it has been a weapon of white Europe to subjugate colored races, and scientific technology has manifestly become diabolical. Along with science, the young discredit the professions in general, and the whole notion of "disciplines" and academic learning. If these views take hold, it adds up to a crisis of belief, and the effects are incalculable. Every status and institution would be affected. Present political troubles could become endless religious wars. Here again, as in politics and morals, the worldwide youth disturbance may indicate a turning point in history and we must listen to it carefully.

Contemporary conditions of life have certainly deprived people, and especially young people, of a meaningful world in which they can act and find themselves. Many writers and the dissenting students themselves have spelled it out. For instance, in both schools and corporations, people cannot pursue their own interests or exercise initiative. Administrators are hypocrites who sell people out for the smooth operation of the system. The budget for war has grotesquely distorted reasonable social priorities. Worst of all, the authorities who make the decisions are incompetent to cope with modern times: we are in danger of extinction, the biosphere is being destroyed, two thirds of mankind are starving. Let me here go on to some other factors that demand a religious response.

There is a lapse of faith in science. Science has not produced the general happiness that people expected, and now it has fallen under the sway of greed and power; whatever its beneficent past, people fear that its further progress will do more harm than good. And rationality itself is discredited. Probably it is more significant than we like to think that intelligent young people dabble in astrology, witchcraft, psychedelic dreams, and whatever else is despised by science; in some sense they are not kidding. They need to control their fate, but they hate scientific explanations.

Every one of these young grew up since Hiroshima. They do not talk about atom bombs—not nearly so much as we who campaigned against the shelters and fallout—but the bombs explode in their dreams, as Otto Butz found in his study of collegians at San Francisco State [*To Make a Difference: A Student Look at America.* Harper. '67], and now George Dennison, in *The Lives of Children* [Random House. '69], shows that it was the same with small slum children whom he taught at the First Street School in New York. Again and again students have told me that they take it for granted they will not survive the next ten years. This is not an attitude with which to prepare for a career or to bring up a family.

Whether or not the bombs go off, human beings are becoming useless. Old people are shunted out of sight at an increasingly earlier age, young people are kept on ice till an increasingly later age. Small farmers and other technologically unemployed are dispossessed or left to rot. Large numbers are put away as incompetent or deviant. Racial minorities that cannot shape up are treated as a nuisance. Together, these groups are a large majority of the population. Since labor will not be needed much longer, there is vague talk of a future society of "leisure," but there is no thought of a kind of community in which all human beings would be necessary and valued. . . .

A special aspect of biological corruption is the spreading ugliness, filth, and tension of the environment in which the

young grow up. If Wordsworth was right—I think he was—
that children must grow up in an environment of beauty
and simple affections in order to become trusting, open, and
magnanimous citizens, then the offspring of our ghettos,
suburbs, and complicated homes have been disadvantaged, no
matter how much money there is. This lack cannot be remedied by art in the curriculum, nor by vest-pocket playgrounds,
nor by banning billboards from bigger highways. Cleaning
the river might help, but that will be the day.

Facing a Religious Crisis

If we start from the premise that the young are in a religious crisis, that they doubt there is really a nature of things,
and they are sure there is not a world for themselves, many
details of their present behavior become clearer. Alienation
is a powerful motivation, of unrest, fantasy and reckless
action. It leads, as we shall see, to religious innovation, new
sacraments to give life meaning. But it is a poor basis for
politics, including revolutionary politics. It is said that the
young dissidents never offer a constructive program. And
apart from the special cases of Czechoslovakia and Poland,
where they confront an unusually outdated system, this is
largely true. In France, China, Germany, Egypt, England, the
United States, etc., most of the issues of protest have been
immediate gut issues, and the tactics have been mainly disruptive, without coherent proposals for a better society. But
this makes for bad politics. Unless one has a program, there
is no way to persuade the other citizens, who do not have
one's gut complaints, to come along. Instead one confronts
them hostilely and they are turned off, even when they might
be sympathetic. But the confrontation is inept too, for the
alienated young cannot take other people seriously as having needs of their own; a spectacular instance was the inability of the French youth to communicate with the French
working class, in May 1968.

In Gandhian theory, the confronter aims at future community with the confronted; he will not let him continue a

course that is bad for *him,* and so he appeals to his deeper reason. But instead of this *Satyagraha,* soul force, we have seen plenty of hate. The confronted are *not* taken as human beings, but as pigs, etc. But how can the young people think of a future community when they themselves have no present world, no profession or other job in it, and no trust in other human beings? Instead, some young radicals seem to entertain the disastrous illusion that other people can be compelled by fear. This can lead only to crushing reaction.

Politics as Affirmation

All the "political" activity makes sense, however, if it is understood that it is not aimed at social reconstruction at all, but is a way of desperately affirming that they are alive and want a place in the sun. "I am a revolutionary," said Cohn-Bendit, leader of the French students in 1968, "because it is the best way of living." And young Americans pathetically and truly say that there is no other way to be taken seriously. Then it is not necessary to have a program; the right method is to act, against any vulnerable point and wherever one can rally support. The purpose is not politics but to have a movement and form a community. This is exactly what Saul Alinsky prescribed to rally outcast blacks.

And such conflictful action has indeed caused social changes. In France it was conceded by the Gaullists that "nothing would ever be the same." In the United States, the changes in social attitude during the last ten years are unthinkable without the youth action, with regard to war, the military-industrial, corporate organization and administration, the police, the blacks. When the actors have been in touch with the underlying causes of things, issues have deepened and the Movement has grown. But for the alienated, again, action easily slips into activism, and conflict is often spite and stubbornness. There is excitement and notoriety, much human suffering, and the world no better off. . . .

Yet it is noteworthy that when older people like myself are critical of the wrongheaded activism, we nevertheless al-

most invariably concede that the young are *morally* justified.
For what is the use of patience and reason when meantime
millions are being killed and starved, and when bombs . . .
are being stockpiled? Against the entrenched power responsible for these things, it might be better to do something
idiotic now than something perhaps more practical in the
long run. I don't know which is less demoralizing. . . .

And I have learned, to my disgust, that a major reason
why the young don't trust people over thirty is that they
don't understand them and are too conceited to try. Having
grown up in a world too meaningless to learn anything, they
know very little and are quick to resent it.

This is an unpleasant picture. Even so, the alienated
young have no vital alternative except to confront the Evil,
and to try to make a new way of life out of their own innards
and suffering. As they are doing. It is irrelevant to point
out that the System is not the monolith that they think and
that the majority of people are not corrupt, just brow-beaten
and confused. What is relevant is that they cannot see this,
because they do not have an operable world for themselves.
In such a case, the only advice I would dare to give them
is that which Krishna gave Arjuna: to confront with non-
attachment, to be brave and firm without hatred. (I don't
here want to discuss the question of "violence," the hatred
and disdain are far more important.) . . .

Religiously the young have been inventive, much more
than the God-is-dead theologians. They have hit on new
sacraments, physical actions to get them out of their estrange-
ment and (momentarily) break through into meaning. . . .

Religion as Strength

It is hard to describe this (or any) religiosity without
lapsing into condescending humor. Yet it is genuine and it
will, I am convinced, survive and develop—I don't know into
what. In the end it is religion that constitutes the strength
of this generation, and not, as I used to think, their morality,
political will, and common sense. Except for a few . . . I am

not impressed by their moral courage or even honesty. For all their eccentricity they are singularly lacking in personality. They do not have enough world to have much character. And they are not especially attractive as animals. But they keep pouring out a kind of metaphysical vitality.

Let me try to account for it. On the one hand, these young have an unusual amount of available psychic energy. They were brought up on antibiotics that minimized depressing chronic childhood diseases, and with post-Freudian freedom to act out early drives. Up to age six or seven, television nourished them with masses of strange images and sometimes true information—McLuhan makes a lot of sense for the kindergarten years. Long schooling would tend to make them stupid, but it has been compensated by providing the vast isolated cities of youth that the high schools and colleges essentially are, where they can incubate their own thoughts. They are sexually precocious and not inhibited by taboos. They are superficially knowledgeable. On the other hand, all this psychic energy has had little practical use.

The social environment is dehumanized. It discourages romantic love and lasting friendship. They are desperately bored because the world does not promise any fulfillment. Their knowledge gives no intellectual or poetic satisfaction. In this impasse, we can expect a ferment of new religion. As in Greek plays, impasse produces gods from the machine. For a long time we did not hear of the symptoms of adolescent religious conversion, once as common in the United States as in all other places and ages. Now it seems to be recurring as a mass phenomenon.

Without doubt the religious young are in touch with something historical, but I don't think they understand what it is. Let me quote from an editorial in *New Seminary News,* the newsletter of dissident seminarians of the Pacific School of Religion in Berkeley: "What we confront (willingly or not we are thrust into it) is a time of disintegration of a dying civilization and the emergence of a new one." This seems to envisage something like the instant decline of the

Roman Empire and they, presumably, are like the Christians about to build, rapidly, another era. But there are no signs that this is the actual situation.

It would mean, for instance, that our scientific technology, civil law, professions, universities, etc., are about to vanish from the earth and be replaced by something entirely different. This is a fantasy of alienated minds. Nobody behaves as if civilization would vanish, and nobody acts as if there were a new dispensation. Nobody is waiting patiently in the catacombs and the faithful have not withdrawn into the desert. Neither the Yippies nor the New Seminarians nor any other exalted group have produced anything that is the least bit miraculous. Our civilization may well destroy itself with its atom bombs or something else, but then we do not care what will emerge, if anything.

But the actual situation *is* very like 1510, when Luther went to Rome, the eve of the Reformation. There is everywhere protest, revaluation, attack on the Establishment. The protest is international. There is a generation gap. (Luther himself was all of 34 when he posted his ninety-five theses in 1517, but Melanchthon was 20, Bucer 26, Münzer 28, Jonas 24; the Movement consisted of undergraduates and junior faculty.) And the thrust of protest is not to give up science, technology, and civil institutions, but to purge them, humanize them, decentralize them, change the priorities, and stop the drain of wealth.

These were, of course, exactly the demands of the March 4 [1969] nationwide teach-in on science, initiated by the dissenting professors of the Massachusetts Institute of Technology. This and the waves of other teach-ins, ads and demonstrations have been the voices not of the alienated, of people who have no world, but of protestants, people deep in the world who will soon refuse to continue under the present auspices because they are not viable. It is populism permeated by moral and professional unease. What the young have done is to make it finally religious, to force the

grown-ups to recognize that they too are threatened with
meaninglessness. . . .

New Protestant Sects

Viewed as incidents of a reformation, as attempts to
purge themselves and recover a lost integrity, the various
movements of the alienated young are easily recognizable as
characteristic protestant sects, intensely self-conscious. The
dissenting seminarians of the Pacific School of Religion do
not intend to go off to primitive love feasts in a new heaven
and new earth, but to form their own Free University; that is,
they are Congregationalists. The shaggy hippies are not nature children as they claim, but self-conscious Adamites trying to naturalize Sausalito and the East Village. Heads are
Pentecostals or Children of Light. Those who spindle IBM
cards and throw the dean down the stairs are Iconoclasts.
Those who want Student Power, a say in the rules and curriculum, mean to deny infant baptism; they want to make up
their own minds, like Henry Dunster, the first president of
Harvard. Radicals who live among the poor and try to organize them are certainly intent on social change, but they
are also trying to find themselves again. The support of the
black revolt by white middle-class students is desperately like
Anabaptism, but God grant that we can do better than the
Peasants' War. These analogies are not fanciful; when authority is discredited, there is a pattern in the return of the repressed. A better scholar could make a longer list; but the
reason I here spell it out is that, perhaps, some young person will suddenly remember that history was about something.

Naturally, traditional churches are themselves in transition. On college campuses and in bohemian neighborhoods,
existentialist Protestants and Jews and updating Catholics
have gone along with the political and social activism and,
what is probably more important, they have changed their
own moral, esthetic and personal tone. On many campuses,
the chaplains provide the only official forum for discussions

of sex, drugs and burning draft cards. Yet it seems to me
that, in their zeal for relevance, they are badly failing in
their chief duty to the religious young: to be professors of
theology. . . .

The young are hotly metaphysical—but alas, boringly so,
because they don't know much, have no language to express
their intuitions, and repeat every old fallacy. If the chaplains
would stop looking in the conventional places where God is
dead, and would explore the actualities where perhaps He
is alive, they might learn something and have something to
teach.

FOLLOWERS OF JESUS [2]

WANTED
Jesus Christ

Alias: The Messiah, The Son of
God, King of Kings, Lord of
Lords, Prince of Peace, etc.

Notorious leader of an underground liberation
movement

Wanted for the following charges:
—Practicing medicine, winemaking and food
distribution without a license
—Interfering with businessmen in the temple
—Associating with known criminals, radicals,
subversives, prostitutes and street people
—Claiming to have the authority to make peo-
ple into God's children

Appearance: Typical hippie type—long hair,
beard, robe, sandals

Hangs around slum areas, few rich friends,
often sneaks out into the desert

[2] From "The New Rebel Cry: Jesus Is Coming!" *Time.* 97:56-63. Je. 21,
'71. Reprinted by permission from *Time,* the Weekly Newsmagazine; © Time
Inc.

> *Beware:* This man is extremely dangerous. His
> insidiously inflammatory message is particu-
> larly dangerous to young people who haven't
> been taught to ignore him yet. He changes men
> and claims to set them free.
>
> *WARNING: HE IS STILL AT LARGE!*

He is indeed. As the words of this Wanted poster from
a Christian underground newspaper demonstrate, Jesus is
alive and well and living in the radical spiritual fervor of a
growing number of young Americans who have proclaimed
an extraordinary religious revolution in His name. Their
message: the Bible is true, miracles happen, God really did
so love the world that He gave it His only begotten Son. . . .

It is a startling development for a generation that has
been constantly accused of tripping out or copping out with
sex, drugs and violence. Now, embracing the most persistent
symbol of purity, selflessness and brotherly love in the history of Western man, they are afire with a Pentecostal passion for sharing their new vision with others. Fresh-faced,
wide-eyed young girls and earnest young men badger businessmen and shoppers on Hollywood Boulevard, near the
Lincoln Memorial, in Dallas, in Detroit and in Wichita
"witnessing" for Christ with breathless exhortations. Christian coffeehouses have opened in many cities, signaling their
faith even in their names: The Way Word in Greenwich
Village, the Catacombs in Seattle, I Am in Spokane. A strip
joint has been converted to a "Christian nightclub" in San
Antonio. Communal "Christian houses" are multiplying
like loaves and fishes for youngsters hungry for homes, many
reaching out to the troubled with round-the-clock telephone
hot lines. Bibles abound: whether the cherished, fur-covered
King James Version or scruffy, back-pocket paperbacks, they
are invariably well-thumbed and often memorized. "It's like
a glacier," says Jesus-rock singer Larry Norman, twenty-
four. "It's growing and there's no stopping it.". . .

Some of the fascination for Jesus among the young may simply be belated hero worship of a fellow rebel, the first great martyr to the cause of peace and brotherhood. Not so, however, for the vast majority in the Jesus movement. If any one mark clearly identifies them it is their total belief in an awesome, supernatural Jesus Christ, not just a marvelous man who lived 2,000 years ago but a living God who is both Saviour and Judge, the ruler of their destinies. Their lives revolve around the necessity for an intense personal relationship with that Jesus, and the belief that such a relationship should condition every human life. . . .

Aims of the Jesus Revolution

The Jesus revolution rejects not only the material values of conventional America but the prevailing wisdom of American theology. Success often means an impersonal and despiritualized life that increasingly finds release in sexploration, status, alcohol and conspicuous consumption. Christianity—or at least the brand of it preached in prestige seminaries, pulpits and church offices over recent decades—has emphasized an immanent God of nature and social movement, not the new movement's transcendental, personal God who comes to earth in the person of Jesus, in the lives of individuals, in miracles. The Jesus revolution, in short, is one that denies the virtues of the Secular City and heaps scorn on the message that God was ever dead. Why?

The enthusiasm is not universal. By no means a majority of the young, or their elders, are soldiers in the revolution—any more than they were flower children or acid trippers. Some call the Jesus movement a fad or just another bad trip. Is it? Is the growing fascination with Jesus a passing, adolescent infatuation? There are obvious fad aspects: Jesus shirts (JESUS IS MY LORD), bumper stickers (SMILE, GOD LOVES YOU), posters, buttons (THE MESSIAH IS THE MESSAGE), and, inevitably, a Jesus-People wristwatch. Some followers are affecting a Christ couture: white pants and tunics, Mexican-peasant style. There are *de rigueur* catch phrases: endless

"Praise Gods" and "Bless Yous." There is even a "Jesus cheer"—"Give me a J, give me an E . . ." Rapidly catching on is the Jesus-People "sign," a raised arm with clenched fist, the index finger pointed heavenward, to indicate Jesus as the "one way" to salvation. "If it is a fad," says evangelist Billy Graham, "I welcome it." . . .

The movement is apart from, rather than against, established religion; converts often speak disparagingly of the blandness or hypocrisy of their former churches, but others work comfortably as a supplementary, revitalizing force of change from within. The movement, in fact, is one of considerable flexibility and vitality, drawing from three vigorous spiritual streams that, despite differences in dress, manner and theology, effectively reinforce one another.

The Jesus People, also known as Street Christians or Jesus Freaks, are the most visible; it is they who have blended the counterculture and conservative religion. Many trace their beginnings to the 1967 flower era in San Francisco, but there were almost simultaneous stirrings in other areas. Some, but by no means all, affect the hippie style; others have forsworn it as part of their new lives.

The Straight People, by far the largest group, are mainly active in interdenominational, evangelical campus and youth movements. Once merely an arm of evangelical Protestantism, they are now more ecumenical—a force almost independent of the churches that spawned them. Most of them are Middle America, campus types: neatly coiffed hair and Sears, Roebuck clothes styles.

The Catholic Pentecostals, like the Jesus People, emerged unexpectedly and dramatically in 1967. Publicly austere but privately ecstatic in their devotion to the Holy Spirit, they remain loyal to the church but unsettle some in the hierarchy. In a sense they are following the lead of mainstream Protestant Neo-Pentecostals, who have been leading charismatic renewal movements in their own churches for a decade.

Together, all three movements may number in the hundreds of thousands nationally, conceivably many more, but

any figure is a guess. The Catholic Pentecostals, often meeting in the privacy of members' homes, may number 10,000,
but some observers believe that they could easily be three
times that. . . .

Spreading the Word

The revolutionary word is also spread by a growing, literally free Jesus press that now numbers some fifty newspapers across the country. Donations are apparently enough
to print 65,000 copies of *Right On!* in Berkeley and 400,000
copies of the *Hollywood Free Paper*, the movement's largest.
Now Berkeley's CWLF [Christian World Liberation Front]
is hoping to start a Jesus news service. There is much to report, in all parts of the United States. Items:

At First Baptist Church in Houston, youth-minded Pastor
Bisagno, thirty-seven, brought in Evangelist Hoag to recruit
the young in a week-long revival. Hoag traveled from school
to school with his plea, and 11,000 young people stepped
forward at Bisagno's church to declare themselves for Jesus.
Now the first few pews at First Baptist are reserved for the
youngsters. While the rest of the congregation mumble their
amens, the kids puctuate Bisagno's sermons with yells of
"Outta sight, man, bee-yoo-ti-ful."

In Chicago's Grant Park bandshell, street evangelist
Arthur Blessitt last month warmed up a crowd of nearly
one thousand with a lusty Jesus cheer, then led them off on
a parade through the Loop, gathering people as they went.
"Chicago police, we love you!" they shouted to cops along
the route. "Jesus loves you!" Blessitt also passed a box
through the crowd, asking for a special contribution: drugs.
The box came back filled with marijuana, pills and LSD; it
was turned over to the flabbergasted cops. . . .

On a cul-de-sac beach at Corona del Mar, California, the
Reverend Chuck Smith recently held another of the mass
baptisms that have made his Calvary Chapel at Santa Ana
famous. Under a setting sun, several hundred converts waded
into the cold Pacific, patiently waiting their turn for the rite.
On the cliffs above, hundreds more watched. Most of the

baptized were young, tanned and casual in cut-off blue jeans, pullovers and even an occasional bikini. A freshly dunked teen-ager, water streaming from her tie-dyed shirt, threw her arms around a woman and cried, "Mother, I love you!" A teen-age drug user who had been suffering from recurring unscheduled trips suddenly screamed, "My flashbacks are gone!" As the baptisms ended, the crowd slowly climbed a narrow stairway up the cliff, singing a moving Lord's Prayer in the twilight. . . .

The Role of Drugs

The path to the movement, in or out of communes, is often littered with drugs. The Way, an eighteen-year-old, offbeat and minor theological group now virtually taken over and greatly expanded by the Jesus People, has two staunch supporters in Wichita, Kansas: prominent lawyer Dale Fair and his wife, who got involved when a Way evangelist helped their daughter off drugs. One of the San Francisco pioneers, Ted Wise, has been so successful with drug cures that he now has a new clinic in Menlo Park. Washington, D.C., movement leader Denny Flanders tells drug users: "You can use drugs after Jesus, but you won't need them. If you become Christians, this is what has to happen." Convert Connie Sue McCartney, twenty-one, of Louisiana, describes how "the devil came to me" and tempted her to return to speed. She had kept some in hand just in case, but she was up to the temptation: "I took it, flushed it down the john in the name of the Father, the Son and the Holy Ghost." Former Houston speed freak Terry Vincent says: "Man, God turned me around from the darkness to the light. That's all I know. That is all I want to know." . . .

Gospel Crusaders

Another major part of the Jesus movement is the highly organized, interdenominational youth movement of the established churches—a sort of person-to-person counterpart of mass-rally evangelism. Though they have been around for decades, supported by local congregations and generous pri-

vate contributors, they are finding a huge new growth in the
Jesus revolution.

The biggest of the straight groups is Campus Crusade for
Christ, twenty-year-old soul child of former businessman
Bill Bright. He still means business: this year's budget is
$12 million, and by next month he will have three thousand
full-time staffers on 450 campuses. Inter-Varsity Christian
Fellowship is a different breed of campus evangelism—more
intellectual, more socially concerned—but it has no lack of
gospel zeal. It conducted a missionary convention at the
University of Illinois last December [1970] that drew 12,000,
probably the largest college religious meeting in North
American history. Young Life, founded in 1941, reaches its
audience with 1,300 clubs, US and foreign. Youth for Christ
began business a few years later with a lanky young evangelist named Billy Graham; it is now in 2,700 high schools. . . .

Catholic Pentecostalism? The name is an apparent contradiction in terms: an austere and ritualized church coupled with a movement characterized in its early years by
unleashed emotionalism—eye-rolling ecstasies, shouting,
jumping, even rolling on the floor. Classic Pentecostalism
has since toned down markedly, but it can still put even an
unwary Catholic into theological shock. Jerry Harvey, who
helped start the growing Catholic Pentecostal group in the
San Diego area, once invited some Protestant Pentecostalists
"to show us how to do it their way. The poor nuns who were
there actually turned white."

The Catholic establishment in the United States has not
blanched, but it has not turned red with enthusiasm, even
though Pope John XXIII himself called upon the Holy Spirit
to "renew your wonders in this, our day, as by a new Pente-
cost." An inquiry conducted in the United States for the
National Conference of Catholic Bishops did find, however,
that Pentecostal experience often "leads to a better understanding of the role the Christian plays in the Church." The
evidence supports that finding. One Los Angeles priest says
that he has stayed in the priesthood because of the "tremen-

dous peace" he found in the renewal movement. Dr. James McFadden, forty, dean of Michigan's pioneering School of Natural Resources, is a Catholic for whom religion "never had an experiential dimension. It was intellectual, the distant Christ of history." But he found "extraordinary" love among the three hundred Pentecostals of the university's Word of God community. "Very few people live as though there really is a God who sent His only son to be a man."

The Pentecostalist fervor has been growing rapidly. From its beginnings at Duquesne University in 1967 ... the movement spread to Notre Dame and Ann Arbor, which have been major forces in it ever since. But there are sizable numbers elsewhere. On Trinity Sunday ... [in 1971], 450 Catholic Pentecostals held a "Day of Renewal" at St. Theresa Catholic Church in San Diego; ... [in June 1971] 3,000 Catholic Pentecostals from all over the country ... [were] expected to gather at Notre Dame for their annual national conference.

Despite the evidence of enriched religiosity, there is enough in the Catholic Pentecostalist movement to account for the hierarchy's reserve. It is casually ecumenical. Its speaking in tongues—glossolalia, a form of prayer that is usually a babbling nonlanguage—is done quietly, but it is done. The Pentecostals have the unhappy faculty of offending both liberals and conservatives in Catholicism: liberals resent their insistent orthodox theology, conservatives their communal life-style.

Passive Versus Ecstatic Believers

The confident conviction of the Jesus revolution (we have the answer; the rest of the world is wrong) irritates many, whatever branch of the movement it radiates from. Dan Herr, publisher of the progressive Catholic bimonthly *The Critic,* calls Catholic Pentecostalism "spiritual chic." Some who turn off may be expressing the natural and inevitable resentment of the passive believer against the ecstatic believer. . . .

Others criticize the absolutism of the Jesus revolution and the complete dependency it creates in some of its adherents. Jean Houston, director of the Foundation for Mind Research in New York City, finds that while "the Jesus trip gives them rich expectations and more rigid values, they also suffer a narrowing of conceptual vision. They become obsessed." She cites the case of one girl who turned to the Jesus movement after a severe family crisis. "She escaped her guilt and horror, but it had the effect of a psychological and social lobotomy. Where once she had been superbly inquisitive, she now could relate things only in terms of her religion—but she had a focal point for all her energy." Sociologist Andrew Greeley calls Catholic Pentecostalism the "most vital movement in Catholicism right now," but warns that it could become "just pure emotion, even a form of hysteria." The Reverend George Peters of the United Presbyterian Church says of the Jesus People: "I see dangers. This biblical literalism. The kids quote verses without understanding them to prove a point. I thought we'd outgrown that. I'd like to see some kind of form."

The established churches may not have the luxury of choosing the youngsters' style. Whatever the excesses or shortcomings of the Jesus revolution, organized religion cannot afford to lose the young in numbers or enthusiasm. In parts of the movement, of course, the churches are not losing them; indeed, they are gaining zealots. Catholic Pentecostals and straight evangelicals are already having an effect; if organized religion embraced the Jesus People as well, the greening effect on the churches could be considerable. Theologian Martin Marty of the University of Chicago Divinity School feels that the Jesus People, frustrated by a complex society that will not yield to their single-minded devotion, may well disband in disarray. But even Marty says: "Five years from now you may have some better Presbyterians because of their participation in the Jesus movement." And the Reverend Robert Terwilliger of New York City's Trinity Institute says longingly: "There is a revival of religion everywhere—except in the church."

WINDS FROM THE EAST [3]

Several serious thinkers have recently attempted to understand the new religious mind of young America, and I think what is most instructive about these efforts is the way they have failed. One must hasten to add that the problem is formidably difficult. The turning of our young people to mysticism and Eastern religion is a phenomenon so various and pervasive, and seems to touch on so many sides of the present crisis of civilization, that one may well despair of grasping its true significance. How much is only the flash of youthful rebellion? the love of anything alien at a moment in time when familiar values are drained of their energy? And how many among us are able to distinguish between the real content of these new teachings and what seems to be the extravagance of their followers? We may have one or two thoughts about Zen, for example, but what or who is Meher Baba, Subud, Krishnamurti, Vajrayana Buddhism or Sufism? Are we obliged to try to understand these teachings at their source, or is it enough to pass judgment on the young people who proclaim them?

In a recent article in the Saturday Review . . . Marcia Cavell, a professor of philosophy at NYU [New York University], wove her case against the new religions around the pronouncements of Charles Manson. "Guilt, as Manson says, is a figment of the imagination. One remembers that Satan's greatest snare has always been the promise of . . . 'paradise now.' A lesson to be learned from the Manson cult, I think, is that dreams of heaven often pave the road to hell." Elsewhere in her article, she admits that her judgments about Eastern religion are those of a superficial observer, but the clear implication is that one does not need to be more than superficial about Eastern teachings to see where they are leading the young.

This is the problem for many of us. It is hard to resist lumping the younger generation's enthusiasm about Oriental

[3] Article by Jacob Needleman, author of *The New Religions. Commonweal.* 94:188-90. Ap. 30, '71. Reprinted by permission.

religion together with drug abuse, occultism and witchcraft with all of its often childish, bizarre or even heinous applications. John Passmore, another philosopher, writing in *Encounter,* sees this "new mysticism" as little more than a puerile urge for instant gratification and feels no need to cite any writer more penetrating than Timothy Leary. "Zen Buddhism," Passmore claims, "positively prides itself on its moral and political irresponsibility." With that, he hastens to remind us that various Nazis also found their inspiration in "mysticism," and then he notes that "Contemporary hippy-mystics are often convinced that they are the recipients of a special divine grace. They display that fanaticism, 'aristocratic' pride and antinomianism which Wesley so feared, setting themselves above all kinds of moral restraint."

At the other extreme, Charles A. Reich in *The Greening of America* sees this new "consciousness" as the great hope for America and the whole Western world. It offers, he says, "the sensual beauty of a creative, loving unrepressed life." Unlike Christianity, which, according to Reich, has become just another form of future-oriented repression, the ideals of the young are read as a force for a complete and immediate transformation.

Only Theodore Roszak, in *The Making of a Counter Culture,* strikes for a sense of discrimination between the counterfeit answers and real questions that this movement of the young brings to us. It is certainly no criticism of Roszak to say that his approach remains bound to Western psychological and sociological categories; it is his notable achievement to have stayed within those categories and yet to have communicated through them a hard sense of the religious that is new to modern man. But even Roszak leaves us with the understanding that the value of the "mystical" lies in its power to satisfy certain ordinary desires of men.

None of these writers ever seriously questions his own understanding of the nature and function of religious training. Yet to provoke such questioning can be the most immediately significant result of the so-called "spiritual revolution." Without this self-questioning, we shall continue to be so fascinated by passing judgment on the young that we may never see the real meaning of what these new teachings can bring us.

In my opinion—and space does not permit me to offer a thorough justification of it—even the harshest critics of our young "mystics" fail to see how enormous is the gap between the practice of a spiritual discipline and the religious activities of these young people. Because they—because we—do not see this gap, because we habitually underestimate the depth of real religious practice and the quality of human effort which it demands, we are blind to the positive value which this movement may possess. This value may be nothing at all like what its young proponents imagine it is; it may be infinitesimal compared to what they claim for themselves. Yet, for all that, it may be real—very small, but real. Does our way of life have even that these days?

New Dimensions

In writing my book, *The New Religions,* I came to the conclusion that these Eastern teachings have brought a new dimension of urgency to our whole society's inability to grasp the purpose of work in the growth and transformation of man. I also tried to show that the Eastern teachings, in reviving the ideas of religious *discipline,* may bring back the sense of the gradations of religious life. For while the all-or-nothing principle of faith communicates the ever-present exigency of the search for God, the equally important principles of compassion (in Buddhism) and catholicity (in Christianity) recognize the great forces of resistance that operate upon man in this search.

Here I can list only one or two other conclusions which my study brought home to me about the future importance of this phenomenon:

—The revitalization of the idea that in a spiritual discipline what we call moral rules are really instruments for the production of certain experiences which make the seeker directly aware of the need for transcendent inner help in the governance of his life. Thus, the external *Thou Shalt* may be organically displaced by an internal understanding of the *reasons* for "sanity" and "balance" in life.

—The Eastern cosmic scheme brings back the idea of *levels* of intelligence and consciousness in the universe. And since man in this scheme is an image of the universe, a real basis is provided for us to ask: at what level of consciousness do *I* exist? and: at what level of consciousness *may* I exist? This then leads to the idea of inner evolution as a result of spiritual work.

These are only a few of the ways these new religions may alter our thinking about man in the universe. The point I wish to make now is one that is only implicit in my book, but which seems to need explicit formulation if we are to understand the value of our young people's new religiosity.

What I am going to suggest may sound very odd to all parties concerned, but it seems to me that the great value of this new "religiosity" is that through it our young people are able to *entertain great ideas*. Surely one aspect of our present crisis as a civilization is that the transcendent ideas which once defined our lives have grown small in our minds. They have become choked and stunted by subjective opinion, interpretation and an impatience to "test" every idea by instantly applying it to solve the overwhelming external problems of human society. Thus we have converted the great ideas of our civilization into mere ideals, which is to say that we no longer know how to take the time to understand ideas before hastily acting upon them.

We no longer believe in the value of merely entertaining ideas, of living with them without expecting anything of them. I think this prevents them from becoming a real force in our lives, something that could help to shape our aims for ourselves and for society. In any event, it is obvious that the followers of the great religious paths come to these paths with more intense an aim than most of us have, whether we are young or old.

A spiritual path thus requires a certain preparation of the mind. I do not think we have that preparation, and neither do our young people. Yet this explosion of interest in the mystical may for many be the first step in such preparation. If so, it is surely mistaken of us either to condemn it by likening it to some of the ways we ourselves have misused religious ideas or naively to extol it by putting it in a class with the great spiritual paths of mankind.

I recently saw the preliminary rushes of a film being produced in California which deals with this whole phenomenon. The makers of the film took their cameras to these groups and teachers without any pretense of judging their authenticity, and a very broad spectrum is thereby revealed: from the silence and seriousness of the young Zen Buddhists in their California monastery to the glazed eyes and dreamy smiles of naked men and women being led in meditation by a man who calls himself a Sufi master. I had previously witnessed much of this first-hand during the writing of my own book, but what made the evening so instructive was that the film-makers had also gone to India to interview some religious leaders. Sandwiched amid all that footage of gurus speaking about "oneness with God" were a few brief frames taken inside some temple of a gaunt *fakir,* his emaciated arms twisted behind him, his legs folded beneath him, his tongue stretched out and down its full length, and his wide-open eyes staring unblinkingly into the brilliant mercury lamp. He did not move a muscle, and one knew he had kept that posture for longer than one would dare imagine.

To the educated Westerner, this fakir would epitomize much that is hateful about religion: the apparent denial of the body, the violence to natural impulses, the withdrawal from life and men. Yet judge it as one may, one instantly recognized *effort.* He was on a *path,* demanding of him a scale of effort which must strike us as staggering. And we must assume that a comparable quality of effort is one way or another required by all psychospiritual disciplines, whether it be in the obedience of a Christian monk, the Herculean pondering of a *jnana-yogi*, or in the transcendent flexibility of a Sufi searching for a new consciousness in the midst of the pulls and shocks of ordinary life.

Opening Their Minds

The contrast is unmistakable between the rigors of a *path* and the activity of our young people. But having sensed even a little of this contrast, we can be freer in our minds to allow them their attraction to the religions of the East, and see it, in part, as a process of opening their minds to new ideas. When we see a group of beardless youths robed in yellow, tendering alms-bowls and chanting "Hare Krishna" along Fifth Avenue, need we assume that they are either following or degrading the path of *bhakti-yoga,* a discipline that demands a lifelong struggle against all the powerful emotions that scatter our lives into a thousand pieces? May we not rather see them, some of them at any rate, as *entertaining* the idea of service as a method of psychological change? They may strike us as absurd or offensive—perhaps because we feel they are only playing at being monks. But what if most of them are only playing? How much of the sorrow of our civilization is due to the fact that *we* do not entertain ideas before acting on them—persuading, institutionalizing, making war in their name?

The phenomenon of "the new religions" therefore points to a flaw in our society of which we may have been unaware: namely, that we lack a means by which new thought can enter into our lives without inner or outer violence. We are unaware of it, because we do not believe it even to be possible. We look for ideas to come at us with proofs, arguments and, above all, with clear prescriptions for action. We seek to be persuaded, compelled or even seduced by ideas: witness our forms of art, our methods of philosophy and the manner in which we have tied scientific speculation to technology. But perhaps it is impossible for transcendent ideas—ideas that come from a more fundamental level of intelligence—to take root in this way.

The new religions, being a call to direct experience, nevertheless compel us to think in a new way about our situation in the universe; warning us against mere thought, they stir our thought. And it is very interesting how thought that has been shaken is no longer "mere" thought, how the shocked intellect is no longer the isolated intellect. I think it can be said that a religion which does not astonish the mind cannot change human life. Conversely, a mind which is insulated against shocks cannot understand the sense of religion. We have grown so accustomed to denigrating religion because of its sentimentality or its comforting fables that we are somewhat at a loss when a religion comes along which has none of these aspects.

So, while admitting the possibility that our young "mystics" are deceiving themselves, admitting that they may often confuse intense experience (whether from drugs, radical politics, sex, or something else) with psychological growth, admitting even that none of them may be able to assimilate the teachings of a few truly extraordinary spiritual masters who have come to the West—admitting all this as possibly true, the outstanding question remains whether we who may not be drawn to these new religions are necessarily more intelligent than these young people. By "intelligence" I mean: the ability to place oneself in the face of great ideas which surpass our understanding, but which demand our best thought.

COMMUNES: THE ALTERNATIVE LIFE-STYLE [4]

Over the past few years, the commune movement has grown at an unprecedented and explosive rate, and there is every indication that this is only the initial phase of a trend that is bound to have far-reaching implications for the function and structure of our contemporary society. Some tra-

[4] From article by Herbert A. Otto, chairman of the National Center for the Exploration of Human Potential, La Jolla, California. *Saturday Review.* 54:16-21. Ap. 24, '71. Copyright © 1971 Saturday Review, Inc. Reprinted by permission.

ditional institutions are already beginning to feel the impact of this explosive growth.

The commune movement has passed far beyond its contemporary origins in hippie tribalism and can no longer be described as a movement for youth exclusively. There are a rapidly growing number of communes composed of persons in their mid-twenties to upper thirties. A source at the National Institute of Health has estimated that more than 3,000 urban communes are now in operation. This figure closely corresponds to a recent New York *Times* inquiry that uncovered 2,000 communes in thirty-four states.

Certain common viewpoints, almost a *Weltanschauung,* are shared by members of the contemporary commune movement. First, there is a deep respect and reverence for nature and the ecological system. There is a clear awareness that 70 percent of the population lives on 1 percent of the land and that this 1 percent is severely polluted, depressingly ugly, and psychologically overcrowded. Commune members generally believe that a very small but politically influential minority with no respect for the ecological system or the beauty of nature exploits all of the land for its own gain. Surpassing the credo of conservationist organizations, most commune members stress the rehabilitation of *all* lands and the conservation of *all* natural resources for the benefit of *all* the people.

Anti-Establishment sentiment is widespread, as is the conviction that a change in social and institutional structures is needed to halt man's dehumanization and to give him an opportunity to develop his potential. Considerable divergence of opinion exists on how social change is to be brought about, but there is general agreement that the commune movement contributes to change by bringing man closer to himself and to his fellow man through love and understanding.

Communes widely accept the idea that life is meant to be fundamentally joyous and that this is of the essence in doing, and enjoying, what you want to do—"doing your thing."

Work in this context becomes a form of joyous self-expression and self-realization. Many commune members believe that existence can be an almost continuous source of joyous affirmation. They usually trace the absence of authentic joy in contemporary society to the confining nature of many of our social institutions, the stifling of spontaneity, and the preponderance of game playing and of devitalized artificial ways of relating socially.

A strong inner search for the meaning of one's own life, an openness and willingness to communicate and encounter, coupled with a compelling desire for personal growth and development, are hallmarks of the movement. A strong anti-materialistic emphasis prevails; it decries a consumption-oriented society. In many communes, what does not fit into a room becomes commune property. A considerable number of communes aim for the type of self-sufficiency through which they can exist independently of "the system."

There is a strong trend toward ownership of land and houses by communes. Leasing arrangements have not proved satisfactory; in too many instances, landlords have canceled leases when community pressures were exerted. The non-urban communes I have visited are strongly aware of ecological factors, and, because of this, members usually had consulted with local health authorities concerning the construction and placement of sanitary facilities. Among the urban communes, toilet and bath facilities were in most cases short of the demand.

Marked preferences for vegetarianism and for organically grown food are noticeable in the commune movement. Many individual members also experiment with different health diets. Roughly 40 percent of the communes I visited were vegetarian; 20 percent served both vegetarian and nonvegetarian meals. The remainder served meat when available—usually two to six times a week. This third group, although not vegetarian by choice, liked their vegetarian meals and expressed very little craving for meat. Whenever possible, communes concentrate on growing and raising their own food. An estimated 60 percent of the urban communes are now purchasing some or most of their supplies from health-food stores or similar sources.

Not surprisingly, the commune has become the repository of repressed man's erotic fantasy. I was continuously told that visitors who come not to learn and understand but to peek and ogle invariably ask two questions: "Who sleeps with whom?" And, "Do you have group sex?" There appears to be much fantasizing by outsiders about the sex life in communes.

Although there is considerable sexual permissiveness, I found a high degree of pairing with a strong tendency toward interpersonal commitment in a continuing relationship. Nudism is casual and accepted, as is the development of a healthy sensuality, and natural childbirth, preferably within the commune, is encouraged. ...

The research team of Larry and Joan Constantine has studied multilateral (group) marriage for the past three years. They have written and published more studies in this area than other behavioral scientists, but have found only one commune practicing group marriage. ...

Interest in spiritual development is a dominant theme in most communes. Study of and acquaintance with Eastern and Western mystics and religious philosophies is widespread. Religiosity and denominationalism were seldom encountered. On the other hand, I was struck by the deep commitment to spiritual search of so many members in all the communes I visited. Many members were trying different forms of meditation, and books on Eastern religions and mysticism were prominent on shelves.

Doing Your Own Thing

I find that although there is some overlapping of functions and categories, a number of distinct types of communes can be recognized and are found in operation.

The Agricultural Subsistence Commune: The main thrust is to farm or till the soil (mostly organic farming) so that the land will provide most, if not all, needs and make the commune independent and self-supporting. Many of these communes cultivate such specialized crops as organically grown grain, vegetables, and other produce, which are then sold to health-food stores, health-food wholesalers, or supermarkets.

The Nature Commune: Emphasis is on supporting the ecological system and on the enjoyment of nature. Buildings and gardening or farming plots are designed to fit into the landscape to preserve its natural beauty. Everyone "does his own thing," and economic support for subsistence usually comes from such varied sources as sale of produce and handicrafts, wages from part-time work, welfare support, etc.

The Craft Commune: One or several crafts, such as weaving, pottery making, or carpentry (including construction or work on buildings outside the commune), occupy the interest of members. They often spend considerable blocks of time enjoying the exercise of their craft with the income contributed to the commune. Many of the craft communes sell directly to the consumer as a result of local, regional, or sometimes national advertisements and publicity. Profit margins vary since the vast majority of such communes do not subscribe to the amassing of profits as the primary aim of their enterprise. Included in this category are the multimedia communes that specialize in light shows, video tape, and film making.

The Spiritual/Mystical Commune: The ongoing spiritual development of members is recognized to be of primary importance. There may be adherence to a religious system, such as Buddhism, Sufism, or Zen, and a teacher or guru may be involved. Studies of various texts and mystical works, use of rituals, a number of forms of meditation (such as transcendental or Zen meditation), and spontaneous spiritual celebrations play key roles in the life of the commune. Several of these communes also describe themselves as Christian and have a strong spiritual, but not denominational emphasis.

The Denominational Commune: There is a religious emphasis with membership restricted to those of a particular denomination. Examples are the Episcopalian Order of St. Michael, in Crown Point, Indiana, and the Catholic Worker Farm, in Tivoli, New York.

The Church-sponsored Commune: Such a commune may be originated or sponsored by a church. There is usually a religious emphasis, but denominationalism is not stressed.

The Political Commune: Members subscribe to or share a common ideology. They may identify themselves as anarchists, socialists, pacifists, etc. Emphasis is on the communal living experience with others sharing the same viewpoint. This is seen as fostering the individual's political development. The commune is rarely engaged in direct social action in opposition to the Establishment.

The Political Action Commune: Members are committed and practicing political activists (or activists-in-training) for the purpose of changing the social system. Classes are conducted, strategy formulated and carried out. The commune may be identified with a minority cause or be interested in organizing an industry, community, or ghetto neighborhood. It often identifies itself by the single word *revolutionary.*

The Service Commune: The main goal is social service. Emphasis is on organizing communities, helping people to plan and carry out community projects, offering professional or case-aide services, etc. Some of these communes include members from the helping professions. There are several such communes in the Philadelphia and New York ghettos; another example is the Federation of Communities, which services several locations in the Appalachians.

The Art Commune: Artists from different fields or the same field come together to share in the stimulating climate of communal artistic creativity. As compared with the craft commune, members of the art commune are often painters, sculptors, or poets, who usually sell their art works independently rather than collectively. There are poetry and street theater communes in Berkeley and San Francisco.

The Teaching Commune: Emphasis is on training and developing people who are able both to live and to teach others according to a particular system of techniques and methods. Communes whose purpose or mainstay is to conduct a school or schools also fall into this category.

The Group Marriage Commune: Although members may be given the freedom to join in the group marriage or not, the practice of group marriage plays an important and often central role in the life of the commune. All adults are considered to be parents of the members' children.

The Homosexual Commune: Currently found in large urban areas, with admission restricted to homophiles. The aim of these communes is to afford individuals who share a common way of life an opportunity to live and communicate together and to benefit from the economies of a communal living arrangement. Some of the communes subscribe to the principles of the homophile liberation movement. . . .

The Growth-centered Commune: The main focus is on helping members to grow as persons, to actualize their potential. There are ongoing group sessions; sometimes professionals are asked to lead these. The commune continues to seek out new experiences and methods designed to develop the potentialities of its members.

The Mobile, or Gypsy, Commune: This is a caravan, usually on the move. Cars, buses, and trucks provide both transportation and living quarters. Members usually include artists, a rock group, or a light-show staff. The mobile commune often obtains contributions from "happenings" or performances given in communities or on college campuses.

The Street, or Neighborhood, Commune: Several of these communes often are on the same street or in the same neighborhood. Ownership of property is in the hands of commune members or friendly and sympathetic neighbors. Basically the idea is of a free enclave or free community. For example, in a recent New York *Times* article, Albert Solnit, chief of advance planning for California's Marin County, was reported at work "on a city of 20,000 for those who wish to live communally." Several neighborhood or city communes are in the planning stage, but none to my knowledge has as yet been established.

Communes: the Major Problems

Among the major problems faced by all communes are those involving authority and structure. Ideally, there is no one telling anyone else what to do; directions are given by those best qualified to do a job. In practice, strong personalities in the communes assume responsibility for what happens, and there is a tendency toward the emergence of mother and father figures. There are, however, a clear awareness of this problem and continuing efforts toward resolution. At present, opposition to any form of structure, including organizational structure, is still so strong that communes have found it almost impossible to cooperate with each other in joint undertakings of a major nature. Interestingly enough, communes with transcendent or spiritual values are the most stable and have the highest survival quotient.

It is my conclusion that the weekly or periodic meetings of all commune members, which are often run as encounter groups, have a limited effectiveness in the resolution of interpersonal problems and issues. Although trained encounter leaders may be present as facilitators, their effectiveness is often considerably curtailed due to their own deep involvement in the issues that are the subject of confrontation. One answer to this dilemma might be to bring in a trained facilitator or for communes to exchange facilitators.

It is difficult to determine to what extent narcotics represent a problem for communes precisely because their consumption is as casual, widespread, and accepted as is the downing of alcoholic beverages in the business community.

Marijuana and hashish are widely enjoyed, while use of such hard drugs as heroin is seldom encountered, especially in the nonurban communes. In a number of communes where drug use was extensive, I noticed a general air of lassitude and a lack of vitality. I also had the distinct impression that "dropping acid" (LSD) was on the decline; among commune members there seemed to be a general awareness of the danger of "speed," or methedrine. A number of communes are totally opposed to the use of narcotics, especially those with members who were former drug addicts.

In most communes the subject of drugs periodically comes up for discussion so that changes in the viewpoint of the commune flow from the experience of the members. Similarly, problems of sexual possessiveness and jealousy appear to be less critical and are also handled by open group discussion. I noticed a tendency toward the maintenance of traditional sex roles, with the women doing the cooking and sewing, the men cutting lumber, etc. Upon questioning this, I repeatedly received the same answer: "Everyone does what they enjoy doing."

Another major problem in most communes is overcrowding and the consequent lack of privacy and alone-time. Rarely does a member enjoy the opportunity of having a room to himself for any length of time. The common practice is to walk off into the woods or fields, but this is an inadequate substitute for real privacy.

Community relations remains a major and critical problem since many communes are "hassled" by authorities or are located amid unfriendly neighbors. As one member described it, the emotional climate in a hassled commune is "full of not so good vibes—you don't know what they will try next, and you keep looking over your shoulder. That takes energy." Today's commune members generally have a clear awareness of the importance of establishing good community relations.

Many of the communes that have got under way this past year or are now being organized are beginning on a sound financial basis. This trend appears to be related to the strong influx of people in their mid-twenties, early or mid-thirties, and beyond. These individuals have financial reserves or savings and are, for the most part, successful professionals and businessmen with families. . . .

There is considerable mobility in communes, which is symptomatic of an endemic wanderlust and search. If people have to leave for any reason, once they have been exposed to communal living, they tend to return. They like the deep involvement with others in a climate of freedom, openness, and commitment. This feeling of belonging has been described as both "a new tribalism" and "a new sense of brotherhood." One young woman with whom I spoke had this to say about her commune experience:

> When a white man walks into a room full of other whites, he doesn't feel he is among brothers like the black man does. In the communes, we are now beginning to feel that man has many brothers. . . . There is a new sense of honesty. You can say things to each other and share things like you never could in the family. I never had so much love in my whole life—not even in my own family.

She also indicated, however, that commune living is highly intense and possibly not for everyone: "In the commune, there is nothing you can hide. Some people can't take it. They get sick or they leave." . . .

We must recognize that the commune movement, as with most other movements, is passing through certain developmental stages. At this stage, there is little readiness for communes to define themselves as laboratories for the exploration of alternative models that might benefit the society of the future. . . .

Although David Cooper, a colleague and disciple of British psychiatrist Ronald Laing, has sounded a death knell in his new book *The Death of the Family*, I believe we are far from writing the epitaph. The traditional nuclear family will continue, although its form, to some extent, may change; in the years to come, possibly as high as 20 percent of the population will explore alternative models of social living.

It would be a mistake to characterize the commune movement as a collection of dropouts who are content to exist like lilies in the field. A considerable number of successful people from all walks of life are now involved; they have merely shifted their sphere of interest and the nature of their creative contribution. We are dealing with a massive awakening of the awareness that life holds multiple options other than going from school to job to retirement.

The commune movement has opened a new and wide range of alternative life-styles and offers another frontier to those who have the courage for adventure. It is the test tube for the growth of a new type of social relatedness, for the development of an organization having a structure that appears, disappears, and reappears as it chooses and as it is needed. Communes may well serve as a laboratory for the study of the processes involved in the regeneration of our social institutions. They have become the symbol of man's new freedom to explore alternative life-styles and to develop deep and fulfilling human relationships through the rebirth and extension of our capacity for familial togetherness.

THE NEW AMERICAN REVOLUTION [5]

The revolution of the twentieth century will take place in the United States. It is only there that it can happen. And it has already begun. Whether or not that revolution spreads to the rest of the world depends on whether or not it succeeds first in America. . . .

I know it is difficult to believe that America—the fatherland of imperialism, the power responsible for the war in

[5] From *Without Marx or Jesus*, by Jean-François Revel, a French philosopher-critic and a columnist for the French news magazine *L'Express*. Excerpts are from the book *Without Marx or Jesus: The New American Revolution Has Begun*, by Jean-François Revel. Doubleday. '71. Translated by Jack Bernard; translation Copyright © 1971 by Doubleday & Company, Inc. Reprinted by permission.

Vietnam, the nation of Joe McCarthy's witch hunts, the exploiter of the world's natural resources—is, or could become, the cradle of revolution. We are accustomed to thinking of the United States as the logical target of revolution, and of computing revolutionary progress by the rate of American withdrawal. Now, we are being asked to admit that our revolutionary slide rule was inaccurate and to face the future without that comfortable tool.

If we draw up a list of all things that ail mankind today, we will have formulated a program for the revolution that mankind needs: the abolition of war and of imperialist relations by abolishing states and also the notion of national sovereignty; the elimination of the possibility of internal dictatorship (a concomitant condition of the abolition of war); worldwide economic and educational equality; birth control on a planetary scale; complete ideological, cultural, and moral freedom, in order to ensure both individual happiness through independence and a plurality of choice, and in order to make use of the totality of human creative resources.

Obviously, this is a utopic program, and it has nothing in its favor, except that it is absolutely necessary if mankind is to survive. The exchange of one political civilization for another, which that program implies, seems to me to be going on right now in the United States. And, as in all the great revolutions of the past, this exchange can become worldwide only if it spreads, by a sort of political osmosis, from the prototype nation to all the others.

The United States is the country most eligible for the role of prototype nation for the following reasons:

It enjoys continuing economic prosperity and rate of growth, without which no revolutionary project can succeed.

It has technological competence and a high level of basic research.

Culturally it is oriented toward the future rather than toward the past, and it is undergoing a revolution in behavioral standards and in the affirmation of individual freedom and equality.

It rejects authoritarian control and multiplies creative initiative in all domains—especially in art, life-style, and sense experience—and allows the coexistence of a diversity of mutually complementary alternative subcultures. . . .

It is evident from the above that the various aspects of a revolution are interrelated—so much so that, if one aspect is missing, the others are incomplete. There are five revolutions that must take place either simultaneously or not at all: a political revolution; a social revolution; a technological and scientific revolution; a revolution in culture, values, and standards; and a revolution in international and interracial relations. The United States is the only country, so far as I can see, where these five revolutions are simultaneously in progress and are organically linked in such a way as to constitute a single revolution. . . .

This revolt, however, is not the only indication of a new revolutionary direction. There has never been another society that faced a situation like that of the United States with respect to the blacks. In the face of this contagious domestic problem and of the demands of the Afro-American community, American society is being divided into factions and is entering upon the path of cultural polycentrism. And this process, of course, is playing havoc with our prejudices concerning the "conformity" and "uniformity" of American society. The truth of the matter is that American society is torn by too many tensions not to become more and more diversified.

The Role of Youth in the Revolution

Another unprecedented characteristic of the American revolution is the revolt of the young—the contagion of which, at both the national and international levels, was so virulent in the years between 1965 and 1970. This is, moreover, a new development within the context of upper-class divisions during revolutionary periods, since these young revolutionaries are mostly students; that is, members of the privileged class. It should be pointed out that this "privileged class" is less and less exceptional; it is a case, so to speak, of mass privilege. The current upheavals are due not only to the great number of young people in proportion to the rest of the population, but also to the great number of students in proportion to young people. Out of a population of 200 million, there are presently 7 million students; and it is estimated that by 1977 there will be 11 million.

It has been said that there are three nations in the United States: a black nation; a Woodstock nation; and a Wallace nation. The first one is self-explanatory. The second takes its name from the great political and musical convention held at Woodstock, New York, in 1969, which has been documented by the film *Woodstock*. It includes the hippies and the radicals. The third nation is embodied in Governor Wallace of Alabama, and is composed of lower-middle-class whites, whose symbol is the hard hat worn by construction workers. Each of these nations has its own language, its own art forms, and its own customs. And each has a combat arm: the Black Panthers for the blacks; the Weathermen for Woodstock; and the Ku Klux Klan and various citizen organizations for Wallace. We could add other "nations"; e.g., members of the Women's Liberation movement, who have declared war on sexism and who take their methods from those of the black power and student power movements. There is also a large group of citizens who are neither black nor particularly young nor especially intellectual. Far from being reactionary, they are sometimes militantly progressive and are vaguely categorized as liberals. This group includes citizens with a wide range of opinion; from what, in Europe, we call the democrats, to the progressives. The liberals often have been able to contribute the appearance of a mass movement to demonstrations that, without them, would have attracted only the extremists. They demonstrated alongside the blacks throughout the great Southern revolt that began in 1952 and against the Vietnam war in the various moratoriums. They are on the side of the students, the Indians, and the Third World. On May 21, 1970, for instance, thousands of New York lawyers—what we might call the governors of the governing class—descended on Washington to protest American intervention in Cambodia. On the same day, the hardhats demonstrated in New York in favor of this intervention, and, still on the same day, prices dropped sharply on the New York Stock Exchange, indicating, according to some American commentators, that the financiers, like the lawyers, were not in agreement with the Administration over the conduct of the war.

No nineteenth century class distinctions are sufficient to convey the nature of these new political classes—which are also sexual, racial, and esthetic; that is, they are based on the rejection of an unsatisfactory life-style. Each of these categories has specific economic, racial, esthetic, moral, and religious or spiritual characteristics; each has its own customs, its own way of dressing and eating—even though, as a whole, they are referred to as a "community." In this instance, the image of a series of superimposed circles rather than of stratified social levels describes the nature of this community.

The Coalescence of Protests

The "hot" issues in America's insurrection against itself, numerous as they are, form a cohesive and coherent whole within which no one of them can be separated from the others. These issues are as follows: a radically new approach to moral values; the black revolt; the feminist attack on masculine domination; the rejection by young people of exclusively economic and technical social goals; the general adoption of noncoercive methods in education; the acceptance of the guilt for poverty; the growing demand for equality; the rejection of an authoritarian culture in favor of a critical and diversified culture that is basically new, rather than adopted from the old cultural stockpile; the rejection both of the spread of American power abroad and of foreign policy; and a determination that the natural environment is more important than commercial profit. None of the groups concerned with any one of these points, and none of the points themselves, would have been able to gain as much strength and attention as they have if they had been isolated from other groups and other points. ...

One of the most striking characteristics of the revolutionary movement in America is that it is the first such movement in which all demands are part of a single front, and are advanced simultaneously on the same program. Demands belonging to the individualist-anarchist tradition, and those referring to the organized political struggle of the oppressed (or of the less nonoppressed, as the case may be), are, for once, all included in one demand.

There is, therefore, a basis common to all manifestations of the American revolt, and to its European extensions. That basis consists in the rejection of a society motivated by profit, dominated exclusively by economic considerations, ruled by the spirit of competition, and subjected to the mutual aggressiveness of its members. Indeed, beneath every revolutionary ideal we find a conviction that man has become the tool of his tools, and that he must once more become an end and a value in himself. The hippies are characterized by a particularly vivid awareness of that loss of self-identity and of the perversion of the meaning of life. A competitive society, for instance, or a spirit of rivalry, is a source of suffering to them. But they do not self-righteously condemn such societies nor attempt to refute them theoretically; they simply refuse to have any part in them. A hippie, therefore, is above all someone who has "dropped out"; a boy or girl who decided, one day, to stop being a cog in the social machine. ...

Certainly, one can make a good case against the hippies for their political indifference and for their naiveté in rejecting every form of violence—for these are the attitudes that distinguish the hippies. One can even fault them for forgetting that the hippie way of life is possible only in an affluent society and because of a surplus in production (even though the hippie personally may be willing to live in comparative poverty). One can make fun of their nebulous ideology, which is a mixture of confused Orientalism and adulterated primitivism (although they are likely to retort that they prefer pop music to ideology). One can jeer at their simplistic confidence in the strength of universal love as the key to all problems. And one can be astonished at their belief that it is possible for an individual to have absolute freedom without infringing the rights of others. All these things are, no doubt, open to criticism from many standpoints; and they are all no doubt very limited concepts.

The fact remains, however, that the hippies' refusal to accept regimentation in any form gives them a mysterious strength and a means of exerting pressure; the same sort of strength and pressure that is exerted by, say, a hunger strike. To those who try to persuade them to give their revolt a political or religious structure, the hippies offer a patient, but absolutely inflexible, resistance. The May uprisings in Paris and the demonstrations at the Renault plant in France all seem to the hippies to be too much the product of the harsh society that they are trying to escape. . . .

Toward an Antipolitical Revolution

Nonetheless, this rejection of solutions that are too immediate and too concrete originates in a basic intuition that one of the foundations of revolution that we most need today is the elimination of pathological aggression. Unless that elimination is achieved, no revolution can do anything but lead to a new form of oppression. We do not need a political revolution so much as an antipolitical revolution; otherwise the only result will be the creation of new police states. Human aggression is a determining factor in human behavior; and it is accepted even more gratuitously, and is even more murderous, than all of the sacred causes by which it justifies itself and on which it bases itself. Unless this root evil is extirpated, the hippies believe, then everything else will be corrupted. By reflecting that belief in their attitudes and behavior, the hippies at very least perform a useful function; they remind us constantly that a revolution is not simply a transfer of power, but also a change in the goals for the sake of which power is exercised and a new choice in the objects of love, hate, and respect. Also, the hippies have the advantage of being able to point out, to those who still talk about "freedom at gunpoint" in a world dripping with blood that has been shed in vain, that this slogan is nothing more than an outdated jingoism....

Never, in any country or at any time, has public opinion, however well informed it may have been (which was hardly ever the case), reflected an element of dissent sufficiently strong to make known its condemnation of its government's abuses in foreign policy, and thereby to create a real political problem. Public opinion can, on occasion, turn against domestic injustices, but it has never before been known to rebel against external crimes. The American student uprisings are directly associated with the students' rejection of the war in Vietnam. And this rejection is not merely the position of minorities—as proved by the state of semi-insurrection that greeted the announcement of the Cambodian intervention, and by the Senate vote on a document recalling the constitutional obligation of a President to consult with the Congress before any commitment of American troops abroad....

Today in America—the child of European imperialism —a new revolution is rising. It is *the* revolution of our time. It is the only revolution that involves radical, moral, and practical opposition to the spirit of nationalism. It is the only revolution that, to that opposition, joins culture, economic and technological power, and a total affirmation of liberty for all in place of archaic prohibitions. It, therefore, offers the only possible escape for mankind today: the acceptance of technological civilization as a means and not as an end, and—since we cannot be saved either by the destruction of the civilization or by its continuation—the development of the ability to reshape that civilization without annihilating it.

III. YOUTH AND OUR CHANGING EDUCATION

EDITOR'S INTRODUCTION

No area of our contemporary life has been more affected by the youth revolt than that of our universities, themselves the site of much of the protest, from the Berkeley uprising in 1964 to the Columbia University riots and the tragedies at Kent State and Jackson State. And none of our cultural institutions has been more changed as a result of the revolt. Again, the issues involved are varied. Although these issues are dealt with here in summary fashion, both sides of the controversy caused by youthful demands for changes in our universities are presented.

In the first selection the renowned American historian, Henry Steele Commager speaks of the causes of student rebellion.

The article on black studies by Eugene D. Genovese, professor of history at the University of Rochester, touches on a problem which has been raised in the last few years by black youth. That particular segment of our youth, in or out of college, has not generally been identified as part of the current youth rebellion. This is by no means to deny the importance of earlier civil rights protests in the South, whether or not they are to be viewed as part of the youth revolt of the sixties. Nor does this deny the importance of the activities of such groups as the Black Panthers, though such groups are perhaps more analogous to the predominantly white radical youth of the Students for Democratic Society (SDS) and others.

The next three selections by representative academicians of varying viewpoints deal with how the university may be changed for the better and to what extent the most radical of student demands can be met. The first of the three selections is by the president of Yale University, Kingman Brewster, Jr., who advocates many reforms to alleviate the feeling of students that they are "captives" on their campuses. Next, Donald Marquand Dozer, professor of history at the University of California at Santa Barbara, would hope to retain the traditional intellectual function of the university. Sidney Hook, professor of philosophy at New York University, sets forth his views on what student rights are, both civil and educational.

In the next selection, a statement by the American Council on Education, the nation's major private coordinating body for higher education, urges that balanced judgments be brought to bear on campus disorders.

Last, the civil rights of secondary public school students are outlined by Richard M. Blankenburg, a member of the department of education at Marquette University. This article touches on a group in which there is much dissatisfaction with the status quo.

WHY STUDENT REBELLION? [1]

At its best, student revolt in America is characterized by idealism, at its worst by bad manners and violence, and almost everywhere by an exasperating combination of logic and irrationality. This is because it is directed not so much against academic as against public grievances, not against ostentatious injustices and oppression as against authority, traditionalism and complacency. . . .

Irrational as is the outburst of student discontent, the explosion of public disapproval is equally irrational and may be more dangerous. To the public, as to the academy, the student revolt is a traumatic experience, and the public reaction to it is just as emotional as is the student reaction to university malpractices. What possesses the young, their

[1] From article by Henry Steele Commager, noted historian, professor of history at Amherst College. *Newsday.* p 7W-8W+. Je. 1, '68. Copyright © 1968, Newsday, Inc. Reprinted by permission.

elders ask. Never, after all, was a generation so pampered. We have given them everything, parents assert—an expensive education; a four-year exemption from toil and responsibility, and even from the military; a guarantee of a privileged position in the American society and economy. And to what end?

One segment of adult society sees in the student revolt nothing but ingratitude. Another looks upon it as somehow a rejection of law and order and morality and a surrender to irresponsibility—a wholesale license to indulge in LSD and sex. Still others darkly suspect a Communist or Black Power conspiracy. . . .

Revolt Against the Parental University

Yet the student revolt is neither an expression of original sin nor the product of a conspiracy, but an overvigorous and overdue assertion of a discontent that has been brewing for years, and that has come to a head—as many things have come to a head—with the Vietnam war.

First, it is a revolt against the anachronistic notion that the university stands *in loco parentis* to students who are physically, sexually, politically and perhaps even intellectually like any other segment of adult society.

There is considerable justice in this complaint and logic in this protest. The university has persisted in the habit of acting *in loco parentis* long after the real justification for it has disappeared. Yet if little is to be said for the current practice, something is to be said for patience with the liquidation of that practice and the working out of some new formula. Universities do not, after all, act as parents out of sadistic instincts. . . .

Gradually during the nineteenth century the age of students crept upwards, but colleges were not prepared to abandon the habits of generations and treat them as adults, nor were parents, who confessed a passion for the prolongation of youth unique to our own country. That passion lingers on: every politician speaks of "our boys" in Vietnam, and it never seems to occur to us that if they are indeed boys they shouldn't be there but in school.

Not only are college students kept in a state of pupillage; they are subjected to the indignity of being treated like high school pupils, hedged in for four years by requirements of courses, credits, majors and minors, attendance, examinations, all of which are, in a sense, vestigial remains from the high school. They are fobbed off with professors who do not teach, or who teach not gladly but badly. They are often denied an effective voice—sometimes any voice—even in the conduct of their own affairs: the organization of student life, discipline, newspapers and journals, the choice of speakers, even the games they play.

Student reaction to all this is just as irrational as university policy. Students reject the parental role of the university but they reject, with equal vigor, the intrusion of the civil authority onto the campus. They defy university limitations on their drinking habits, sexual freedom, use of drugs, or privacy, but they are outraged at the notion that in all these matters they should be subject to the same disciplines, the same laws and the same penalties that apply to all other members of society.

Nor do most of them know what to do with student freedom when they have it. We have, in a sense, so corrupted them that they love the chains that bind them. They do not want freedom from the tyranny of courses, but more courses —courses, now, in sociology, now in the ghetto, now in Negro history, now in the Vietnamese war. They do not want to rid themselves of examinations and credits and attendance and faculty control of their sports; instead they often demand more of all this. They want to be part of the university enterprise, even to have representatives on boards of trustees, but show little interest in the scientific and intellectual functions of the university—the library, for example, or laboratories— and little initiative in the cultivation of music and the arts.

The Revolt Against Bigness and Irrelevance

Second, students are revolting against bigness—bigness which reduces the individual student to a computerized number, denies him access to professors, or even to his fellow students, weakens instead of strengthening his sense of individuality, and threatens to fit him into a kind of benevolent academic Brave New World. They are revolting against the university which is quite ready to take their (or their parents') money but which subjects them to inferior instruction from graduate students; which houses them in glorified barracks, or worse yet, houses some of them in fraternity and sorority houses and others in barracks—and wraps all of them in a cocoon of rules and regulations.

Here, again, some of the fault is their own making. Students could insist on good instruction—or stay away from bad. They could, but do not, clamor to be housed in cluster colleges that are somehow manageable. They could certainly do away with the inequities and anachronisms of fraternity and sorority which mirror and even exaggerate the inequities and discriminations of secular life.

Third, students are protesting against what seems to them the irrelevance of much of the education imposed upon them —education justified chiefly by tradition, or by habit, or by the convenience of professors or, still more dubious, by the supposed requirements of the business community or of a government whose standards students do not respect.

So much for the discontents that concern the students themselves, discontents with the internal character and operations of the academy. But these, though they may be most persuasive, are not the most profound.

Be it said to the credit of our students that what disturbs them most deeply are public rather than private wrongs; what chiefly alienates them from the university is not its failure as an educational institution, but as a public institution; not its intellectual miscellaneousness, but its moral obtuseness.

A great many students are indeed, in the fatuous phrase of their critics, alienated intellectuals, and they have much to be alienated from. They are alienated by the spectacle of the deep inequalities in a society dedicated to equality, and they are convinced that the academy shares responsibility for creating and perpetuating these inequalities. Now they demand, with a kind of desperate impatience, that the university make up for past sins and lost time: that it admit twice as many blacks as ever before, that it provide special tutoring and social facilities for them and concede them special privileges and power. They do not seem to realize that all this is a form of racism, nor that in their passion to do justice to the blacks they forget the many other neglected victims of our society and our economy. They are ashamed that great urban universities have, for the most part, been content to go about their business without giving thought to their neighbors or neighborhoods, and they ask that the university abandon its isolation and its aloofness, and take an active part in slum clearance, neighborhood rehabilitation, improvement of schools, legal aid and similar things.

To the argument that preoccupation with current and immediate problems will distract the university from concentration on future and general problems, they answer that the university is already using a large part of its resources on current problems—but on the wrong ones. For they are outraged by the readiness of the university to ally itself with the business, political and military Establishment, to train businessmen and scientists prepared to serve corporations on almost any terms, to lend their intellectual resources and their academic facilities to almost any branch of the Government or the military that claims them. . . .

The Basis for Distrust

Nor is it only the university as an institution that they distrust; they distrust, as well, professors who go whoring after lucrative contracts of power and prestige, who are prepared to serve almost any governmental agency in almost any capacity, prepared even to accept limitations of secrecy in scientific research. The readiness of the university to lend its facilities to corporations and to Government has been dramatized, for students, on every campus in the land by the uncritical eagerness of universities to welcome "recruiters" on campus. The extent to which the university has been assimilated to the business and governmental community has been dramatized on a hundred campuses by the readiness of universities to act as employment agencies for these interests.

The university does not preempt the office of the Pentagon or of Dow Chemical Company for interviewing prospective students or faculty, but thinks it quite proper to lend its facilities to "recruiters" who wish to interview students for prospective jobs. Students know that their universities are under no more obligation to help the CIA recruit employees or to help Dow Chemical make money than they are to help authorities license cars or help *Playboy* get advertisements. And they listen, with undisguised cynicism, to university authorities invoking high-sounding principles like "an open campus" or "freedom of information" to defend policies that have no relation to either.

Because they are young they cannot remember, and do not know, that in World War II every university cooperated with the military and with Government in every conceivable capacity, and that no one then argued the impropriety of academic participation in the Manhattan Project, in radar, in the Office of War Information, the Office of Strategic Services, or in military government, nor, for that matter, the propriety of Government recruiting on campus. They should be reminded of this. University authorities should not have to be reminded that they are not prisoners of precedent, and that there is a difference between a war which the entire community regards as involving the very survival of civilization and one which a major part of the community—certainly the academic community—regards as hateful and immoral.

Student rebellion, then, takes on a pattern quite different from that of most rebellions with which we are familiar. It is primarily a rebellion against conditions outside the campus —against practices which students regard as immoral: the war in Vietnam with its accompaniment of napalm and potentially lethal gas and concentration camps; vast expenditures for future wars at a time when the nation is starved for essential social services; the power of the military-industrial-labor-university complex which seems unlimited; racial discrimination and urban decay and police brutality; the cruel waste of human and of natural resources.

In other circumstances we would call this an idealistic protest. But the methods with which it is conducted are far from idealistic.

What shall we say of these methods—the bad manners, the stridency, the destructiveness, of the student protest—but that it is deplorable, and not only deplorable but absurd. Students deplore violence violently; they use the arguments not of reason but of force to persuade the university to abandon the sponsorship of force and return to the path of reason. In the name of freedom they deny freedom of speech or of conduct to the majority of their fellow students. They call impatiently on Government to cultivate patience and yet they champion tolerance with brutal intolerance. They are, in short, tiresomely inconsistent.

But let us keep in mind the wise words of the Reverend William Ellery Channing about the Abolitionists: "The great interests of humanity do not lose their claims on us because sometimes injudiciously maintained." Injudicious may seem what Theodore Roosevelt once called a "weasel word," but the principle is the same, and students can retort that most of the words that come from trustees and university presidents are weasel words.

Besides, those who are most vociferous in charging students with lawlessness and violence do not come into court with clean hands. Students can, and do, retort that it is their elders, and betters, who have set the examples that they now follow.

Who are you, they fairly ask, to counsel reason and moderation? Is it reason and moderation you have displayed in your policies towards Vietnam!

Who are you to deplore violence, you who have poured more bombs on little Vietnam than were rained on either Germany or Japan during the last war!

Who are you to plead the cause of law and order, you who are even now waging a lawless war with lawless weapons, violating the Charter of the United Nations and flouting international agreements on the uses of gas and of weapons of indiscriminate destruction!

Who are you to counsel patience, you who have displayed so little patience with Communist China, and who were so impatient to plunge into Santo Domingo with your Marines before there was any evidence of danger there!

Who are you to counsel judiciousness, you who launched the Bay of Pigs attack on a sovereign nation, and who were prepared to condemn the world to a nuclear war at the time of the missile crisis!

Who are you to deplore with such anguish the flouting of civil laws, you who have flouted the provisions of the Fourteenth and Fifteenth Amendments for a century!

Who are you to decry student intransigence about the draft, you who stood idly by while one half the states of the Union openly nullified almost every civil rights act on the statute books!

Who are you to bustle about arresting draft resisters with such a show of outraged patriotism, you who failed so conspicuously to arrest Governors Barnett or Wallace when they resisted the decisions of the Supreme Court by force, and who have failed to enforce those decisions against a thousand others who defy them!

One violation of the law does not excuse others, but it is hypocritical of our society to insist on a double standard of morality—one for students, and another and very different one for Government itself—and to deplore student violence as a prelude to revolution while standing idly by when local and state officials indulge themselves in open violence.

The answer to student protest and revolt is not hysteria and it is not suppression. Students have something to say—something important for all of us, and we should not deny ourselves the benefit of their protest or their advice because we do not approve of their manners. Nor should we take refuge in that habit of bewilderment and outrage that is the professional mark of the middle-aged. Let us take reassurance, rather, from the reflection that when older and more respectable elements of society were silent, students spoke up.

And let us ask ourselves whether we would rather have a generation of students too indifferent to care about the grave injustices of our society, or too timid to protest against them.

THE ROLE OF BLACK STUDIES [2]

The demand for black studies and for special black studies departments needs no elaborate explanation or defense. It rests on an awareness of the unique and dual nature of the black experience in the United States. Unlike European immigrants, blacks came here involuntarily, were enslaved and excluded from access to the mainstream of American life, and as a result have had a special history with a profoundly national-cultural dimension. Unlike, say Italo-Americans, Afro-Americans have within their history the elements of a distinct nationality at the same time that they have participated in and contributed immensely to a common American nationality. Despite the efforts of many black and some white scholars, this paradoxical experience has yet

[2] From "Black Studies: Trouble Ahead," by Eugene D. Genovese, professor of history at the University of Rochester. *Atlantic*. 223:37-41. Je. '69. Copyright © 1969, by The Atlantic Monthly Company, Boston, Mass. Reprinted with permission.

to be explored with the respect and intellectual rigor it deserves. . . .

The duality of the black experience haunts the present debate and leads us immediately into a consideration of the ideological and political features of the black studies programs. It is, at best, irrelevant to argue, as DeVere E. Pentony does in the April 1969 issue of the *Atlantic,* that all professors of history and social science bring a particular ideology and politics to their classroom and that a black ideological bias is no worse than any other. There is no such thing as a black ideology or a black point of view. Rather there are various black-nationalist biases, from left-wing versions such as that of the Panthers to right-wing versions such as that of Ron Karenga and other "cultural nationalists." There are also authentic sections of the black community that retain conservative, liberal, or radical integrationist and antinationalist positions. Both integrationist and separatist tendencies can be militant or moderate, radical or conservative (in the sense generally applied to white politics in relation to social questions). The separatists are riding high today, and the integrationists are beating a retreat; but this has happened before and may be reversed tomorrow.

All these elements have a right to participate in the exploration of black historical and cultural themes. In one sense, the whole point of black studies programs in a liberal arts college or university ought to be to provide for the widest and most vigorous exchange among all these groups in an atmosphere of free discussion and mutual toleration. The demand for an exclusively black faculty and especially the reactionary demand for student control of autonomous departments must be understood as demands for the introduction of specific ideological and political criteria into the selection of faculty and the composition of programs. Far from being proposals to relate these programs to the black community, they are in fact factionally based proposals to relate them to one or other political tendency within the black community and to exclude others. The bloody, but by no means isolated, feud between black student factions on the UCLA campus ought to make that clear.

One of the new hallmarks of white racism is the notion of one black voice, one black experience, one black political community, one black ideology—of a black community without an authentic inner political life wracked by dissension and ideological struggle. In plain truth, what appears on the campuses as "what the blacks want" is almost invariably what the dominant faction in a particular black caucus wants. Like all people who fight for liberation, blacks are learning the value of organizational discipline and subordination to a firm and united line of action. Sometimes, the formulation of particular demands and actions has much less to do with their intrinsic merits or with the institution under fire than with the momentary balance in the struggle for power within the caucus itself. . . .

Black Studies as Political Schools

The pseudorevolutionary middle-class totalitarians who constitute one temporarily powerful wing of the left-wing student movement understand this dimension, even if few others seem to. Accordingly, they support demands for student control as an entering wedge for a general political purge they naively hope to dominate. These suburban putschists are most unlikely to succeed in their stated objectives of purging "reactionaries," for they are isolated, incoherent, and without adequate power. But they may very well help to reestablish the principle of the campus purge and thereby provide a moral and legal basis for a new wave of McCarthyism. The disgraceful treatment of Professors Staughton Lynd and Jesse Lemisch, among many who have been . . . purged from universities by both liberal and right-wing pressure, has already set a tone of renewed repression, which some fanatical and unreasoning left-wing militants are unwittingly reinforcing. If black studies departments are permitted to become political bases and cadre-training schools for one or another political movement, the door will be open for the conversion of other departments to similar roles; that door is already being forced in some places.

Those blacks who speak in harsh nationalist accents in favor of all-black faculties, departmental autonomy, and student power open themselves to grave suspicions of bad faith. The most obvious objection, raised sharply by several outstanding black educators in the South, concerns the systematic raiding of black colleges by financially stronger white ones. The shortage of competent black specialists in black history, social science, and black culture is a matter of general knowledge and concern. Hence, the successful application of the all-black principle in most universities would spell the end of hopes to build one or more distinguished black universities to serve as a center for the training of a national Afro-American intelligentsia.

One need not be partial to black nationalism in any of its varieties to respect the right of black people to self-determination, for this right flows directly from the duality of their unique experience in the United States. Even those who dislike or distrust black nationalism as such should be able to view the development of such centers of higher education as positive and healthy. If there is no place in the general American university for ideological homogeneity and conformity, there is a place in American society for universities based on adherence to a specific ideology, as the Catholic universities, for example, have demonstrated.

Responsible black scholars have been working hard for an end to raiding and to the scattering of the small number of black professors across the country. Among other obstacles, they face the effort of ostensibly nationalist black students who seek to justify their decision to attend predominantly white institutions, often of high prestige, by fighting for a larger black teaching staff. The outcome of these demands is the obscurantist nonsense that black studies can and should be taught by people without intellectual credentials since these credentials are "white" anyway. . . . What has to be resisted firmly is the insanity that claims, as in one . . . instance, that experience as a SNCC [Student National Coordinating Committee] field organizer should be considered more important than a Ph.D. in the hiring of a professor of Afro-American history. This assertion represents a general contempt for all learning and a particular contempt for black studies as a field of study requiring disciplined, serious intellectual effort—an attitude that reflects the influence of white racism, even when brought forth by a black man.

The demand for all-black faculties rests on the insistence that only blacks can understand the black experience. This cant is nothing new: it forms the latest version of the battle cry of every reactionary nationalism and has clear antecedents, for example, in the nineteenth century German Romantic movement. To be perfectly blunt, it now constitutes an ideologically Fascist position and must be understood as such. . . .

Universities and Black Identity

We might mention here the problem of the alleged "psychological need" of black people to do this or that or to be this or that in order to reclaim their manhood, reestablish their ostensibly lost dignity, and God knows what else. There is a place for these questions in certain kinds of intellectual discussions and in certain political forums, but there is no place for these questions in the formation of university policy. In such a context they represent a benevolent paternalism that is neither more nor less than racist. Whites in general and university professors and administrators in particular are not required to show "sympathy," "compassion," "understanding," and other manifestations of liberal guilt feelings; they are required to take black demands seriously—to take them straight, on their merits. That is, they are required to treat political demands politically and to meet their responsibility to fight white racism while also meeting their responsibility to defend the integrity and dignity of the university community as a whole.

Only if the universities have a clear attitude toward themselves will they be able to fulfill their duty to the black community. Our universities, if they are to survive—and their survival is problematical—must redefine themselves as institutions of higher learning and firmly reject the role of cadre-training schools for Government, business, or community organizations of any kind. Blame for the present crisis ought to be placed on those who, especially after World War II, opened the universities to the military, to big-business recruitment, to the "fight against communism," to the CIA, and to numerous other rightist pressures. If Dow Chemical or ROTC belongs on a college campus, so does the Communist party, the Black Panthers, the John Birch Society, the Campfire Girls, or the Mafia for that matter. Students have a clear political right to organize on campuses as Democrats, Republicans, Communists, Panthers, or whatever, provided their activities are appropriate to campus life, but the universities have no business making special institutional arrangements with this or that faction off campus and then putting down other factions as illicit. And Government and business represent political intrusions quite as much as do political parties. The same is true for the anachronistic and absurd practice of having American universities controlled by boards of trustees instead of by their faculties in consultation with the students. In short, the black studies question, like the black revolt as a whole, has raised all the fundamental problems of class power in American life, and the solutions will have to run deep into the structure of the institutions themselves. . . .

No matter how painful some of the battles are or will become, the advent of black studies programs represents a momentous step toward the establishment of relations of equality between white and black intellectuals. But, if these programs are to realize their potential in support of black liberation and in the fostering of genuinely free and critical scholarship, our universities must resolve honestly the questions of limits and legitimacy. Those who blindly ignore or cynically manipulate these questions, and the reforms they imply, corrupt the meaning of black studies and risk the destruction of institutions necessary to the preservation of freedom in American life.

TOWARD THE VOLUNTARY UNIVERSITY [3]

If we do not succeed in achieving a campus which is more voluntary than most of ours now are, if we do not restore a widespread faith in the openness of society, then I think our present troubles will seem as nothing compared to what lies ahead. . . .

My elders and betters, my peers and contemporaries are backed to the wall, then driven up the wall, eventually driven up and over it, by students who are often fundamentally anti-intellectual; who are impatient with learning and research; who think there are social ends other than the advancement of learning which a university should serve; and who see no reason why the majority vote of students should not dictate what those ends are and how they should be pursued.

It was an SDS [Students for a Democratic Society] member at Berkeley who first woke me up to the reason why so many seek to divert the university from its primary mission: "Like don't give me that stuff about how I'm here to learn," he said, "I'm here because I have to be; so if I have to be here against my will, why shouldn't I have a say in running the place."

He might have been talking about the draft, or about parental insistence that he go to college, or about the university seeming to be an indispensable hiring hall for those who would escape the menial levels of drudgery.

Whatever he meant it was clear that his determination to take the place over was motivated in large part by the sense that he was trapped in it by forces beyond his own

[3] From an address at Michigan State University, by Kingman Brewster, Jr., president of Yale University. Text from *Christian Science Monitor*. p 9. Ja. 14, '70. Reprinted by permission of the author.

choice or control. On the whole, this reaction is not without noble precedent. It is in areas where freedom of choice, including freedom to escape, is not possible that we are more insistent that self-determination shall be gained collectively, by democratic participation or representation.

A university, too many of whose members feel captive, is corrupted, distracted, and fouled for all its members. Higher learning cannot work if it is involuntary. And the judgments which universities and their faculties must make about degrees and about appointments cannot be made by a process which allows the judged to out-vote their judges.

The most dramatic distortion of the motivation for going to college is, of course, the result of the draft. . . . But even if the shadow of the draft in an unpopular war were lifted, there would be powerfully coercive pressures driving young men and women to universities in a hang-dog, involuntary mood.

Parents and schools are likely to think that somehow, something is wrong with the son or daughter who doesn't want to go right on to college after high school, or who doesn't want to go through college in four consecutive years. Now some of this is economic—the desire to get them off the family's back, to put it bluntly. But most of it is pure conformity to the pace of the conventional escalators of success.

Parental concern is whetted, of course, by the fear that once off the escalator the son or daughter might never get back on. The dreadful word "drop-out"—quite appropriately pejorative at the elementary and high-school level—has been allowed to frustrate sensible plans for splicing academic and nonacademic experience. It makes it harder to think of taking off for work or social-action involvement between school and college, or in the middle of college.

The Educational Lockstep

It is the excessive lockstep continuity of learning, from age five to twenty-five, which stultifies the motivation of some of the most gifted students. Easier escape and easier reentry would do much to make the campus a voluntary community once again.

Then there is the growing notion that to be really accomplished it is necessary to have an advanced degree, preferably a doctorate. Here I do place the blame on the employers, professional, semiprofessional, business, financial, and governmental. Its most absurd extreme is the decision of the great Harvard Law School to follow the lesser sheepskins and allow me to convert my LL.B. to a doctorate by mail application and the payment of an appropriate fee! No doubt there are corporations, state governments as well as the Federal Government, which will automatically reward this "higher degree" with a higher job rating, and several thousand dollars of higher salary. The package, not the product, seems to be what counts.

Nothing would be healthier for the voluntary campus atmosphere than for prestigious employers to make a deal with universities whereby a talented college senior could count on returning to the campus when he needed it, any time within ten years after graduation. Then he could go to work right after college. He could be confident that, if more specialized training would help his advancement, his employer would be able to send him back to study. Even better, he would know that if he decided he did not like the field he was working in, he could go back to the university and equip himself for another specialty or profession.

A person should not be made to feel that he must get all his formal education in the first twenty-odd years of his life. Nor should he be made to feel that once he picks a line of work he has forever forfeited a chance to change his mind and tool up for some other career. There must be more chance to recycle back through the university, if we are to retain the sense of continuous freedom of career choice. . . .

It would be far better for the campus atmosphere and the academic ethic if the university were a resource for men and women of all ages, if, but only if, they really want what it has to offer. . . . Of course, this ideal can never be completely achieved, but I submit that the approach to the ideal of the all-volunteer campus is worthy of much more attention, energy, and ingenuity than it has received.

UNIVERSITIES FOR LEARNING [4]

"We will take control of your world, your corporation, your university," Mark Rudd, leader of the rebellion at Columbia University, wrote to President Grayson Kirk in the spring of 1968. "There is only one thing left to say," Rudd concluded. "Up against the wall! This is a stick-up!"

Since then, Rudd's defiance of higher education has been echoed by thousands of militant students, nonstudents, and their faculty supporters. They have terrorized university presidents. They have intimidated faculties and have shattered traditional curricula. They are threatening the future of higher education in America.

In the first eight months of 1969 campus disruptions caused property damage estimated at $8.9 million. According to studies made by Alexander W. Austin, research chief for the American Council on Education, 155 out of 195 campuses which his team surveyed experienced disruptive student incidents between September 1968 and February 1970. Of these, 175 incidents were directed against aspects of the college or university itself on 84 of the campuses; the remaining 260 incidents on the 71 other campuses involved protests against Vietnam, pollution, the "Chicago Seven" trial, and the like. Between January and March 1970 more than thirty cases of arson occurred on college campuses with total damage exceeding $500,000. Sather Gate in Berkeley, Morningside Park in New York City, University Hall in Cambridge, Massachusetts, and Isla Vista in Santa Barbara, California, have become bywords for rioting and mindless destruction with higher education as their targets.

[4] Article entitled "Right On—Up With Higher Education!" by Donald Marquand Dozer, professor of history at the University of California at Santa Barbara. *University Bookman*. 12:3-13. Autumn '71. Reprinted by permission.

Serious as the physical destruction has been, far more serious has been the damage to morale of faculty and students. "We are parents of a student at your campus," runs a letter written to a campus newspaper in California. "We were so proud when our daughter was accepted . . . at your beautiful and excellent school. We are no longer proud. We are appalled that the majority of students . . . would allow a few radicals to ruin the reputation of such a fine school." Higher education is alienated from the public. It is also undergoing a crisis of self-confidence, as faculties and administrators themselves confess their lack of faith in the values they have professed to represent.

The alienation of colleges and universities from society has been mainly self-induced and self-propelled. The cause for it is not to be found in student acts of defiance; these acts have merely exposed the hollowness of much that masks itself as higher education. Long before students began to voice their complaints about the political involvements of institutions of higher education, colleges and universities—both public and private—were mirroring the concerns and preoccupations of contemporary society. They committed themselves to the ideology of a state-structured society which would be exclusively political and salvationist. Through their willing identification with Government policies they accepted political criteria as measure of their success as educational institutions, they permitted erosion of their educational integrity, and they forfeited their capacity for academic balance and real dialogue. Drawn by the magnet of political power, institutions of higher learning thus accepted the responsibility of living entirely in the "now," but they still have not moved fast enough into the "now" to satisfy the new "now" generation. As they transformed themselves into political institutions they became the spoils of political opportunists who now desire to use them for their own ends.

In the judgment of modern militants, the university—and perhaps also every other institution—that does not supply the "correct" answer to all problems of the present does not deserve to survive. If they gain control over the university, they will assuredly mold its mission to respond to the fad of the present; they will relate its program directly and exclusively to solving the "now" problems. They demand that traditional structures be reconstructed in such ways as to produce the new world and the new man of the future. To them, therefore, nothing of the past is valid or sacred. As a means of accomplishing their objectives, they are resorting to the kinds of sabotage and terrorism that disrupted universities in Spain in 1936 before Franco and in Cuba in 1959 before Castro.

The thrust of the protest movement in higher education is purportedly directed against the Establishment, by which is meant the organization that has been built and that is being maintained by the older generation. But in a broader sense it is directed against both the structure of society and the principle of form and management in society. To "hang loose" is to reject the need for order in life. The cry for the reconstitution of higher learning demands the denigration of the management function and the abolition of structure. If it succeeds it will convert the matrix of society into a spongy formless thing. To call this movement simply a counterculture is seriously to underestimate its revolutionary potential.

The gravity of the current malaise in institutions of higher learning and of its spreading infection into high schools cannot be obscured by well-meaning efforts of school officials to excuse these symptoms as a natural result of manifest grievances which are now being called to their attention spectacularly for the first time. These officials respond with breast-beating confessions of guilt and with frantic efforts to alleviate the alleged causes of the complaints. But they are failing almost everywhere to come to grips with the real problem.

Administrative Breakdown

The current impasse in higher education can be partially accounted for by the breakdown in administrative authority, by the soft line which college and university authorities have chosen to follow. In 1966, the latest year for which full data are available, the current-fund expenditures of all institutions of higher education in the United States totaled $12.6 billion. In that year those institutions enrolled more than seven million students and their investment in physical plant alone amounted to the enormous sum of $35.7 billion. In the campus riots since 1966 college and university authorities have failed even to discharge their minimal responsibility of preserving public buildings and other public property.

A tragic gap has thus been disclosed between the legal responsibility of university trustees, regents, presidents, chancellors, and deans, and the degree of authority which they have chosen to exercise in coping with critical problems. Among them, retreat is the order of the day and heroism is a commodity in short supply. Higher education seems to have bred a generation of administrative poltroons who are acting out a death wish for the institutions which they head.

One such university chancellor even personally paid the bail of the militants because he "did not want to lose communication with the student body." The president of Kent State University of Ohio charged that the grand jury which acquitted the National Guard of responsibility for the shooting of four students on that campus showed "a frightening misunderstanding of the role and mission of higher education in an American society dedicated to progress." By implication at least he thus suggested that the university's mission includes rioting, destruction of public property, and complete administrative resignation permitting even anarchy. "The methods of these militants are extreme," admitted another high university official, "but isn't it wonderful that these students are committed?" He failed to point out that the objective of their "commitment" was clearly stated in the declaration of one of the leaders of the student riots at Columbia University in early 1968, "If we don't have enough strength to destroy the nation, by God we can at least destroy Columbia."

It is the duty of administrators to administer, of faculties to teach, and of students to learn. This division of authority in higher education has been allowed to go sadly awry. Through default of administrative leadership by presidents, chancellors, and deans, administrators jump through hoops at the command of student extremists and faculties meet in almost continuous hand-wringing sessions to the neglect of their students and of their classroom duties.

The example set by permissive university presidents and chancellors in yielding to student demands has had the effect of prostituting grading practices in their institutions and of making classroom showmanship and popularity with students the principal measure of the success of the members of teaching staffs. The deterioration of professionalism in academic life is further attested by the proliferation of courses which are offered on a mere pass-fail basis and by the system which has been introduced on the Irvine campus of the University of California allowing students to reject a certain number of their final course grades. This system, the chancellor of that campus has boasted, has had a remarkably beneficial effect upon student morale! And why not?

By and large, universities have long since ceased to dedicate themselves to the pursuit of academic excellence. In this state of academic demoralization higher education has rapidly shed its pose of intellectualism and has declined into a bathos of emotionalism, "relevance," and "democracy."

Students have long known that if they parroted back the "liberal" views of their professors in courses in the social sciences they would receive A grades, but grading practices have now become so lax that even in the so-called "hard" sciences —the physical sciences—students almost never receive failing grades and even in large introductory lower-division courses in such subjects as physics and chemistry students who rank in the lowest 10 percent of their class are given passing grades of C.

In a course in South American Indians at the University of California, Santa Barbara, students received a final mark of A for dyeing pieces of cloth. In another course the professor, for his final examination, handed out blank sheets of paper to the members of his class, and said, "Write your names on this paper. I will put two words on the blackboard. If you answer *True* you will get a grade of A in the course. If you answer *False* you will get a grade of A minus; and those who helped me distribute papers during this quarter will receive A pluses." On this campus the grade-point average for all students has risen to a substantial B grade or 3.133 on a basis of 4.0. Is it any wonder that under these conditions approximately one fourth of the members of the entire senior class qualify for membership in Phi Beta Kappa?

At the American University in Washington, D.C., President George Williams and a majority of the faculty expressed their sympathy with the so-called National Student Strike, and the administration issued a statement recognizing "the legitimacy of the political concerns raised by the strike." This declaration was countered by one heroic member of the faculty, William F. Fuchs, who served notice on his students in a letter to the editor of a Washington newspaper that he was "staging his own demonstration—a demonstration for society, law, and order, common sense, and discipline. My protest will appear on your report cards. It will look like this—'F.' " He continued, advising his students: "Your major undertaking ought to be passing your courses—not passing judgments on the President of the United States, Congress, the Supreme Court, Dow Chemical, everybody over the age of thirty, and everybody under the age of thirty who doesn't agree with you."

A university is a place where a certain discipline is required. That discipline must not be made subject to "democratic" controls, to what Chancellor Samuel Gould [formerly of the State University of New York] has called the "authoritarianism of the amateur." The principle of majority rule, which is one of the essential characteristics of democracy, can have little place in a true university community. The mission of the university is (a) to impart knowledge; (b) to conserve knowledge; and (c) to advance knowledge. The only one of these missions which is susceptible to even a modicum of student participation is the first. In the classroom situation continuous responsiveness between teacher and student is a vital necessity, but if teacher and student exchange places, the rationale of education evaporates. In the current reversal of roles between teachers and learners the rich and essential disciplines of education are lost, and teachers vie with each other in efforts at influence-peddling with students.

A department of economics at one of the campuses of the University of California has responded to pressures, from both a frightened administration and threatening students, for student voting privileges at departmental meetings by announcing that once each quarter the department will schedule a general meeting of faculty, graduate students, and undergraduate majors at which students will be expected to contribute discussion, suggestions, and questions. But, the department announcement continues firmly, "Student participation will remain advisory. The Department of Economics is not a government nor is it in any way analogous to a government. Individual faculty members were not elected as representatives but were appointed by virtue of skill, training, experience, and accomplishments. . . . Therefore the Economics Faculty reserves the right to conduct its deliberations, discussions, and votes in private session."

In a true university the hierarchy of values will be preserved. In such a university, the past, the present, and the future meet; and those who have experienced the human situation meet and talk with those who have only begun to experience it. It is a place where recipes for successful living of those who think they possess them and those who think they want them can be exchanged and critically examined. Since in this context the learned and the learners do not occupy the same level of learning, a university must operate to some extent hierarchically. It must maintain within its own boundaries the principle of professional elitism which respects the leadership role of the learned on the one hand and the necessary disciplining of the learners on the other.

Constant vigilance must be exercised, however, to prevent this professional elitism from shading into professional snobbery. Like all members of institutional groups, educators tend their own herd of sacred cows. One of these, "Everyone who disagrees with us is an ignoramus," is likely to get loose and wreck the entire barn. Another one, whose name is scarcely even softly whispered, is called "The public be damned." Another is sanctimoniously called "Freedom to live in an ivory tower."

Irving Kristol has pointed out that "when an institution no longer knows what it is doing, it starts trying to do everything." The university, as its name implies, has universal interests and is dedicated to the investigation of all things under the sun. But it is not, therefore, a place for all men. It must be, above all, a place where mind meets mind, and positions in it for both teachers and taught must be reserved for the mentally fit. Those who cannot meet this elementary qualification should seek help in other places, for the university should not be thought of as a relief agency dedicated to salvaging damaged or improvident lives. When such people are brought into the university they find themselves in an uncongenial environment, they soon conclude that they are "sons of the stranger," and they strike back at the forces that placed them there. Even the best-equipped and best-intentioned institution of higher learning must fail if it attempts "to make a silk purse out of a sow's ear."

Teachers as Activists

This truism has been lost sight of in the demands for the universalization of higher education to which colleges and universities have enthusiastically responded since World War II. As these institutions have become objects of mass invasion by the sons and daughters of John Q. Public, they have

shown themselves incapable of providing the learned faculties needed to justify their role as citadels of higher education. In substitution they have put at the head of classrooms
young instructors who were already indoctrinated in the
techniques of political activism and who, unable to carry
on classroom dialogues in their own learned discipline, have
simply imposed their immature political opinions upon their
classes. They have taken advantage of the sincere idealism of
the young people under their charge and have induced them
with inflammatory rhetoric and impassioned illogicalities
to share their own frustrations and to serve their own destructive purposes. To them are attributed many of the depredations committed by militants on college campuses.

A professor of philosophy at Yale University urges a student audience to launch a nationwide student strike. "Go
back to your communities and organize," he commands.
"Make a summer of organized resistance against oppression."
When professors, under the aegis of academic freedom, teach
such irresponsible and subversive doctrines to young, highly
impressionable people, they must expect to pay a price for
their antisocial exercise of this freedom. By such utterances
they reduce higher education to lower education, and they
should be separated from the university community. The
freedoms of education—academic freedom—must be exercised
under the law.

Into the vacuum formed by the apathy of chancellors,
presidents, and boards of trustees, some "liberal" professors
whose teachings through the years have created the climate
for student rebellion and have in some cases triggered actual
acts of violence, have moved in an attempt to salvage their
positions of authority over the students, to ingratiate themselves with an outraged public, and to disguise themselves as
honest academicians. The best that can be said for them is
that, provided their own conversion is now truly sincere, they
have literally been hoist with their own petard, they have
been failing through the years to perceive the full implications of their own teachings, and they must be characterized

now as slow learners, and, as such, too stupid to serve further as mentors of the young.

Students are not entitled to demand "relevance" from their teachers. It has been one of the glories of higher education in America that it has provided a wide range of educational opportunities from which young people could freely choose subjects most conducive to their own growth. This has been considered to be an indispensable attribute of a free society, but it is now being seriously limited by the demand for relevance. Young people must themselves assume the responsibility of supplying the relationship, if any, between their classroom experience and their own career interests. When students demand that educators supply the relevance in their lives they are asking for more than they are entitled to ask and more than any system of formal education can give them. The late Bishop James Pike once stated that every course that he had taken in college "was relevant, including Greek grammar." The university can only say, "Here I stand embodying certain social values and equipped with certain techniques and procedures and with the facilities and the disposition to discover better ones."

Reasserting Civilized Values

Institutions of higher learning which have allowed themselves to become advocates of suicide, destruction, nihilism, and chaos, which have assumed political roles, which have transformed themselves into universal service institutions, and which have opened their doors with the proclamation "come one, come all," have overextended themselves. Under the assaults which are now being mounted against them and which they are failing to withstand, they would do well to retreat to more defensible positions. Grim as the plight of higher education is, the only hope lies in a reassertion and revitalization of values which have been the casualties of conflict and which now lie discarded in the debris. Those values are the values of civilization itself.

First, colleges and universities must set forth their institutional objectives clearly and simply and restore conditions under which freedom to learn and freedom to teach again become possible. These two freedoms define the limits of academic freedom, which is merely the right of intellectual dissent but does not include any other form of dissent.

Second, public institutions of higher learning must be dissociated from politics to the maximum extent possible within the context of public tax policies, and private institutions of higher learning must dedicate themselves once more to the pursuit of independent education of the traditional type, divorced from political and public influences.

Third, college and university facilities must not be used for activities that do not advance the purposes of higher learning.

Fourth, campuses must not be treated as sanctuaries from the law.

Fifth, the criteria for appointment, retention, and promotion of faculty members must be broadened to include not only scholarly competence and proven teaching ability but also matters of professional conduct, and faculty members who fail to meet these criteria must be dismissed.

Sixth, universities must not appoint or retain faculty persons who are members of an organization which requires its members to accept its orders in violation of the principle of free inquiry inherent in the doctrine of academic freedom.

Seventh, existing faculty imbalances must be corrected to permit consideration of all sides of controversial questions. There is always hope when people are given opportunities to listen to all sides; when they are denied such opportunities errors harden into prejudices.

Eighth, policy-making authority which has been delegated to academic senates and faculties should be converted into a mere advisory power which will be given due consideration by officials responsible for the administration of public colleges and universities.

Ninth, the principle must be maintained that students are admitted to the university at the invitation of the university and that membership in its society is a privilege, not a right. If, on the contrary, access to higher education continues to be construed as a right, then all placement tests must be abolished, and all admissions offices in colleges and universities must be closed. The young man or young woman who comes up to the university and is duly admitted to its privileges should be explicity put on notice both orally and in writing:

> You are now entering into an institution which has been established for the purpose of offering you an academic education. We shall do this to the best of our ability according to rules of discipline applicable to both faculty and students. Should anyone disagree with any part of our programs he should present his grievance to proper officials of the university for consideration. Criticisms whenever justified will be appreciated and the appropriate rectifications will be made. During the course of the year we will not permit demonstrations or clamorous dissent that tends to constrain civil liberties in any manner, and persons who act in that way will be expelled or dismissed.

Tenth, when a student submits himself to the university experience under these conditions, he and the university enter into a voluntary contractual relationship which can be ended by the failure on the part of either to abide by the terms of the contract. For this reason the university can and should require the student to deposit a bond for his good behavior and respect for its property and other physical facilities.

Compliance with these ten points is essential to enable colleges and universities once more to perform their primary task, which is to instill in young people a deep conviction of the need for critical intellectual inquiry into the human situation and a steadfast determination to cling to those values which are demonstrably true.

WHAT STUDENT RIGHTS IN EDUCATION? [5]

What are the specific rights students may legitimately expect, and in their continued absence, may legitimately demand, in conjunction with their enjoyment of academic freedom? These rights seem to me to fall within two generic classes—social and educational. Let us consider each in turn.

There is a growing recognition that students should be entrusted with the power to regulate their social life through their own organizations. As far as possible, students should be treated as adults and allowed to assume the responsibilities of governing themselves. But they must be held responsible for the abuse of those responsibilities. Moreover, they should not be deprived of rights they would enjoy as citizens where the exercise of such rights does not interfere with the educational mission of the university.

Although this should be a general rule, even in this area the faculty cannot abdicate all responsibility. With respect to student life and student organization, the faculty must retain the ultimate power of veto, when basic issues of educational policy or human rights are involved. If any action of the organized student body or of any student group threatens the educational mission or goal of the university, whether on campus or off campus, the faculty must be prepared to intervene.

For example, suppose students decide to establish fraternities or sororities. Normally a decision of this sort would fall within the jurisdiction of student authority and its representatives. But if these societies were organized along racial or religious or secular lines that interfered with the educational process or the right to learn, the faculty would be under an obligation to veto the proposed action.

In any situation in which the majority of students deprive a minority of its rights, after all appeals to the conscience and goodwill of the majority have been exhausted,

[5] From *Academic Freedom and Academic Anarchy*, by Sidney Hook, professor of philosophy at New York University. Cowles. '70. p 58-68. Copyright 1969, 1970 by Sidney Hook. Reprinted by permission of the publisher.

the faculty must intervene to curb the dictatorship of the majority and to defend the right to learn or the academic freedom of the minority. Student bodies in the South a few years ago displayed racist prejudices and elsewhere they have been known in the past to be susceptible to the spirit of vigilantism.

In the present days of tension, as students take over control of their own social life on campus, often resorting to the tactics of confrontation to implement demands they make against administration and faculty, it is advisable for the faculty to stipulate in advance certain guidelines to permissible limits of dissent. In the nature of the case, these must consist mainly in indicating what conduct cannot be tolerated if any individual or group wishes to remain a member of the academic community. After several recent shocking incidents, some students blandly insisted that there were no explicit provisions condemning disruptive sit-ins, and that any punishment for their action was *post hoc* and unfair.

Universities and Punishment

One curious aspect of current debate about disciplinary measures for the disruption of the educational process has been the contention of some civil libertarians, sympathetic to student activism, that university punishment of students' actions that also fall under the sphere of competence of the civil authorities is a form of double jeopardy, and hence a violation of the student's constitutional rights.

Students have also taken up this cry and denounced as paternalist tyranny or worse any effort of the university to enforce its own penalties over and above those laid down in the criminal code for *all* citizens. This claim has not prevented them on occasion from demanding that the university intervene on behalf of students who have run afoul of the law in order to get criminal trespass and even more serious charges dismissed.

The contention that any university punishment, whether sanctioned by student organization or faculty and administration, for an offense punishable under the law places the individual in double jeopardy is odd on its face. For the punishments by the university, which run from censure to expulsion, are never of the same order as civil punishments.

A student who breaks into a print shop off campus to steal university examination papers for sale to his fellow students, when apprehended and convicted, is punished for breaking and entering. If the university punishes him—as it always has in such cases without a murmur of protest ever having been heard—by suspension or expulsion, is this double jeopardy?

A student arrested on the campus for pushing drugs to fellow students is punished under the law. Should he, therefore, be exempt from university punishment? There is such a thing as conduct unbecoming a student or member of the academic community. Such conduct may or may not be subject to the sanctions of the criminal code. But that has nothing to do with the legitimacy of university discipline enforced in a nonarbitrary fashion through academic due process.

The fact that a practice has been long established does not testify to its wisdom or its justice. When challenged, its rationale must be explored in the light of current needs and conditions. It should be obvious, however, that if nothing punishable by law can be punished by the academic community by relevant educational measures, and if everything legally permissible were educationally permissible, the university could not function as a genuine educational organization. Plagiarism either by students or faculty members of something in the public domain is not a legal offense. In fact, it may have constitutional protection under the First Amendment. Would it, therefore, be unjustified to impose some academic sanctions for gross and deliberate intellectual dishonesty?

Another curious feature of contemporary agitation over student rights is that although the movement for the abolition of course requirements is growing, students seem oblivious to the compulsion, often outrageously abused, involved in the imposition of student activity fees that run into hundreds of dollars in the course of their academic career. These fees are collected by the university and turned over to official student organizations that disburse them as they see fit.

In some eastern colleges, student organizations elected by a handful of students have donated thousands of dollars to the Black Panthers and SDS [Students for a Democratic Society], whose views are strongly opposed by the majority of students. They have also underwritten the traveling expenses and speakers' fees of crusading propagandists for causes quite foreign to the interests of those whose money has been conscripted. Although such situations can be remedied, the possibility of abuse would be greatly reduced, if not eliminated, if all such fees were made voluntary. Extracurricular activities would then reflect the genuine interests of the mass of students rather than the interests of special groups whose members have managed to slip into the strategic positions of influence and power.

Privacy of Student Life

Academic freedom for students in determining their social life is subject to a great many complications flowing from the fears of parents about the morals of their daughters, restrictions of towns concerning the consumption of alcohol, and the controls of state legislatures on the budgets of colleges and universities. In one college, a suit by the irate parents of a pregnant sixteen-year-old coed, on the ground that the college had failed to exercise the proper supervisory care of its dormitories, was narrowly averted because of the fear of publicity.

The uneasy relations between town and gown can easily be exacerbated by public and conspicuous consumption of drugs and liquor. Budgetary reprisals by legislatures may cripple the educational future of the university. Usually the legitimate demands of students to determine their social life can be granted without fuss and feathers if provocative actions are avoided. Most students are sufficiently sensible to proceed with discretion in situations where the state of public opinion is such that public reaction may damage the quality of their educational experience. However, the responsibility of faculty and administration is primarily to make the alternatives clear to students so that they are aware of the consequences of their decisions. In the end, it is the students who must make the choice about their personal lives.

What Educational Rights?

What does academic freedom for students mean with respect to strictly educational matters? On this question, confusion abounds. The divisions of opinion run in all directions.

My own view is that students are justified in presenting three kinds of demands wherever a situation exists that makes these demands relevant. First, students should have the right of educational participation in the form of *consultation*. They should have the right to be heard, to receive explanations, to present their own views concerning *any* educational measures that affect them. This should apply to proposals to increase tuition, to requirements for graduation, to the use and modification of grading systems—even to the content of their courses.

Actually, although it has become customary to use the language of "rights" concerning participation of this kind, it is an imperative of effective teaching. Any scholar or administrator worth his salt would welcome such interest and discussion, and greet with enthusiasm this active participation and consultation by students. For in this way they can be more readily motivated and inspired to begin the processes of self-education and independent judgment.

Unfortunately, in the past students have been profoundly indifferent to educational matters. There is reason to believe that their present interest is belated and transitory, and that few students have as yet developed a sustained sense of the importance of pedagogical questions. Concerns that have moved students into confrontations have, with the exception of some aspects of the black studies program, never been strictly educational questions.

To those fearful members of faculty and administrative staff who are dubious about discussing these matters with students and inviting them to present alternative solutions to problems, one may address a single question: "If you have a good reason for making or refusing to make some administrative or curricular change, if you are not acting arbitrarily but reasonably, on what possible ground can you refuse to justify the position taken?" Students have sometimes been known to make valuable suggestions or counterproposals. The exercise of their right to consultation can itself become a vital educational experience introducing them to a complex of interesting social problems, and motivating them in an authentic and hopefully lasting way.

Consultation, discussion, dialogue, even debate with students on educational questions are one matter. The power of *decision* on educational questions is something else again altogether. One of the sorriest aspects of the contemporary chaos is the confusion between the two. Even some normally levelheaded persons in the academy have become infected with strange notions about what democracy in education means. The SDS, of course, on ideological revolutionary grounds makes the vehement routine demand that students should have the power "on an equal footing with the faculty" to make decisions on all educational matters. Sometimes its members speak as if students should have the preponderant power. This means that the students, or their representatives, would have the power to outvote or at the very least veto the faculty on any proposed curricular change, and nullify the decisions of any professor who seeks to organize his course in a manner they disapprove of.

Well, why not?—For many reasons. First, this is to draw an equation between the authority of ignorance and that of knowledge, of inexperience and experience, of immaturity and maturity. To be sure, there are some students who in all these respects are precocious and some teachers who have slipped through the professional safeguards against incompetence and are inglorious mediocrities. But it would be absurd to base a general policy on rare and exceptional instances. There are ways of containing the incompetence of teachers, and a perceptive teacher can grant to specially qualified students the opportunity to determine their own educational projects. But the decision to do so must lie in *his* discretion, and his discretion alone.

The Authority of Teaching

Is it arbitrary to assume that there is a presumptive authority that attaches to the teacher's function?—No more so than it is arbitrary to assume that the master craftsman in any field should exercise the authority of his superior skills. In what field does the apprentice enjoy the same authority as his teacher to determine the order of studies and the nature of the disciplines required to become a master journeyman? This is obvious if one considers the student as potentially an apprentice teacher, or assumes that every student may someday qualify for a professorship so that he is a potential colleague—a very large assumption, indeed. How much more obvious with respect to those who, so to speak, are just passing through the subject or field, oblivious to the depth, riches, and lasting values of the subject matter of the teacher's specialty?

A second reason for leaving the *decision* as to what factors constitute the necessary and sufficient conditions for the achievement of a liberal-arts education or any other kind of university education, general or professional, to faculty bodies is that by law and custom *responsibility* is vested in them for granting the degrees and certification of competence.

Everyone in the community has a stake in maintaining the best standards of education and in safeguarding against their erosion. One need not overdramatize the possibilities, but even an incompetent medical or laboratory technician may imperil a person's health or life. The student who receives a degree carries with him the judgment and reputation of the faculty "to whom it may concern," and it concerns a great many.

It is not for nothing that degrees from different colleges are rated differently by those in the know. The differences reflect the different standards of the faculties. Were students to share as coequals in the planning, execution, and evaluation of their curriculum, their degrees would be debased. Invidious distinctions—much worse than those current today —would develop, reflecting the degree of involvement of students in the evaluation and certification of their education. The best students will not attend universities in which their fellows are the peers of their teachers.

A third and even more weighty reason for leaving the decisions on curricular matters to the faculty is that concern with its basic problems normally is a life-long commitment. Students come and go every four years. And if they are well educated, they have more intellectual humility, are more aware of what they don't know, when they leave college than when they enter.

Most teachers grow old in their profession. The range of evidence open to members of the faculty is of an altogether different dimension from what is available to any one student generation. The judgment of the relative importance of different social factors, the assessment of future developments, the immunity to fads and pressures of public opinion and popular culture—whether mediated by alumni or government or the mass media—as these bear on the construction and necessary revision of curricula of study require a historical perspective that only the faculty can acquire. Having fought, over a half century, for curricular reforms inspired by John Dewey's philosophy of education, I can testify that on occasions faculties have lacked historical perspective, and oscillated between the extremes of holding on to fixed curricula inherited from the past (whose excellence was proved in their eyes by the fact that they had been nurtured by them) and a willingness to add anything to the curriculum that would draw enrollment and subsidies. But unfortunately no group exists—neither trustees, nor administrators, nor alumni, nor students—that can supply historical perspective if the faculty lacks it. The only improvement possible to an educational institution suffering from the weaknesses of a poor faculty is to develop a better faculty, not to elevate the students to positions where they preempt the role of the faculty.

Students as Equals

Finally, because the class concept has recently been introduced into the discussion of higher education, and the relation between student and teacher assimilated into the class struggles of industrial society, it cannot be stressed too strongly that the educational interests of teachers and students in the colleges are common. Every piece of new knowledge won, every problem clarified, every intellectual power sharpened and developed, every original insight or vision that lights up the darkness, is a gain for all. One excellence does not exclude another. All intellectual values are shared. That is why when students have won the right to consultation, they can with good conscience and good sense leave the ultimate or final decisions on educational matters to the faculties. There is no spiritual inequality among those who constitute the academic community of teachers, learners, and administrators in virtue of the differentiation of status and functional roles anymore than there is in a family where mother, father, older and younger children accept different tasks and responsibilities.

If the right to consultation is granted students, beneficent changes are sure to result—if we do not confuse ourselves and others by smuggling into the concepts of consultation and communication the notion of decision, too. Unfortunately this confusion is very much in evidence in recent measures adopted by some faculties who feel themselves threatened by student unrest, and, in order to head off confrontations on campus, have rushed to put students as *voting members* in key curriculum committees, or have made them an integral part of the faculty senate with the same privileges with respect to decisions on curricular affairs as the senior members of the faculty. This has the consequence—in the event of a divided faculty vote—of giving unqualified students the strategic balance of power in deciding issues of the gravest educational importance.

These decisions have been reached in haste, and are justified by the invocation of the weasel expression, "Giving students the right to help determine educational policy." The operating word here turns out to be "policy"—whose ambiguity is the key that opens the door to educational absurdity. If the students have the right to consultation and participation, this certainly gives them the right to help determine educational policy to the full extent of their rationality, ingenuity, and persuasiveness. More than this is not required. But if, as is only too often the case, the right to help determine educational policy is construed as the right to help make the decisions, to cast votes just as members of faculties do, the upshot is likely to be continued and intensified educational disruptions.

One can write the scenario in advance. Once faculties have yielded on the principle of student decision on educational matters, the students will demand a more equitable representation on faculty committees and faculty senates. It will not be long before the SDS or the Peace and Freedom party or some other would-be revolutionary student group captures the student seats as they so often have done with respect to student-editorial and student-government posts, whenever they set out to do so. An issue will arise, or one can easily be created, on which the students will be defeated. They will then take their case to the general student body agitating for greater if not equal representation. . . .

Even without the potentialities of political embroilment, there are dangers flowing from the presence of students on committees dealing with matters in which, in the interests of *other* students, strict privacy is desirable. At Oberlin College, notable for its liberalism and high academic standards, in the spring of 1969 student members of the Oberlin Committee on Admissions, unable to convince faculty members of the wisdom of one of their proposals, published confidential material from student-admission folders; and shrugged off the charge that they were guilty of a grave breach of ethics and a disgraceful violation of the rights of privacy.

There are certain inescapable risks involved even in student participation but they are worth taking because of the immense possible educational advantages. But there are no compensating advantages in the risks incurred when students are given the powers of *educational decision*.

That is why with respect to the first legitimate demand for student rights, we must say: "Consultation, yes—decision, no."

A DECLARATION ON CAMPUS UNREST [6]

The unprecedented, comprehensive, and often unpredictable changes that are taking place in this age both disturb and alarm large segments of our society. Most of the changes and attendant alarms affect the operations of our institutions of higher learning. They are also related to the values, concerns, and behavior of our young people. In coming to grips with the compelling issues, all who would think seriously about them must recognize that present-day society —in America and in many foreign lands—is in serious trouble on many fronts. We see around us racial conflict, continued poverty, and malnutrition midst unparalleled prosperity and seemingly unlimited promise. We are confronted by pollution of our environment, decay of our cities, the continuation of wars and the threat of war, and everywhere a vague but widespread discontent with the general quality of life.

[6] A statement formulated by a group of educational administrators, trustees, and foundation officers who met April 4-5, 1969, under the auspices of the American Council on Education. (The statement was subsequently approved by the Council's Board of Directors.) The Council. 1 Dupont Circle, Washington, D.C. 20036. Reprinted by permission.

These problems affect all of society, not the university alone or the young alone. We must all be concerned to deal intelligently and responsibly with these problems that are neither the exclusive discovery, nor the sole responsibility of the young. Yet the depth of feeling among young people in many countries today about the issues, their general dissatisfaction with the slow-moving ways of society, and the extreme behavior of a small minority of students are evidence of the profound crisis that involves our entire society and, specifically, the university community.

The university itself has often become the immediate target of student discontent, sometimes couched as legitimate complaints about the deficiencies of the universities, sometimes devised as a softening-up exercise for assault on the wider society.

How to deal with campus crises arising from the widespread protests has become a major public issue and the cause of confused and angry debate. That there should be deep anxiety about the course of the conflict and its possible outcome is understandable. No social, racial, or age group that perceives itself and its values to be seriously threatened will fail to strike back. Increasingly there are backlash temptations to enact strong, often ill-considered, and largely futile measures to cope with a youth rebellion that none of us fully comprehends, not even the youth themselves.

Searching for Balanced Judgments

Certain balanced judgments are proper to make, however, as we search for understanding and solutions:

1. It is important for the public to understand that, despite the nationwide publicity given to student disorders, the great majority of American campuses have remained peaceful. On campuses where conspicuous disorders have occurred, educational programs generally have gone along their normal ways. Most students and faculty have continued

to carry on their regular work. In the main, good teaching and good research, as traditionally defined, have been uninterrupted.

2. On the undisturbed campuses and among the majority of orderly students, however, there are widely shared discontents which extremists are at times able to manipulate to destructive ends. Moreover, even in the absence of violence, there has developed among some of the young a cult of irrationality and incivility which severely strains attempts to maintain sensible and decent human communication. Within this cult there is a minute group of destroyers who have abandoned hope in today's society, in today's university, and in the processes of orderly discussion and negotiation to secure significant change. Students and faculty are increasingly aware of the true nature of this group and are moving to deal with its destructive tactics. The necessity to deal with extremists, however, is placing an extraordinary burden upon the whole educational enterprise and upon those who man it. Consequently, universities are having to divert their energies and resources from central educational tasks in order to deal with student unrest in its various forms.

3. The spectacular events precipitated by the extremists should not be allowed to obscure the recent accomplishments of those students, faculty, and administrators who have serious interest in constructive changes in society and in the university. They have broadened the curriculum and improved teaching. They have moved toward a more open and participating pattern for university governance. And they have begun to make the work of universities more meaningful in dealing with the problems of society. Those efforts must continue. Reform and self-renewal in higher education are ongoing imperatives.

4. Meanwhile, the speed and scale of social change have imposed many kinds of demands upon educational institutions for which their programs, their capabilities, and their

funding are not always adequate. Moreover, universities are increasingly asked to perform functions for society, particularly in reshaping the behavior, values, and life-styles of the young, on which the family and other social institutions have already had major influence—or lack of influence. Some of society's expectations for universities are quite unrealistic. Insofar as these expectations can be dealt with, they involve a sharing of responsibilities among diverse social institutions. Many of society's demands require new resources and fresh approaches to old and new problems.

Historic Concerns of the University

5. Recognizing the right of and even the necessity for constructive dissent—and allowing for inevitable arguments over what is in fact constructive—certain axioms must be accepted as basic to the operation of any university:

(a) Disruption and violence have no place on any campus. The academic community has the responsibility to deal promptly and directly with disruptions. If universities will not govern themselves, they will be governed by others. This elementary reality is increasingly becoming understood by all components of the university community. Student and faculty groups, including the American Association of University Professors and the National Student Association, have recently joined in efforts to improve disciplinary procedures and to formulate clear and realistic codes for dealing with misconduct, and more particularly with violence and disruption. Also, by involving students and faculty effectively in the governance of the university, it can be demonstrated that there are better ways of getting views considered and decisions made than by disruption.

(b) The historic concern of the university community with academic freedom needs to be restated, reaffirmed, and vigorously defended against all, within or without the university, who would obstruct the right of scholars to investigate, teachers to teach, or students to learn. This reiteration is not to claim for the university special privileges that put it above the law or that free it from critical public appraisal—rather it affirms that the university must maintain a basic institutional integrity to function as a university.

(c) Violations of criminal law must be dealt with through the ordinary processes of the law—and universities must attempt to deal with disruptive situations firmly before they reach the stage of police action. Governmental attempts to deal with these problems through special, punitive legislation will almost certainly be counterproductive. Meanwhile, students and faculty whose consciences demand that they express dissent through law violation must be prepared to accept the due processes and the penalties of the law. They should not be encouraged to expect amnesty from the effects of the law. Such an expectation would be the ultimate use of the *in loco parentis* concept against which many young activists passionately protest. Nor should they expect amnesty from academic discipline, which is the most effective sanction in disruptive incidents.

6. The education community needs to undertake a far more comprehensive effort than ever before attempted to study the underlying bases of youthful discontent and alienation and the broad social problems to which they are related. As social critic, the university must help society understand and solve such problems.

7. All universities should give particular attention to a continuing search for ways, including new social inventions, by which the life of rationality and civility, shared concern, and mutual respect may be supported and strengthened within the university community. The survival of the university and its long-term contribution to society depend upon the ability of the institutions to make their everyday life reflect that spirit and pattern.

THE RIGHTS OF PUBLIC SCHOOL STUDENTS [7]

Lately student protest and activism have raised serious questions concerning the rights of public school students. Because of recent litigation by some students or their parents, the courts have been forced to delineate student rights. . . .

Actually, the term "civil rights" has a legal connotation. Civil rights means the rights the individual has under the law. A brief legal definition is: "Civil rights are such that belong to every citizen of the states or the country, or in a wider sense to all its inhabitants." And that includes children. Also civil rights is "a term applied to certain rights secured to citizens by the Fourteenth Amendment and by various acts of Congress" (including the Civil Rights Act of 1964 which has been cited in recent cases dealing with students excluded from school because of long hair) .

In looking at the difference between the public schools and the private schools relative to civil rights, it is important to look at the legal relationship between the school and the student. In a public school the relationship is one of government. The public school is an extension of the state. The relationship is one of government and citizen. This is very important in civil rights because the antithesis of civil rights is police power. Police power is defined as "that inherent and plenary power in the state over persons and property which enables the people to prohibit all things inimical to comfort, safety, health, and welfare of society."

Public schools, as an agency of the government, possess police power; this differentiates the relationship between school and student in a public school situation from that in a private school situation. In a legal sense the relationship between the private school and the student is one of contract. It is, however, important to realize a person cannot be deprived of his civil rights by contract; a person cannot contract away

[7] From "Civil Rights of Public School Students," by Richard M. Blankenburg, a member of the department of education at Marquette University, Milwaukee, Wisconsin. *Teachers College Record.* 72:495-503. My. '71. Reprinted by permission.

his constitutional rights. And, of course, even in a private school, students and administrators are obliged to respect the comfort, safety, health, and welfare of society.

Schools No Longer Parents

But the public school represents a direct government-citizen relationship. There have been times when the courts have decided on the civil rights of public school students, which many parents and administrators recognize as justified in terms of the legal issues, but question whether the conclusions are in the best interest of the educational operation. For example, for years school teachers have contended, and the courts maintained, in the absence of parents that teachers become a kind of legal parent for the time the student is in school. The legal terminology is *in loco parentis.*

A Nefarious Doctrine: A recent decision made by a Wisconsin circuit court shocked many citizens. A male student had been excluded from school because his hair was too long. The judge ruled in this case there was no evidence a male student who allows his hair to grow long is a threat to society. He refused to accept the argument that the school acting *in loco parentis* had a right to determine the length of the student's hair. He stated:

> The argument that school authorities stand in *loco parentis* to the student is a tired, worn-out slogan. . . . That nefarious doctrine, *in loco parentis,* has been employed to heap adult abuse against children by judges and courts as well as teachers in the schools. The prejudice and frustration of people in power cannot be given unbridled license as practiced against children under the hypocritical disguise that the acts committed against them are for the children's own good. *(Wisconsin ex rel. Koconis v. Fochs, October 14, 1969.)*

Most parents and educators would have to concede the judge was correct in stating long hair is not a real threat to society or public education. But the same individuals, arguing on educational issues rather than legal ones, would insist that civic pride in their school would be enhanced considerably if all the male students were closely and neatly trimmed. (And some would contend shorn students are better behaved.) However, those charged with making these final decisions concerning the liberty of the individual citizen must weigh the civil rights of the accused on one side of the scales of justice and the police power of the state on the other side of that scale. In this case the balance swings in favor of civil rights. It is not a matter of majority rule (that would truly be mob rule), but of the unalienable right of the individual.

Most high school classes study civil rights and the Constitution quite thoroughly, and it would be paradoxical for teachers to advocate unalienable rights and then insist that students wait until after graduation to experience them. This seems to be what the judge in Wisconsin was saying—a student is a citizen with all the rights of a citizen under the Constitution. Recently the court trend has been in favor of male students expelled for long hair.

Armbands as Symbolic Speech

Black Armbands: In an important Supreme Court case, *Tinker v. Des Moines Independent Community School District* (1969), students of a school district wore black armbands to protest Vietnam war policy. The principals in the district held a meeting, after the initial wearing of the armbands, and enacted a rule prohibiting their use. The Tinker children continued wearing the black armbands, however, and with others were suspended for disobeying the rule. The Court was called upon to rule on the reasonableness of the suspension.

The Court ruled against the school district in this case. In its decision the Court declared that the wearing of an armband was a symbolic act; its purpose was to express certain views. Wearing the armbands, the Court said, was symbolic speech, the kind of free speech protected by the Constitution. (Of course, all speech is not protected by the Constitution. Justice Oliver Wendell Holmes once said shouting "Fire" in a crowded theater would not be a form of free speech protected by the Constitution.) In this case the Court found no evidence that students wearing armbands had created any disruption of classroom activities whatsoever. And because this symbolic display had not caused any disruption, it was judged free speech, of the kind protected by the Constitution.

Secondly, the Court found evidence that the principals' edict against armbands was based upon viewpoints connected with the Vietnam war. The principals simply disagreed with the armband wearers' opinions and reacted by issuing the ban. As a matter of fact, the court found students were allowed to wear other political symbols, such as political badges. Some students were even allowed to wear iron crosses (which the Court felt also had some political symbolism). The Court declared:

> The school officials banned and sought to punish petitioners for a silent, passive expression of opinion unaccompanied by any disorder or disturbance on the part of the petitioners. There is, here, no evidence whatever of petitioners' interference, actual or nascent, with the school's work or of collision with the rights of other students to be secure and to be let alone. Accordingly this case does not concern speech or action that intrudes upon the work of the school or the rights of other students.

In another place, the Court said:

> In our system undifferentiated fear or apprehension of disturbance is not enough to overcome the right to freedom of expression. Any departure from absolute regimentation may cause trouble. Any variation from the majority's opinion may inspire fear. Any word spoken in class, in the lunchroom, or on the campus that deviates from the views of another person may start an argument or cause a disturbance, but our Constitution says we must take this risk. . . . In our system, state-operated schools may not be enclaves of totalitarianism. School officials do not possess absolute authority over their students. Students in school as well as out of school are persons under our Constitution.

Teachers and Free Speech

Free Speech: Another recent Supreme Court case, *Epperson v. State of Arkansas* (1968), also involved free speech. This case deals with the teacher's free speech which, in essence, affects students, since restriction of the teacher's freedom limits the knowledge made available to students. Arkansas had a law that prohibited teaching the theory of evolution. Because the science textbook included this theory, the teacher would be guilty if she taught from it. The teachers brought this case to court to question the constitutionality of the law.

In striking down the Arkansas statute, the Supreme Court for the first time used the term academic freedom in reference to a public elementary or secondary school. The courts previously had talked about academic freedom in regard to universities, where historically there is a precedent for academic freedom; public schools were not organized to do original research as the university was, and consequently, public schools did not warrant traditional academic freedom.

In the *Epperson* case the Court held: "The vigilant protection of constitutional freedoms is nowhere more vital than in the community of American schools and this Court will be alert against invasions of academic freedom." Apparently, what the Court had in mind was the right of the student to information, stating farther along in its decision: "As this Court said, the First Amendment does not tolerate laws that cast a pall of orthodoxy over the classroom."

In Defense of Conscience: In recent years the Supreme Court has also defended the conscience of public school children by ruling that religious services conducted in public school violated the constitutional guarantee of freedom of religion. . . . Yet it was not until 1963 that the Supreme Court ruled Bible reading (in the form of religious exercises) was an unconstitutional infringement of the children's religious freedom. The Supreme Court in *School District of Abington Township v. Schempp* held Bible reading ceremonies in public schools violated two clauses of the Constitution: the guarantee of the free exercise of religion and the prohibition against the governmental establishment of a religion. The Court went on to say, however, "Nothing we have said here indicates that . . . a study of the Bible or religion, when presented objectively as part of a secular program of education, may not be effected consistent with the First Amendment."

An earlier case, *Engel v. Vitale* (1962), concerned a prayer which the New York State Board of Regents required be said aloud by each class at the beginning of the school day. The prayer was: "Almighty God, we acknowledge our dependencies upon Thee and we beg Thy blessings upon us, our parents, our teachers, and our country."

The United States Supreme Court decided this statute had the effect of establishing a state religion and as such violated the First Amendment to the Constitution prohibiting the establishment of a religion by Government. . . .

What Freedom to Loiter?

Loitering: In many states the legislatures have been very quick to enact statutes to control the behavior of persons on school grounds, including especially the behavior of students. California, like most other states, enacted a statute which prohibits loitering in the vicinity of the school. In the case of *Huddleson v. Hill* (1964), the defendants challenged the constitutionality of the statute claiming the statute was too vague to enforce. To paraphrase the statute, it stated that loitering in the vicinity of the schools would be punishable by six months imprisonment or a $500 fine.

The term *loitering* is defined as to be slow moving, delay, linger, saunter, or lag behind. In the *Huddleson* case, the court decided: (1) If you interpreted the statute in the literal sense, it was too vague to be enforced; (2) When a court can adopt a broad or restricted construction of the statute, and the restricted one would make it a valid statute, then the restricted construction of the statute is the one that the court should adopt; and (3) What the statute in its entirety meant, and what the legislatures intended it to mean, was individuals should be prevented from loitering in the vicinity of schools to commit a crime.

The court specifically defined the meaning of the statute as follows:

As proscribed by the statute, the word *loiter* obviously connotes lingering in the designated places for the purpose of committing a crime as opportunity may be discovered. . . . Loitering as forbidden includes waiting, but mere waiting for any lawful purpose does not constitute such loitering.

The court then concluded:

Therefore, as we construe the state statute before us, persons who merely sit on park benches, loll on public beaches, pause in the vicinity of schools, and public areas frequented by children cannot be reasonably considered as loitering within the compass of the statute. It is only when the loitering is of such a nature that from the totality of the person's actions and in the light of the prevailing circumstances, it may be reasonably concluded that it is being engaged in "for the purpose of committing a crime as opportunity may be discovered," such conduct falls within the statute.

It would appear from this wording that if a student is excluded from school, and he returns to wait on the sidewalk after school for one of his friends, he is not guilty of loitering. The court's definition of the term *loitering* does throw a different light on the statute; the court has provided a more definitive right of a student in cases where the student is "loitering" in the mind of educators, but not within the interpretation of the statutes.

Students and Privacy

Privacy: Another recent case related to the civil rights of students took place in Mount Vernon, New York. The initial case, *People v. Overton* (1967), concerned Carlos Overton, a student in the public high school. Detectives from the police force came to the school and informed the vice principal they had a warrant to search the boy and his locker; the vice principal opened the locker for the police. Marijuana cigarettes were found there, and the cigarettes were used as evidence to convict the boy. It was later discovered that the search warrant of the police officers was not a valid warrant. The prosecution insisted that the validity of the search warrant was not important because the vice principal had the authority to open the boy's locker at any time necessary. The highest court in New York supported the prosecution.

Yet in an appeal to the Supreme Court of the United States, the Court in *Overton v. New York* (1968), overturned the highest court in New York on the basis of more recent Supreme Court decisions. Basically, the Supreme Court held that a person cannot, on the basis of an invalid search warrant, obtain access to the locker of a student after the student has been assigned the locker for his own personal purposes, and obtain evidence from that search to convict the student. The Court did not say a student can grab marijuana cigarettes and run down the hall pursued by the vice principal and the police department, throw the marijuana in his locker, slam the door, and then demand a search warrant. When there is obvious reason to believe evidence of a crime is concealed in a locker, and there is a danger involved in waiting to obtain a search warrant, a school official would be obligated to open a student's locker. What the Supreme Court does say is this: A police officer cannot lie to a student and say he has a valid search warrant when he doesn't, and by these means obtain evidence which can be used to convict the student. The Court also seems to be suggesting that a principal or vice principal must have good cause to invade the privacy of a locker assigned to a student for personal use.

The Right to Due Process

Due Process of Law: Another aspect of student civil rights, which the courts have been concerned with recently, is the constitutional guarantee that an accused person has "due process of law." The Fifth and Fourteenth Amendments state a person cannot be deprived of life, liberty, or property without "due process of law"; however, due process has not been specifically defined in the Constitution, and the courts have had to determine what actually constitutes due process. A recent case involving students and the due process clause of the Constitution is *In the Matter of Gault* (1967).

In this case, a young man on the basis of his own testimony was declared a juvenile delinquent in a juvenile proceeding and was committed to a state institution. Neither he nor his parents were adequately notified of the charges, nor was he adequately represented by legal counsel. The juvenile authorities contended that cases dealing with juveniles were of such a sensitive nature that some elements of due process cannot always prevail.

The Court held that juvenile proceedings which may lead to commitment to a state institution must be regarded as "criminal proceedings" for purposes of applying the privilege against self-incrimination. Unless a confession meets all the requirements of "due process" (notification of the right to attorney and the consequences of confession), commitment of a juvenile to a state institution cannot be sustained in the absence of sworn testimony and the opportunity for cross-examination.

The Court refused to accept the contention of the authorities that juvenile proceedings, because of their sensitivity, did not require procedure consistent with judicial due process. The Court declared: "Neither the Fourteenth Amendment nor the Bill of Rights is for adults alone. . . . Due process requirements do not interfere with provisions for the processing and treatment of juveniles separately from adults."

A hearing in connection with a juvenile court adjudication of delinquency need not conform to all the requirements of a criminal trial, the Court stated, but it must have all the essentials of due process and fair treatment. The Court declared, "Under the United States Constitution, the condition of being a boy does not justify a kangaroo court."

Madera v. Board of Education of the City of New York (1967) involved a suspended public school student who was the subject of a school "Guidance Conference." The meeting was attended by the child, the parents, the principal, the superintendent, the assistant superintendent, the guidance counselor, and the school-court coordinator assigned to the district. The conference is not a criminal proceeding, no record is kept, nor is any statement from the conference used in any subsequent criminal proceedings. As a result of such a conference, the student could be reinstated, transferred to another school, or with parents' consent, transferred to a special school for socially maladjusted children. The student contended he had been denied due process because he had been refused the right to be represented by attorney.

The court decided that a "Guidance Conference" did not represent a hearing which required ordinary legal procedure. The purpose of the hearing, the court reasoned, was to consider only educational matters; its consequences, therefore, were not sufficiently serious to require the adversary system ordinarily utilized in court proceedings.

In juvenile hearings which could have serious consequences to the student, it would appear that every care should be taken to guarantee him "due process of law." Boards of education hearings on expulsion would certainly be considered a case of serious consequences to the student. Yet many such hearings do not contain the elements of due process. For example, in many hearings, especially those involving young witnesses, the opportunity for cross-examination is not allowed. Obviously, the effect of an attorney interrogating a young child under the rules of adversary procedure would be difficult to defend. However, there is always the possibility of indirect cross-examination; questions to be directed to the witness could be submitted to the hearing officer by the defense, and then directed to the witness by the less aggressive hearing officer (who could also rule on the relevance of the questions). In this manner the individual could be provided with due process, and the due process could be adapted to juvenile proceedings.

Another aspect of due process relates to how a school handles police investigations of students in the school building. A booklet, *Academic Freedom in the Secondary Schools,* published by the American Civil Liberties Union, outlines the procedure advocated by the ACLU. The booklet states:

Where disciplinary problems involving breaches of law are rampant, schools cannot be considered sacrosanct against police and the proper function of law officers cannot be impeded in crime detection. Whenever police are involved in the schools, their activities should not consist of harassment or intimidation. If a student is to be questioned by the police, it is the responsibility of the school administration to see that the interrogation takes place privately in the office of a school official in the presence of the principal or his representative. Every effort should be made to give a parent the opportunity to be present. All procedural safeguards prescribed by law must be strictly observed. When the interrogation takes place in school, as elsewhere, the student is entitled to be advised of his rights, which would include the right to counsel and the right to remain silent.

IV. WHAT POLITICAL ROLE FOR YOUTH?

EDITOR'S INTRODUCTION

There can be no doubt that the youth movement of the past decade has had a significant impact politically. If the civil rights marches in the South are considered as one aspect of the movement, the impact is even more obvious. What has been called the New Left of the middle sixties did not, however, offer new political theory or action which proved viable or of great political moment. But with the eighteen-year-old voting privilege now a matter of law, it can certainly be said that a new political role for youth is at hand.

The first article in this section provides an overall survey of the influence of youth on politics in recent years and points also to some of the false promises that have been encountered. Two teachers of political science at the University of California at Berkeley, John H. Schaar and Sheldon S. Wolin, make the assessment. This is followed by a short note on whether or not certain youthful political groups of recent years have been inspired by neo-Communist philosophy.

The remainder of the section comprises articles pointing to more recent activist concerns of youth. Whether youth and the Establishment can cooperate was investigated in 1970 by a Task Force on Youth in a study conducted by the Daniel Yankelovich Organization for John D. Rockefeller 3rd. A press release reports on this research.

Two articles discuss the new eighteen-year-old voting privilege: one by Mary Goddard Zon, research director of the AFL-CIO Committee on Political Education; and the second by Guy Halverson, staff correspondent of *The Christian Science Monitor*. In the latter article reference is also made to the potential new legal rights that may accrue to eighteen-year-olds as a consequence of their enfranchisement.

What has appeared to many observers as a waning of the youth revolt may in fact disguise a redirection of youthful energies from public demonstrations into political and social action of a more meaningful nature. In the section's concluding article, the consumer advocate Ralph Nader comments on the opportunities open for student activists.

YOUTH IN POLITICS [1]

During the sixties, the young achieved a distinctive status for themselves, a status almost as sharply defined as that of other accursed or blessed groups, such as blacks, Jews, Junkers, and right-wing deviationists. The young demanded and received recognition of their distinctiveness as a group bearing its own values, possessing a unique culture, and dedicated to its own ends. Youth made a deep impact on politics, education, fashion, art, and the consumer economy. The entire nation was aware of the new presence: a Gallup Poll of March 1969 reported that campus disorders had replaced the Vietnam war as the primary concern of Americans. . . .

It is too early yet to assess the full impact of the youthful politics of the sixties on the larger political system, but some things can be said.

Over the course of its first ten years, the New Left failed to create [a] new radical theory beyond both liberalism and socialism. . . . Although the New Left gradually has moved away from the single-issue, basically reformist outlook of the early sixties over toward a general indictment of the system, that movement was not powered or accompanied by an increasingly coherent and comprehensive theory. Rather, it is a mood, a feeling of rage and revulsion, which is increasingly impatient with theory, or even thought and argument. The anti-intellectualist strain which was present in

[1] From essay entitled "Where We Are Now," by John H. Schaar and Sheldon S. Wolin, professors of political science at the University of California at Berkeley, authors of *Berkeley Rebellion & Beyond: Essays on Politics & Education in the Technological Society. New York Review of Books.* 14:3-10. My. 7. '70. Reprinted with permission from *The New York Review of Books.* Copyright © 1970 NYRev, Inc.

the movement from the beginning has triumphed. Theory on the New Left is now reduced to the vulgar Marxism and Maoism of Progressive Labor, or to the Weatherman view of white radicals as a suicide squad providing cover for black urban guerrillas, the true vanguard of the revolution.

Nor was the New Left able to develop a conception of political action coherent and effective enough, over the long pull, to sustain its members in a political vocation—to answer the questions: What does a radical look like in American politics, and how does he define himself in action which goes beyond the episodic and theatrical? Even the heroes, the ego-ideals, of the New Left are drawn from Cuba and China, despite the fact that the only indisputable statement that can be made about any future American revolution is that it will not look at all like any foreign revolutions we have read about. To mistake the many sporadic outbursts and uprisings of the past decade for *the* American Revolution is to misunderstand the nature of the political system within which these events have occurred, and to underestimate the capacity of that system to assimilate or to suppress anomalies.

Many modes of action have been tried by the New Left —civil rights work, community organizing, on-campus organizing, antidraft unions, factory organizing, political action as guerrilla theatre, even electoral politics—but none offered a decisive lever for radical change. There are now few hopeful projects on the left, and the only likely alternative life-styles seem to be Weatherman adventurism and the Yippie freakout. Maybe the only hopeful possibility for action—perhaps it was always the best one—is [German student activist] Rudi Dutschke's "long march through the existing institutions."

Youth Movement or Radical Politics?

But that means that the New Left would have to become less a student and youth movement and more a radical political grouping drawn from and able to work within many sectors of society for many different but unspectacular goals. The goals chosen would be those with high potential for accentuating evident contradictions in particular institutions, thereby undermining their present structures and challenging their present policies.

The New Left, so far, has shown little taste for such patient and pedestrian strategies. New Left radicals, for example, despite their own argument that the knowledge industry is the key industry in advanced societies, never developed much in the way of a theory and practice of countereducation. The "Free Universities," for example, have accomplished little; and most student efforts toward radical experimentation within the established universities have been suppressed or assimilated. The campuses are quieter now, because their managers have raised the ante on disruption and become more efficient at suppression, because few new leaders have appeared in the New Left since the early sixties, and also because people have learned that episodic outbursts, powered by indignation and hope but not sustained and directed by theory, are ineffective.

Despite these failings, the political impulses of the young during the sixties have had decisive consequences for the larger political order. The young opened up many closed questions, forcing them into the arena of public controversy, and making it "safe" and politically profitable for the middle forces in American politics to adopt them as issues. Thus while the young have not stopped the Vietnam war, they have reduced its scope and changed its objectives. Not many years ago only a handful of public men dared to oppose the war. Now opposition is so respectable that any overt attempt to spread the conflict to Laos and Cambodia would encounter strong official and popular resistance. Furthermore, debate about the war has also opened the question of American imperialism and neocolonialism, a question closed in the public mind since the Spanish-American War.

Many other questions were opened to public debate by the young people of the sixties: civil rights and racial justice;

conscription and the impact of militarism on American life; the structure and content of higher education, and university complicity with the military and corporate establishments. The young radicals publicized the issues of impersonality and bureaucracy, and sensitized their peers to the subtlety and ubiquity of the modes of bureaucratic control. It was the young who offered a serious and widespread challenge, for the first time, to the values associated with technology, rationalism, objectivity, and bigness. And now the question of ecology has also been opened. (We shall return to this.)

Safety for the Middle

The young opened all these questions, and made them safe for the middle. In order for the Muskies, McGoverns, and Fulbrights to criticize the Vietnam calamity with political safety, many of the young have been jailed or forced into exile or the underground. In order for civil rights and racial justice to become part of the nation's agenda, the young —black and white alike—have risked their careers and their lives. In order for the biases and hypocrisy of the legal system to become matters of public concern, and for the institution of the police to be seen as a political problem of the first order, the young have paid heavily in their freedom, security, and dignity.

In order for sexual mores to become more than a matter of polite discussion, the young have been driven to experiments in which they have taken on burdens and undergone experiences beyond their capacities. In order for the colleges and universities to reappraise the meaning of education, the young have had to disrupt their own educations and to pay the price in ignorance. In order for the ethic of technocracy and the cult of objectivity to be questioned, a whole generation had to blow its collective mind in self-experimentation.

What is fantastic about the politics of the sixties is that this crazy compound of wild energy, bizarre experiments, and the large number of lives whose promise will never be ful-

filled has all gone toward getting the moderates of America
to address themselves to the problems which have been tear-
ing the society apart. The young may not have radically
altered the system, but they have probably saved it, though
only at a terrible cost to themselves. This, apparently, is
what it takes to move the system.

The impact of the young on the political order does not
end with the list of issues opened and made safe for America
not as a gift but as a burden. . . . [The young] refused the
roles and identities prepared for them by their fathers, and
. . . still feel themselves to be superfluous in the future which
they are told is theirs. That is why New Left politics and
the cultural revolution were in large part struggles for identity. That is also why the demands and the style of the young
in this period were met with such bitter resistance. For the
young rejected the gift, and you do not do that without earning the hatred of the giver. That is new in American politics,
and it is one of the ways to state the defining impact of the
New Left on the old system.

So there has been a difference, even a great difference.
But underneath, it is possible to see forces within the system
that seem implacable to change, ineluctably working out a
logic deeper than the conscious intentions of either Right
or Left. Nixon's State of the Union message of January 22,
1970, offers some clues to those forces, and perhaps shows the
tendencies of the present and foreseeable future. . . .

A New Politics of Ecology?

That the longest and most significant part of the speech
was devoted to "the great question of the seventies," the
natural environment, was a recognition not only of the intrinsic importance of these problems but also of their great
interest to the younger generation. As the President noted,
the restoration of nature "is the cause of particular concern to young Americans. . . ."

By this move Nixon captured the issue which might
allow for peace between the political system and the younger

generation. . . . As the President's speech made clear, the terms of the new consensus would have to be consistent with the logic of technological society. He promised both technological progress *and* a better environment. "The answer is not to abandon growth but to redirect it." . . .

This new preoccupation with the natural environment means that for the first time since the early sixties, when civil rights agitation reached its crest, an issue exists which can connect the energies and ideals of the young to the policies and machinery of the system. Past controversies over the war, the draft, and educational reform sharply divided the young activists from their governors and elders. Now, on the broad ground of environment, they stand in common cause with the power elite. It is the kind of issue which is particularly appealing when the disappointments and abrasions of political encounters become too much, for it permits a full catharsis of moral indignation without seriously altering the structure of power or the logic of the system. Outrage can be directed against enemies whose evils are manifest, enemies who pollute and dirty, enemies who turn out to be the old foe of pastoral America, the corporations and monopolies.

It was predictable that the first target chosen by the Government in its new zeal for nature would be that ancient enemy, Standard Oil, which had polluted the waters of New Orleans. It is also predictable that future policies will not be implemented—any more than the Sherman Act was—to transform the corporate structure. We may expect, instead, ingenious devices for passing on to the consumer the costs of cleanliness.

The wide support commanded by the ecology problem is probably due to its uniquely ecumenical qualities. It is not an issue which provokes class conflict or widens generation gaps. Everybody wants clean air and water and open space. Another soothing feature of ecology is that it promises to remove the growing antagonism toward science evident in the student generation of the sixties. Students have begun to blow their minds with talk of ecosystems, recycling, and biospheres, apparently unaware that the concept of nature held by most biologists is not that of John Muir, but is as abstract and mathematical as the nature conceived by atomic physicists.

The political implications of the new and benign consensus appear most clearly when it is contrasted with the consensus pursued by the Johnson Administration. It is not accidental that at the same time as the Nixon Administration is using environment to forge a new unity, it has been shelving, retarding, or neglecting most of the previous policies dealing with blacks, the poor, education, and the cities. Johnson's vision of the Great Society lacked nobility, but it never excluded the disadvantaged. The Nixon consensus, by placating the silent majority, is also capitalizing upon the despair of the confused minority of activists who had struggled for racial justice and economic improvement and who now, by their commitment to nature, were tacitly conceding that racial and economic injustice were ineradicable facts of American society.

A Revulsion Against Politics?

The evolution of student activism, from the involvement of the sixties to the pastoral innocence of the seventies, bespeaks a growing revulsion toward politics. "Our politics," writes Jerry Rubin, is "our music, our smell, our skin, our hair, our warm naked bodies, our drugs, our energy, our underground papers, our vision." . . . The revulsion against politics is all the sadder because it is being expressed by a generation which taught itself to be the most deeply political one in recent history.

"Let us get America moving again," President Kennedy had exhorted. The struggle of the sixties demonstrated how difficult and costly that task could be. In casualties, it may be likened to World War I, where Europe lost a whole generation of young men. The high price of change is inherent in the basic features of the political system and its surrounding technological culture.

First, the institutions of our national Government have become bureaucratized to an extraordinary degree. They are huge in size, hierarchical in structure, and impersonal in their ways. As they become distended, they also become less amenable to control and coordination. Change is not typically defeated by a bureaucratic conspiracy but by the normal methods of the system. The tendency of any bureaucratic organization is to assimilate an important change of policy into its routine ways of proceeding, with the result that change is accommodated to the needs of the organization, instead of the organization accommodating itself to the demands of change. Add the interlocked bureaucracies of Government, business, and the military, and their extension throughout the world and into outer space, and it is apparent why it takes so much to move the system. One must literally move heaven and earth.

Second, since the Civil War, the system has steadily evolved into a mechanism for blurring choices. The party system works to make both parties identify the same issues and define their programs in very similar terms. At the same time, the dynamic supplied by competition between interest groups reinforces the main thrust of the system because the legitimacy of the groups themselves depends upon their accepting the rules of the game and striving for limited, incremental objectives. There is a powerful and persistent mainstream in American politics which fixes the limits of reform. Successful reform movements of the twentieth century, such as the New Freedom and the New Deal, have accepted the prevailing assumptions and proceeded to improve the going system. As others have pointed out, FDR's New Deal did not save capitalism, but it did save the corporations.

Third, the evolution of the American economy into a corporate structure with large-scale and interconnected units of finance and production has been accelerated by the tech-

nological revolutions of the twentieth century, especially
the revolution in electronics. This development has an important bearing upon the possibilities of change. On the
one side, the economy of the technological society is continually in process of innovation. It is governed by a rhythm
of incessant change, constantly producing new techniques,
equipment, and products. On the other side, technological
society has a logic and a set of imperatives which confine
change within narrow limits. It needs adaptable, technique-
oriented persons to operate its systems. It needs a society
which will not cling to traditions and customs. It needs a
public which has a bottomless appetite for consumption
and whose patterns of need and desire are easily altered.
Given the dynamic of change encapsulated in a certain logic,
the result is a paradox: a society dominated by the rigidities
of change; a society in which constant innovation conceals
a persistent direction. The difficulties encountered in changing this type of society are measurable by the apparent impossibility of resolving racial problems, reducing poverty
and class inequities, reviving the cities, coping with the
destruction of the environment, and redefining education.

The Politics of Technology

This form of society is evolving its own politics, one
adapted to the needs of technology. To begin with, the
present polarization actually works to the advantage of those
who are attempting to govern. The dialectic between Left
and Right provides a dynamic which an uncharismatic President would otherwise lack. The rhetoric, tactics, and de-
meanor of the young, together with the militancy of some
blacks, have activated the Right and kept it in motion. The
majority may be silent, but they are also resentful, fearful,
and ready for mobilization. The tactic of the Nixon Administration is to play off these dynamics in different ways. The
President feeds the fantasies of the Right by allowing his
Vice President and attorney general to fulminate and, occasionally, to crack down on dissenters. He gives the Right
an atmosphere of toughness and the Left a few martyrs, while

distracting the mass media by crude threats. At the same time, the President moves to undercut the Left whenever its objectives are taken over by political moderates. He will champion ecology, guaranteed annual income, a more rational welfare system, and peace in Vietnam. He will then process these causes to the point of blandness so that the Right can digest them, while the Left remains hungry but unsure of the reasons why.

There are signs that the President is winning the respect of the journalistic connoisseurs of American politics. And those barometers of approaching success, the social scientists, have begun their trips to the back door of the White House. The President is being praised as a shrewd pragmatist who possesses a superb sense of timing and is careful with his political capital. It is possible, however, that what is being admired in the President is more than the politics of opportunism, which is hardly new, but a new art form growing out of the demands of technological society. Perhaps the cunning of history has brought to the highest office in the land a man whose genius is nonleadership. The President himself has characterized his style as one of low visibility, and has asked for a politics of lowered voices. His ideal seems to be a republic whose public space would be filled by silence, or, at most, by the "lowered profile" of a rarely seen leader, conducting low-key politics for a silent majority.

The new politics reflects the fragilities of technological society. Such a society is made anxious by instabilities and tensions, passions and animosities. As it comes to see itself more and more as a vast electronic circuit, it is tempted to define its unity in nonpolitical language, to seek values like "economic growth" and "clean water" which are safely "above" politics. "Restoring nature to its natural state is a cause beyond party and beyond factions. It has become a common cause of all the people of this country."

Beyond these dimensions, there is another aspect of technological society which has interesting political implications. It is a commonplace that technological society increasingly deprives men of useful and satisfying work. Despite all of the inquiries into the psychology and sociology of factory life, for example, it is evident that there is no way to alter substantially the routinized and uncreative nature of work in the factories. The same is largely true of clerical work and of much that passes for technical and even intellectual work.

This is the future awaiting the increasing number of young people who are being educated and encouraged to develop unsatisfiable expectations about their adult roles. A superfluous population is being produced, one that cannot be absorbed and simultaneously fulfilled. Moreover, education is designed to increase dissatisfactions. It encourages self-consciousness and critical awareness, and nourishes hopes of a better life with beauty and dignity. . . .

As yet, technological society has not figured out how to cope with its superfluous human beings. Without being too fanciful one might suggest the following possibility. The governors of the technological order could combine repressive legal measures with a welfare system which would produce euphoric demoralization. Such a welfare system would merely have to extend many elements already present or probable, such as a guaranteed annual income and unemployment compensation. Subsidize the arts so that music would blare throughout the land, and then take the final step of relaxing drug controls. This seems incredible, but no more so than Senator Goldwater urging the relaxation of marijuana laws. When the incredible becomes credible, then the system will have systematically introduced juvenicide as public policy.

ARE STUDENT REBELS NEO-COMMUNISTS? [2]

At the time of the students' revolt in Paris, in May and June 1968, a number of Gaullists said it was dominated by the Communists, and General de Gaulle himself opened his

[2] From "Neo-Communism and the Students' Revolts," by Maurice Cranston, a reader in political science at the London School of Economics and Political Science. *Studies in Comparative Communism.* 1:40-54. Jl./O. '68. Reprinted by permission.

election campaign by saying: "The danger is communism."
Others thought differently. Many supporters of the students'
revolt argued that the Communists had sabotaged it, and
Jean-Paul Sartre after the election blamed the Communist
party for the triumph of the Gaullists.

There seems to me to be some truth in all these contradictory utterances, and I think that something may be learned
about the connection between political movements and the
students' revolts, not only in France but throughout the
world, if the contradictions can be unraveled. This is not to
say that the students' revolts are simply political phenom-
ena or that they are wholly explicable in terms of political
and ideological pressures, but I do suggest that such pressures
are an important feature of those revolts, and one that is not
always well understood. . . .

The Varieties of Communism

It is necessary here, I think, to give some thought to what
is meant by communism. After having had, until the Russian
Revolution, a fairly wide and loose meaning, the word "communism" has since gained a distinct, and I feel a useful,
precision in common usage as the name of the doctrine up-
held by the Communist parties attached to Moscow. . . .
Although the breach between Moscow and Peking, and the
repudiation of what is now called Stalinism, have produced
a little unsteadiness in the use of the word, I think that clarity
demands and that common convention still authorizes the
use of the word "communism" *tout court* exclusively for the
Moscow-type doctrine. Various neologisms are available to
designate the variant and deviant types. I propose in this
paper to adopt the expression "neocommunism," but to argue
that there are at least two very dissimilar types of neocommunism, though both are connected with student revolts in
different parts of the world.

The connection between communism *tout court* and the
student revolts has been minimal. Sartre's complaint against
the French Communist party that it hindered rather than
helped the students' movement is, from Sartre's point of view,

a fair complaint. Sartre argued that the Soviet Union was satisfied with the carve-up of the world at Yalta and did not want to see the balance of power disturbed. This may or may not be true, but it is clear enough that the Soviet Union, and the French Communist party which it dominates, would rather see de Gaulle than moderate Socialists like Guy Mollet in charge of France; and however much de Gaulle may attack the Communists, the Communist party in its heart does not detest him, for he pursues a left-wing foreign policy more effectively than a Popular Front government could be expected to do. As for domestic policy, the French CP is the party of the trade unions, and what it wanted most from the strikes of May and June 1968 was economic concessions to the workers. . . .

What Sartre [stands] for is not communism but neocommunism in one of its most potent present forms. But before we consider this particular ideology, it is important to isolate it from another form of neocommunism which flourishes in Eastern Europe, and which has a definite connection with the student revolts that occurred in Czechoslovakia, Poland, and Yugoslavia in 1968.

The theory of East European neocommunism has been given its most elaborate expression by the Polish philosopher Adam Schaff. It is sometimes also known as Socialist humanism, and its main features are these: (1) it is against bureaucracy; (2) it is against censorship and police surveillance; (3) it favors the use of science and technology for the improvement of the people's conditions of life; (4) it favors free contacts and "dialogue" with the inhabitants of capitalist countries; (5) it believes in peaceful coexistence; (6) it believes that individuality can be reconciled with the economic exigencies of socialism, and nationalism with internationalism. In short, East European neocommunism is a liberalized communism. . . . The unvarnished demand for . . . liberty is simply "not on" in Eastern Europe; the only way of asking for it is in the Socialist humanist or neo-Communist package. . . .

The Theorists of Neocommunism

The kind of neocommunism which flourishes in the West, and which has played a conspicuous part in Western students' revolts, is quite unlike the East European neocommunism, and in some respects it is its very antithesis. . . . Among its theorists we might usefully single out three: Herbert Marcuse in the United States, Sartre in France, and R. D. Laing in Great Britain. All these men are scholars of high distinction, although their backgrounds are different, Marcuse being a philosophical sociologist, Sartre both a literary man and a philosopher, and Laing a psychiatrist. They are all avowed Marxists, but what is no less important is that they are also all in one sense or another Hegelians. Their Marxism is *not* that of the Communist party or of the orthodox Leninist school. The Marx they follow is not so much Marx the econo-mist, the later Marx, the author of *Das Kapital*, as he is Marx the sociologist, the author of the early philosophical manu-scripts. Their Marx is, like themselves, a Hegelian of sorts, a metaphysician, not a positivist, not a scientific determinist. Their Marx is the philosopher of "alienation."

This association of neocommunism with the reformula-tion of Marxism may account in part for its appeal to in-tellectuals, for orthodox communism or Marxism-Leninism (whether or not it is connected with the name of Stalin) is open to devastating objections, which no educated person can easily overlook: the economic analysis contained in *Das Kapital* has been proved by events to be false. But if Marx is discredited as an economist, Western neocommunism rescues him from criticism by presenting him instead in the role of a philosopher, where his position is less readily assailed. . . .

This conception of a Hegelian Marx has some exponents in Eastern Europe, the most notable being, of course, [the late] Gyorgy Lukacs in Hungary. But in the main, East European neocommunism rejects the Hegelian Marx and upholds an ideology which stands squarely in the positivist tradition of the French Enlightenment against the German metaphysical tradition which Hegel represents. This distinction might seem to be of interest only to professional philosophers; but its importance is in truth more extensive. . . .

Consider the question of violence. The ideology of orthodox communism plays down its role. Communist *practice,* of course, involves violence—war, sabotage, torture, assassination, and the rest—in the pursuit of its aims. But as much as possible such violence is veiled. . . . The three theorists I have named are all champions of violence. . . .

Sartre as an existentialist-Marxist is perhaps a less fashionable philosopher among the present generation of students than he was, as a straightforward existentialist, among students just after the war, but he remains the outstanding intellectual of the unorthodox Left, and his ideas continue to influence indirectly many young people who may not be aware of their provenance. Sartre has long believed in the necessity of political violence. . . . In his most substantial work of political and social theory, *Critique de la Raison Dialectique,* Sartre argues that all political societies rest on institutionalized terror. Indeed what he offers is really a modernized version of Hobbes' social contract theory, according to which all men are enemies (because of the scarcity in nature) and can be held together in societies only if they pledge to subordinate their private ends to the social end and if their pledge is enforced by terror. Unlike Hobbes, however, Sartre hints that if scarcity were removed, men might cease to be each other's enemies, and that in a world of Socialist abundance, when violence would no longer be necessary, a new and more pleasing species of man might emerge. However, Sartre takes care to emphasize that since scarcity has governed all history hitherto, it is impossible for us to conceive the nature of such a possible better world.

R. D. Laing, a Scots psychiatrist who is also a Hegel scholar, is by way of being a disciple of Sartre's. He is a youngish man, only a little over forty, whereas Sartre is sixty-three and Marcuse is over seventy. He is a less original theorist than the other two, but from the point of view of the young he is in many ways more appealing. Laing has adapted Sartre's existential psychoanalysis to therapeutic use in psychiatric practice; he has also published (with Dr. D. Cooper) an abridged English translation of Sartre's *Critique de la Raison Dialectique* under the significant title *Reason and Violence*. Laing also provides an important link between the theory of Western neocommunism and the ideology of the psychedelic hippie movement, since he is one of the most persuasive defenders of the use of mind-expanding drugs.

This liaison is of particular interest in connection with the student revolts. In theory the neo-Communists and the hippies are sharply at variance with one another: the hippies believe in dropping-out, in withdrawing from society, whereas the neo-Communists believe in changing society by revolutionary action; the hippies are pacifists, noisily dedicated to nonviolence and love, while the neo-Communists, as we have seen, believe in violence; the hippies believe in intuitive wisdom aided by drugs, while the neo-Communists believe in dialectical reason. But in spite of these seemingly insuperable differences, the neo-Communists and the hippies are in fact united by shared antipathies toward the bourgeois, the established, and "old" (that is, those no longer young), and united also by certain shared sympathies for the colored, the oriental, and the metaphysical. It is these sympathies, often diffuse and obscure, to which Laing in his writings gives a vivid articulation; his book *The Divided Self* analyzes the concept of alienation, so elusive in the works of Hegel and Marx, in a way which many young people find relevant to their own condition, even without understanding it.

But Laing remains more or less limited by the frontiers of his own subject, psychology; and the theorist who has come forward as the leading ideologue of the students' protest movement is Herbert Marcuse, at once the most austere and the most extreme exponent of neocommunism. There are doubtless several reasons why Marcuse is more popular than Sartre among the present generation of students. For one thing, Sartre has a marked element of authoritarianism in his thinking; in the lifetime of Stalin he was a steadfast defender of the Soviet Union against liberal critics. Marcuse, on other hand, has always been critical of Stalinism and his form of neocommunism includes, however paradoxically, a good deal of anarchism. Marcuse believes that the existence of a nonrepressive civilization is a possibility; he does not regard the word *utopian* as a word of reproach. Indeed Marcuse's theory offers a platform for reconciliation between Marxists and anarchists, and anyone who was puzzled to see the Black-and-Red Flag flying beside the Red Flag over the Sorbonne during the student occupation might gain some insight into that strange alliance by reading in succession Marcuse's *Reason and Revolution,* a Marxist book, and his *Eros and Civilization,* an anarchist book.

A German scholar who found refuge in the USA from Nazi persecution, Marcuse has been a professor at several of the best American universities. Nevertheless, his hostility to the American political system and to American civilization is intense. He describes the advanced industrialized, democratic, affluent society as exemplified in America today as hell. In such writings as *One-Dimensional Man* and *A Critique of Pure Tolerance* Marcuse explains why the affluent society is hell: it is hell because most of the people who live in it have been so deceived and corrupted by it that they actually like living in it and consider themselves to be free men, whereas in truth, Marcuse insists, they are slaves. In a society where most people are thus perverted by the comforts and illusions the system produces, a democracy which entails accepting the decisions of the majority is, Marcuse says, unacceptable. The majority of people need to be saved from themselves; they are the victims of their own "false consciousness" and need to be given "true consciousness."

Is Liberalism Dead?

Furthermore, Marcuse asserts that the liberal tradition of freedom and human rights has exhausted itself, and that

Western democratic societies of today are barely distinguishable from totalitarian ones. In these circumstances, Marcuse argues that a new doctrine of toleration is needed: toleration of the Left, toleration of revolutionary violence, toleration of subversion in affluent societies, but intolerance of the Right, intolerance of the Establishment, intolerance of any opposition to socialism. He explains that the scope of this policy of intolerance "would extend to the stage of action as well as discussion and propaganda, of deed as well as of word." Indeed, Marcuse belives that intolerance of what he calls "repressive" movements should be instituted forthwith:

Withdrawal of tolerance from repressive movements *before* they can become active; intolerance toward thought, opinion, and word, and finally intolerance in the opposite direction, that is, toward the self-styled conservatives, to the political Right—these antidemocratic notions respond to the actual development of the democratic society which has destroyed the basis for universal tolerance.

For the Gandhi-King types of nonviolent resistance movement, Marcuse has only contempt. "To refrain from violence in the face of vastly superior violence is one thing, to renounce *a priori* violence against violence, on ethical or psychological grounds (because it may antagonize sympathizers), is another." Nonviolence, he adds, is "a necessity rather than a virtue" and "normally it does not harm the case of the strong." Like Sartre, Marcuse claims that violence is a feature of all existing regimes. "Even in the advanced centers of civilization," Marcuse writes, "violence actually prevails."

What is usually known as the force behind the law, Marcuse calls the violence that is used to uphold domination. Consequently this is the kind of violence he disapproves of. But violence used *against* the established authorities is another matter. . . .

In short, Marcuse holds that so long as violence comes from below, from the have-nots, from the oppressed, it is a good thing. But this raises a difficult question. Who in the democratic, affluent society are the people below, who are the have-nots and oppressed? Clearly not the proletariat as defined by Marx, the industrialized working classes. Marcuse shares Sartre's despair of the workers of Europe and North America, who, as a result of technical progress and trade union organizations, have acquired such a generous share of modern affluence that they are content with the status quo. Sartre sees the possibility of a new proletariat emerging among the colored races, the inhabitants of "neocolonial" states in Asia, Africa and South America, a new proletariat which could enact the historic revolutionary role assigned by Marx to the Western working classes. Sartre develops this thought in his preface to Frantz Fanon's book *Les Damnés de la Terre*. Marcuse also believes in the revolutionary potentialities of colored people, and, again like Sartre, looks hopefully to such guerrilla movements as those of Castro and Che Guevara, notwithstanding the fact that Castro and Guevara and most of the known guerrilla fighters in Latin America have been the sons of middle-class families and by no means either have-nots or *les damnés de la terre*.

The Affluent Underdogs

Marcuse's new proletariat, however, is rather more extensive than Sartre's. Even within the affluent society itself, he observes, "underneath the conservative popular base is the substratum of the outcasts and the outsiders, the exploited and persecuted of other races and other colors, the unemployed and the unemployable." With this extensive category, many protesting students find it easy to identify themselves. Marcuse's theory offers them a place within the new proletariat which is to revolutionize the world.

Older readers may see only absurdity in the reasoning by which students, as a class, can think of themselves as underdogs. But it is necessary to remember that the social condition of the student as such has changed considerably in recent years. Before the last war, undergraduates formed a privileged minority among the young, and they were conscious of their privilege both in their immediate enjoyment of college life and in the prospect of places of advantage in society when they graduated.

But with the extension of university education to a vastly enlarged proportion of the young, a privilege tends to be transformed into a right; only unfortunately, especially in ever more overcrowded places like the state universities of America, the miserably underfinanced French and Italian universities and the English "redbrick" colleges [British universities or colleges other than Oxford and Cambridge—especially, any of the newer ones in the provinces] the experience of being a student has lost many of its former joys and former prospects of advantage. In such a situation, an appeal to the underdog of the kind that Marcuse makes can strike an immediate response in students who feel *deprived* —deprived, if nothing else, of the consciousness of privilege.

It is no accident that Marcuse's smallest following has been in those rich universities such as Oxford, Cambridge, Harvard, Princeton, and Yale where the undergraduates are still manifestly privileged. . . .

Student Grievances

Many students today have real grievances. But it is surprising how seldom those grievances figure in the public utterances of student leaders in protest movements. Some of their grievances are necessarily incurable; it is logically impossible for a university education to be at the same time a universal right and a special privilege. Other grievances of students are deeply felt but inarticulate—a feeling of almost religious discontent with the materialism of modern civilization is not uncommon among the youth of today. At the same time one should not fail to notice that many of the students' grievances are grievances which could be remedied by practical means—given sufficient funds and sufficient imagination on the part of those responsible for the running of universities.

One of the most telling objections to the spread of neo-communism among students is that it stands in the way of such practical reforms. The events at Columbia provide an especially forceful illustration of this; the demonstrators at Columbia pushed their activities to a point where it was obvious to everyone including themselves that they were doing irreparable injury to the very institution they were supposed to want to improve. The comment of the neo-Communist activist on this was candid: "Better no university at all than a university dominated by the Establishment." . . .

Neocommunism, having no faith in either the popular majority or the industrial working classes, is driven to the position of striking at the Establishment in any way it can.

Like the nihilists and the anarchists of the nineteenth century, it favors action rather than words, and it interprets "action" as deeds of destructive violence. To students as students, neocommunism has nothing to offer.

To students who transform themselves in imagination into members of the revolutionary "new proletariat" it offers the romantic satisfaction of joining a struggle against an abstraction which is scarcely intelligible, "alienation," and toward an objective which is barely conceivable, let alone achievable, a socialist-anarchist utopia.

YOUTH AND ESTABLISHMENT COLLABORATION? [3]

Initiative and leadership will be required on the part of the Establishment if there is to be any prospect of effective collaboration between young activists and the Establishment. . . .

[This is one of] the major conclusions of a large-scale survey of youth and the Establishment conducted by Daniel Yankelovich, Inc., for John D. Rockefeller 3rd and a "task force" he assembled [in the spring of 1970]. The purpose of the task force is to find ways to bring together the nation's young people and the Establishment, mainly business leaders,

[3] From a press release issued December 18, 1970, by Daniel Yankelovich, Inc. The release is a report on research done by this organization for John D. Rockefeller 3rd and the Task Force on Youth. Reprinted by permission.

to generate new programs and institutions aimed at pressing social problems.

The study, in which in-depth interviews were conducted among 872 students from 35 colleges as well as 408 business executives and other Establishment leaders, analyzed the attitudes of college students and business executives toward mutual cooperation to determine the obstacles standing in the way of collaborative efforts, and to test several specific project ideas.

The study revealed a near balance between positive and negative influences on the possibility of collaboration between youth and the Establishment.

On the positive side, the study shows that (1) both groups are concerned about similar domestic issues; (2) there is genuine interest by both groups in working together; (3) there is a mutual willingness to devote time and effort to the solution of social problems.

The study lists as major obstacles to collaborative efforts: (1) the emergence of a set of new values among college students; (2) the radical diagnosis of society held by many students, which is not shared by the business executives; (3) a general mistrust of each other.

Overall, it would seem that these positive elements are largely offset by the negative ones which have so effectively contributed to a national mood of suspicion and fear.

However, the study indicates that a meaningful working alliance can be created if:

I. Student participants come to believe that (1) more than a dialogue is involved and concrete results can be achieved; (2) Establishment participants have no ulterior motive such as appeasing them or distracting them from getting work done; (3) they are equal partners in the undertaking; and (4) Establishment participants will not "cop out" when their own parochial interests are at risk.

II. Business leaders come to feel that (1) students are serious and constructive; (2) students are prepared for a partnership based on mutual concerns arrived at through discussion and analysis; (3) students are willing to accept some of the experience and know-how of the business leaders and not just their financial support for projects with which business may or may not be sympathetic; and (4) students are not unduly impatient or unrealistic in the kinds of results they anticipate.

Areas for Cooperation

The study cites four areas of need that are most promising for cooperative effort by young people and business leaders—poverty, pollution, social justice and reform of party politics.

The students most likely to devote themselves to social change—and those who are influencing the vast changes the study foresees in our life style—are the 44 percent of students on our college campuses the study describes as Forerunners—students with a new set of values who put social contribution and meaningful work ahead of income, success and security.

In order to test reactions to specific forms of cooperation in these and other areas, the study asked students and Establishment leaders whether they would support four project concepts developed by the task force.

All four of the approaches proposed by the task force were found acceptable by both the students and business leaders. Most acceptable to both was the idea of a "university consortium" in which students from several neighboring colleges create an organization to work on a single major problem of the region—such as cleansing a river valley, upgrading ghetto schools, housing, transportation, crime, drug addiction, etc.—with cooperation, organizational assistance and direction from their schools' faculties and administrations.

Second choice of students was helping elect candidates to political office. This was the third choice of business leaders, who had reservations about the students' lack of judgment and capacity to tolerate failure and the potential divisiveness the project might create.

The business leaders preferred as a second choice holding Dialogue Weeks in various cities across the nation—with discussion among students and business and community leaders focusing on causes, effects and actions needed to eliminate poverty in each community. This was the last choice of students, who felt the sessions would be "all talk and no action" and that a week is insufficient time for concrete accomplishment.

The other approach considered, which business leaders approached with reservations, calls for a program for using the existing system—the laws, the courts, stockholder meetings, congressional inquiries, etc.—to produce meaningful social change in much the same way Ralph Nader has evolved an effective public service strategy in the area of consumerism. This was ranked as the third choice of students, who voiced concern that business leaders would back off from anything controversial, and the businessmen ranked it last because they feared student naiveté, overzealousness and lack of constructiveness.

On student willingness to work on projects such as those proposed, the study disclosed that nearly half the Forerunners (projecting to about 1.5 million young people) and one in four of the other students (projecting to an additional million young people) say there is an 80 to 100 percent chance they will commit at least six months of their lives to such projects.

The students—even the more dissident Forerunners—voiced a three-to-one preference for working with the Establishment to achieve change rather than with protest organizations.

Among businessmen, three in four are interested in and willing to collaborate with students and are willing to work on any project. Two thirds say they are ready to help sponsor and devote personal time to such endeavors. And more than one third feel an alliance with the students will create a common ground of understanding between the two groups and improve general communication between youth and the Establishment.

Attitudes of Today's Youth

The study, given broad scope by the free-form style of the in-depth interviews, also revealed a number of insights into the thinking and attitudes of today's youth. Among the disclosures are:

1. Most students are opposed to violence. Some 68 percent feel the burning of the Bank of America Building at Isla Vista [California] was unjustified. Another 28 percent hold doubts about its justification and only 4 percent feel the act was justified.

2. Student anger and frustration over the Vietnam war is high. Half the Forerunners and four in ten of all students feel strongly that the war is "pure imperialism." There is rapidly growing resistance to fighting any war designed to contain Communists, maintain our position of power or fight for our honor. And more than half the students would like to see fundamental reforms in the military while one in four of the Forerunners would like to see it abolished.

3. Signifying their feelings of alienation, more than half the Forerunners and four in ten of all students feel their personal values and points of view are "not shared by most Americans."

4. Most students would like to see either moderate change or fundamental reform in virtually all institutions in our society—big business, the military, the universities, trade unions, political parties, the mass media, the Congress, the FBI, the Supreme Court, the lower courts, the penal system, the high school and the Constitution.

5. Forerunners generally hold even greater contempt for these institutions. Notably, half this group would like fundamental reform of the present two-party political system while one in four would like to see it abolished.

6. Some 61 percent of all students feel business is too concerned with profits and not public responsibility. Another 34 percent partially agree.

7. Nearly half the students feel our nation's foreign policy is "based on our own narrow economic and power interests." Another 40 percent partially agree.

8. More than half feel we are a racist nation. Another one third partially agree.

9. Most students feel Black Panthers, radicals, hippies, college protesters, and conscientious objectors cannot be assured of a fair trial in the United States. Most Forerunners add drug addicts, Weathermen, and moratorium leaders to the list.

10. Two in three students feel radicalism will increase in the years ahead.

Offering an incisive picture of the Forerunner group, the study notes that they are less willing to accept restraints or prohibitions—regarding marijuana, disagreeable laws, police authority, employer authority—than other students or groups in the population. Two in three express sympathy with the goals of activists, though not with all of the activist tactics such as resisting or disobeying the police, assaulting the police, ultimatums, blockades and holding authorities as captives.

As a group, most Forerunners are fully or partially convinced that our social systems ought to be replaced by an entirely new one, that computers and other advanced technology are creating an inhuman and impersonal world, that severe economic recession and depression are inevitable with our type of economy, that economic well-being is unfairly distributed and that today's American society is characterized by "injustice, insensitivity, lack of candor and inhumanity." One in three, the study shows, feels the American system of representative democracy cannot respond effectively to the needs of the people, and another 54 percent partially agree.

In a further description of the Forerunners, the study notes that "we are struck by two motivations that enjoy exceptional strength among the Forerunner students: One is private, directed at personal self-fulfillment, self-expression and creativity. The other is public, directed toward a vision of what a just and brotherly society might be." The study contends the latter should not be mistaken for "youthful idealism," contending that "these young people will not change their basic outlook once they are out of college."

THE YOUTH VOTE [4]

Twenty-five million people between the ages of eighteen and twenty-four, who will be eligible to vote in their first presidential election on November 7, 1972, are now the subject of intense study, speculation and a spate of carefully hedged predictions.

The forty-seven-year-old Dayton housewife, made famous by Dick [Richard M.] Scammon and Ben [J.] Wattenberg as the archtypical component of the 1970 *Real Majority* [a study of how the silent center of the American electorate chooses its President, published by Coward-McCann] is now largely ignored by the pulse-feelers and reflex-measurers who are concentrating on youth.

Compared to the interest shown this year in young voters, the 12 to 12.5 million voters who "came of age" in each of the three previous presidential elections were virtually ignored. The sheer size—25 million—of this year's body of new potential voters fascinates election watchers. That is about the total number of votes cast for FDR in each of his four elections, and 6.5 million more than the total for all candidates when Woodrow Wilson was elected in 1916.

Politicians in both parties mull over a more recent statistic: a switch of 225,000 votes from Richard Nixon to Hubert Humphrey in 1968 in the three key states of Illinois, California and Ohio would have elected Humphrey. In 1972 there will be ten times that number, or 2.3 million newly eligible voters among the eighteen- to twenty-year-olds in those three states.

[4] From "The Youth Vote: How Many, Which Way?" by Mary Goddard Zon, research director of the AFL-CIO Committee on Political Education. *AFL-CIO American Federationist.* 78:12-17. N. '71. Reprinted by permission.

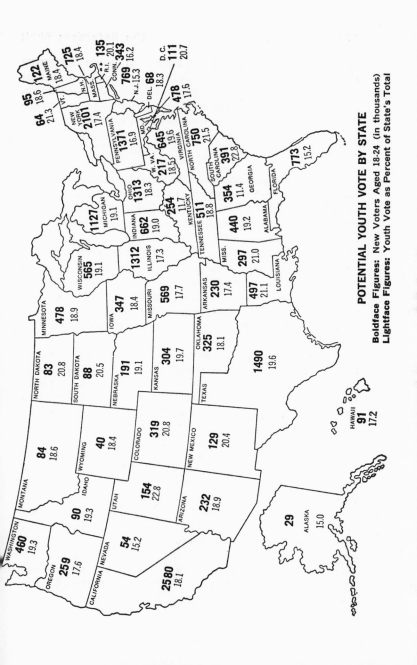

POTENTIAL YOUTH VOTE BY STATE

Boldface Figures: New Voters Aged 18–24 (in thousands)
Lightface Figures: Youth Vote as Percent of State's Total

Elaborate charts and maps have been drawn comparing the number of new voters with voting pluralities in recent presidential, congressional and gubernatorial races and projecting the possible impact of the new voters on the outcome of the 1972 elections. The impact could, of course, be enormous if a sufficient number of that 25 million is added to the pot of 73 million voting for President in 1968 and if they come down in significant numbers on one side or the other. Even if those conditions are not met, the impact could be decisive in a close election when any group can justly claim a decisive role. But most current interest centers on discovering who these young people are and guessing how many of them will vote and how they will vote.

Of the 25 million, 13.9 million would have been eligible to vote in 1972 even if the voting age had not been lowered, and 11.1 million were enfranchised in July 1971 when ratification of the Twenty-sixth Amendment to the United States Constitution lowered the voting age to eighteen.

Together they represent the largest number of voters likely to enter the electorate at one time in the future. In addition to spanning seven years, they were born between 1948 and 1954, the peak of the post—World War II baby boom. After 1972, new presidential-year voters will again span only four years, and the number will decline as the US birth rate declined, dipping in the 1960s to the levels of the Depression years in the 1930s.

The Effects of Education

In addition to any kinship engendered by this circumstance, they share a higher level of educational attainment than any preceding US age group.

Nearly 8 million are now in college—3.9 million among those who [are or] will be twenty-one by election day and 4 million in the younger group. That is an important fact, and its most important aspect may be that it means that almost 18 million, two thirds of the total, are not college students. They are job holders, job seekers, housewives, members of the armed forces and high school students.

Of the 8 million college students, only a small fraction are enrolled at the prestigious schools whose students receive the most attention. Many more attend junior colleges, community colleges and those schools whose unfamiliar names receive mildly jocular treatment on the Saturday night roundup of football scores.

Even though the great majority of young people have had no college experience, the general level of education has risen dramatically in recent years. In 1970, for the first time, the average voter was a high school graduate. While about one out of four (23.7 percent) aged twenty-one to twenty-four had one or more years of college experience in 1960, nearly two out of five (37.5 percent) had at least one year of college in 1970.

In 1970, over half (55.2 percent) of the population aged twenty-five and older finished high school, while 80.5 percent of those aged twenty to twenty-four had high school diplomas. The general rise in scholastic attainment can be expected to continue and to figure prominently in predictions of expected voter turnout.

Since the franchise has traditionally been exercised most by those at the top of the educational scale and since the better-educated products of the baby boom will continue to swell potential voter lists in the next few years, some observers believe that 1972 will witness the debut of a new, continuing, cohesive force in American politics which will in time become the New Real Majority. Shared educational experience and the Vietnam trauma are listed as the bases on which a voting majority may be welded to replace the New Deal coalition, over which last rites have been said periodically for at least twenty-eight years.

Education is the keystone of predictions of a large turnout of young voters. It is the added factor which permits the big youth vote theorists to discount or downgrade the disappointing turnout of women in 1920 following ratification of the Nineteenth Amendment and the limited number of blacks immediately added to the voting rolls following intense agitation and the passage of new legislation in the 1960s.

The large-scale failure of the 29.5 million newly enfranchised women to exercise the right to vote in 1920 is still reflected in our sorry turnout at the polls. Before 1920, the number of potential voters casting ballots hovered around 70 percent. In 1920, it plummeted to 49 percent and has never risen above 64 percent. And today, women of voting age are in the majority, 64 million to 56 million.

That the votes of those women who did venture to the polls in 1920 disappeared into the general electorate without a trace has been attributed by social scientists to sex-role dependence, an awkward way of saying that most women voted as their husbands did. Even the most militant feminist cannot dispute a certain mutuality of economic and social interests and goals between a husband and wife; so that tendency is not necessarily as witlessly docile as it is ordinarily represented to be. Over the years, public opinion polls have recorded some divergence of opinion. More women, including trade union wives, supported Eisenhower. Fewer women, including trade union wives, supported Wallace.

It should be remembered that women were not accorded the franchise by the benign generosity of the male electorate. A militant minority—roughly equivalent to today's militants in proportion to the total youth vote—marched, carried banners and suffered the discomforts of jail to win the vote for themselves and their ungrateful sisters. The extension of the franchise to women was, therefore, attended by considerable controversy and hoopla and subject to a degree of interest and conjecture not unlike that which now surrounds the youth vote.

While people actually died to extend the vote to blacks in the South, cumbersome registration procedures reduced the number voting where interest was highest and the lack of interest among Negroes elsewhere was attributed, probably correctly, to economic and educational factors, since most registration and voting laws and regulations make voting most difficult for the poor and the unlettered.

The theorists betting on a big youth vote in 1972 also discount the experience in four states, Alaska, Georgia, Hawaii and Kentucky, where voters under twenty-one were enfranchised before ratification of the Twenty-sixth Amendment. In 1968, fewer than 40 percent of the under—twenty-one potential in those states actually voted. Nationally, only 52 percent of the first-time presidential voters between twenty-one and twenty-four actually voted, compared to a 62 percent national average.

Since these two groups—those under twenty-one in four states and those twenty-one to twenty-four nationally—share almost the same educational experience as the current crop of new voters, various theories are advanced to explain their poor 1968 turnout. None is as persuasive, however, as the notion that voting is an acquired habit.

Census figures for the past two presidential elections show voter participation rising in stages to peak at those aged forty-five to sixty-five before beginning to drop. The sixty-five- to seventy-five-year-olds still vote more heavily than twenty-five- to thirty-four-year-olds and a higher proportion of those over seventy-five still make it to the polls than do those in the twenty-one- to twenty-four-year-old group. Blacks and Chicanos have been discouraged from acquiring the voting habit by mobility and other factors. There are low voter turnouts even among middle-income, educated whites in the District of Columbia, where the right to vote is relatively new.

In the general population the big difference in voting performance is not age but education. But here too the voting habit is reflected since a higher percentage of those twenty-four and over vote at every level of schooling than do the new voters aged twenty-one to twenty-four.

Since the educational level is rising steadily and since voter participation has been in direct ratio to educational achievement, the odds are improving on the number of

young people whose votes will be counted in 1972. But college students . . . will still be heavily outnumbered by their
elders and by their less schooled peers. Louis M. Seagüll, an
assistant professor of political science at the University of
Pennsylvania, notes in an article in *The Annals of the
American Academy of Political and Social Science* that

education sets the young apart from their parents [and also]
provides a basis for political cleavage within the younger generation itself. . . . Thus, it is a mistake to consider today's youth
as a monolith; it is less a class than it is two distinct population
segments which are likely to act differently, politically.

The Gallup organization, commissioned by *Newsweek*
magazine, estimates that, based on the October 1971 level of
interest, 42 percent of the 25 million newly enfranchised
young people will vote in 1972. That is 10 million ballots,
enough to engage the interest of both major political parties
and the respectful attention of presidential contenders.

Educated or not, they are not expected to march in lock
step to the registration places and on to the voting booth.
They are being pursued by campaign staffs and a growing
number of organizations, dedicated wholly or in part to making it easier for them to vote—by whipping up interest at
rallies, by engaging the services of entertainers, by frequently
successful efforts to permit students to register and vote
where they go to school and handing them pens that write
under water so they can register without leaving their surf-
boards.

Apparently, the more leftist the new voters, the more
ardently they are wooed. Some Democrats threaten that if
they don't approve of the deportment of other Democrats
they will decamp and start a new party into which, they
claim, young voters will hurl themselves with unbridled
enthusiasm.

Efforts to Register Youth

One organization is reported urging young people to register as the first step toward election as delegates to the 1972
Democratic National Convention—a chance to win four fun-

filled days in Miami, fighting Mayor Daley in air-conditioned comfort.

These appeals ignore the 17 million young people who are not in college, and they are directed to a tiny minority of the 8 million new voters who are college students. A number of organizations, including COPE [AFL-CIO Committee on Political Education], are working to register the great majority of new voters who are not in this category.

In Congress, in state legislatures and in the courts, the AFL-CIO has traditionally supported the extension of the franchise. Labor strongly backed voting rights legislation for Negroes, legislation to standardize a thirty-day maximum residency requirement in national elections and passage of the Twenty-sixth Amendment. The AFL-CIO is now supporting proposals for a uniform registration law to make it easier for everyone of every age to vote.

To reach young voters, some local COPEs have set up organizations of young union members. A number of state COPEs and international unions are conducting a census to find young members of union families so that they may urge and assist them to register. National COPE and state COPEs support other nonpartisan groups working to register the millions of young people who work for a living, keep house, go to high school or commute to college.

Nationwide, the various registration drives aimed at young voters have been wildly successful in some places and have fallen flat in others, for no apparent reason.

Mixed Results

The following are random samplings of newspaper accounts of voter registration drives in various states:

California: Perhaps the most successful youth voter registration drives in the nation have been conducted in California, where the Los Angeles *Times* reported as many as 100,000 youth aged eighteen-twenty registered in Los

Angeles County alone. Statewide, estimates are also high on the number registered among the state's 1.1 million new young voters.

Maryland: The Baltimore election board announced that 15,408 of the city's 62,727 voters aged eighteen-twenty, or about 25 percent, had registered. In a special 1971 congressional election held in Maryland's largely rural Eastern Shore district, election officials said 35 percent of the voters aged eighteen-twenty had voted—about twice the turnout of all voters. But only 6 percent of those aged eighteen-twenty were registered for the election.

Massachusetts: The Boston registrar said some 8,000 voters under age twenty-one had registered ahead of the deadline for the Boston municipal elections, but said the registration was "surely not as strong" as it should be. Also in Massachusetts, the Young Democrats, reporting that thirty-five organizations were already "tripping all over themselves" in registration drives aimed at the youth vote, said the group would instead concentrate on "the working-class voter, the union member and minority groups."

Connecticut: As the books closed for the November 2 city and town elections, the Connecticut secretary of state said 28,029 voters aged eighteen-twenty had registered, or about 20 percent of the state's 153,000 eligible. Registration was reported heavier in smaller cities than it was in Hartford.

Alaska: By September 1, some 4,000 of the state's 29,000 voters aged eighteen-twenty had registered.

New Jersey: The eighteen- to twenty-year-old registration was reported at only one fifth, or about 67,000 registered out of the state's 350,000.

Colorado: A compilation by the Denver *Post* of the first 5,000 new voters aged eighteen-twenty to register showed

58 percent registered as independents. The registration totals were reported as "relatively small" statewide.

Illinois: The Chicago board of election commissioners reported that a special September registration drive had enrolled 34,693 voters, 20,936 of them under twenty-one. That brought the total under—twenty-one registration to 42,000, or about 24 percent of Chicago's 175,000 potential.

Virginia: As registration closed for Virginia's November 2 special election for lieutenant governor, estimates were that "a small portion, perhaps 25,000 to 50,000" of the state's 300,000 new voters were registered.

New York: A New York *Times* reported registration of voters aged eighteen-twenty was generally sparse upstate —such as 18,460 out of 150,000 registered in Buffalo and 2,682 out of 16,000 in Albany. But in New York City about 221,000 out of 383,000, or 57 percent, had registered by September 1, the *Times* said.

North Carolina: Just under 10,000 of the state's 341,000 eligible voters aged eighteen-twenty had registered by September, the secretary of the state election board said, and he predicted a total of about 65,000 to 75,000 next year.

Michigan: Only 2,600 of a potential 22,000 Michigan State students registered in a three-day drive as the fall semester began. However, East Lansing officials blamed the low total on lines that caused a twenty- to thirty-minute wait.

Newsweek figures that by the end of October 1971, one fourth of the total had already registered and an additional 38 percent said they were certain to register. That would be a total of 65 percent, compared to 75 percent of the general population now registered.

What Party Affiliation?

In general young voters registering Democratic have far exceeded the number registering Republican. In Orange County, California, for example, where Republicans mounted a youth registration drive in the expectation that parental influence in this strongly conservative area would produce a GOP majority, young people were registering three to two Democratic at the latest check. Republicans have expressed the hope that the likelihood of hot Democratic primary contests is, at least in part, responsible for heavier Democratic registrations.

At the same time, the number of young people describing themselves as "independent" has accelerated an already conspicuous trend in the same direction in the general public. "I don't vote for the party, I vote for the man," and "I may not agree with what he says, but I admire him for speaking his mind," have already earned permanent standing as political clichés, intending to convey, as they do, a degree of thoughtful analysis of the political scene far beyond the Pavlovian response of pulling a party lever. Some observers, however, translate them to mean, "I don't really know what is going on and I don't much care."

Pollsters think the young "independents" may reflect some of this, but they also count in that number the radicals at both ends of the political spectrum and, especially among the better educated young people, a rejection of the legitimacy of party labels in the absence of any real party responsibility. Young liberals don't see why they should publicly identify with the party of James Eastland and young conservatives don't think the Republican party is big enough to accommodate them and Peter McCloskey.

According to the Gallup study in *Newsweek,* 18 percent of the new voters regard themselves as Republicans, compared to 27 percent of all voters; 38 percent say they are Democrats, compared to 45 percent in the general electorate; 42 percent say they are independents, compared to 28 percent of all voters. Thirty-six percent of those electing independent status say they are liberal or radical, 44 percent consider themselves middle-of-the-roaders and 13 percent identify with the conservatives.

Those farthest to the Left and Right in political philosophy are what one political analyst calls "small-base—high-intensity" voters. They are most likely to register, vote and work for the candidates of their choice. And they are most likely to follow the "If-we-can't-have-everything-precisely-our-own-way-we-won't-play" Pied Pipers. Their decibel count is as high as their intensity, sometimes misleading observers into overestimating their numbers.

By their own account, the great mass of new voters are somewhere between the two extremes.

When Gallup examines young voters' priority issues, the New Deal coalition seems less likely to die than to welcome millions of new voters to membership in the club. In order of descending importance, the top seven issues listed are: air and water pollution, job training for the unemployed, crime, schools, Medicare, housing for the poor and increased Social Security benefits.

And, in spite of all the talk about the "issues-oriented" young people, the suspicion grows that they are as frequently swayed by a pretty face as anybody else.

A January 1971 *Life* magazine poll placed Robert Kennedy and John Wayne among the top four of the "most admired" among the young, along with astronaut Neil Armstrong and comedian Bill Cosby. In the *Newsweek* poll, Ted Kennedy far outstrips any other Democratic contender among new voters, significantly depleting the Wallace vote, and George McGovern "was not included in the trial heats because of his low recognition and appeal" among the generation whose political responses were supposedly fixed forever by their opposition to the Vietnam war.

Computing the youth vote on the basis of an estimated 42 percent turnout and applying the current estimate of 60 percent voting Democratic, 30 percent Republican and 10 percent for Wallace, *Newsweek* applied the figures for the

new voters to the 1968 election returns and found that Nixon
would still be President if they had been present and voting
four years ago. Humphrey would have received a plurality
of the popular vote, but only Missouri's electoral votes would
have switched, leaving Nixon with 289, enough to win.

In summary, young voters seem to be somewhat more
likely to vote than earlier first-time voters, somewhat more
liberal than the general electorate and somewhat less inclined
to accept a party label.

Like the women who preceded them into the voting lists,
a great many will share the political goals of other voters
of the same economic and social experience—if not those
of their own parents, those of somebody's parents.

Most issues that concern them are not peculiar to their
age or to their generation.

They are not immune to the appeal of style and appearance.

And if they like attention, and who doesn't, they are
going to have an awfully good time in the next twelve months.

WHAT RIGHTS FOR EIGHTEEN-YEAR-OLDS? [5]

The massive army of American youth is starting to flex
its political and legal muscles. The result, most experts agree,
is that the United States will never again be quite the same.

The new youth thrust is on two fronts:

Securing increased legal rights through so-called age-
of-majority statutes at the state level, as happened in Wisconsin . . . where the Legislature enacted a "youth" law with
only seven dissenting votes in the lower house.

Stepping up political activism through the new Twenty-
sixth Amendment, which lowered the voting age to eighteen. . . .

[5] From "U.S. Youth Refocuses Activism," by Guy Halverson, staff correspondent. *Christian Science Monitor*. p 1+. F. 11, '72. Reprinted by permission from *The Christian Science Monitor*. © 1972 The Christian Science
Publishing Society. All rights reserved.

In Illinois, as well as elsewhere, youth organizers are scrambling to thwart voter registration challenges against young people.

All told, some 25 million young adults between the ages of eighteen and twenty-three . . . [could] be voting in their first presidential election this year—11.4 million of whom are registering for the first time. This massive group constitutes the one new—but totally unknown—factor in the 1972 presidential election.

Legal Issue

The legal issue—such as the age-of-majority statute just enacted in Wisconsin, and California, where the law . . . [took effect in March]—is inexorably linked to the political issue of youth voting, argues George Bell, research director of the Council of State Governments, a national research, action group. "The argument now seems to be that if one is old enough to vote, one is certainly old enough to exercise all the legal rights and privileges of majority," he says.

Adds Brevard Crihfield, executive director of the Council: "This is just one of those waves that hits fast. Within five years most of the states will have taken some kind of action on age of majority."

Already in the past two years some nine states—Illinois, Michigan, New Mexico, North Carolina, Tennessee, Vermont, Washington, California, and now Wisconsin—have lowered the age of majority, in effect giving nineteen-year-olds important legal rights. These rights include the right to own property, make wills, and execute contracts. In all of these states but one, eighteen-year-olds can marry without parental consent.

In at least twelve other states, moreover, according to the Council of State Governments, other legal restrictions also have been removed from young people.

Still, it is clearly the political activism of young people that is most intriguing to observers at this time. According to a recent survey of some 102 key metropolitan areas made by the Washington, D.C., based Youth Citizenship Fund

(YCF), at least 36 percent of the 11.4 million new voters between eighteen and twenty are already registered, and the presidential election is still nine months away.

"I think we're all going to be quite surprised at the total number of young people registered—particularly with the residency barriers breaking down," says Ken Guido, a university law instructor now associated with Common Cause [a citizens' lobby founded by John Gardner concerned with making government more responsive] in Washington.

Just what the youth vote will mean for the presidential race, of course, has all the pundits chewing their pencils at this time. Polls continue to indicate most young people consider themselves more "liberal" and Democratic than "conservative" and Republican, though there are also more "independents" among the young than among the general voting population. Moreover, it is not expected that young people will vote as any kind of bloc. Some analysts, in fact, even doubt that more than half of the youth vote will even vote in the general election.

Size of Youth Vote

But the important fact, say the experts, is the sheer size of the youth vote—a formidable constituency whose presence can't be taken lightly. For President Nixon in particular, the youth vote could be an important element. In 1968 Mr. Nixon carried some five key states by a smaller plurality than the number of new young voters now being registered.

Youth-group organizers are pleased that legal barriers to registration are quickly falling throughout the nation, particularly in college communities, where student populations often equal or outnumber the general voting-age population, and where adults are apprehensive about youth votes. According to Mike Cole, national director of the Youth Citizenship Fund, some thirty-one states—by statute, court opinion, or by an attorney general's opinion—now give students the choice of where to register.

Only some nine states currently require students to register at the home address of parents.

Since passage of the Twenty-sixth Amendment, at least forty court cases have grappled with the issue of registration sites, says Mr. Cole.

Meanwhile, a recommendation that would have allowed students to vote in their college towns, rather than their home towns, was sent back to committees at a meeting of the house of delegates of the American Bar Association (ABA) . . . [in February 1972]. . . .

What most concerns Mr. Cole and other youth organizers is that registrars in college communities might let young people register and then "wait until three or four days before the election to challenge them." Challenges against young people are already under way in some communities, such as at Menomonie, Wisconsin, and Champaign, Illinois.

Common Cause, the Youth Citizenship Fund, the American Civil Liberties Union, and other groups are hoping to build a backlog of court tests on challenges during the months ahead to thwart any last-minute registration challenges.

Important decisions upholding the right of student registrations have already been decided in Kentucky (in a Federal court, December 12, 1971) and California and Michigan (by the supreme courts of these two states, both on August 27, 1971). In addition there have been court orders in at least ten other states.

STUDENT ACTIVISTS [6]

If college students woke up to the world around them in the sixties, the seventies may be when they organize systematically to get something done. The campus demonstrations of recent years have subsided. But in their place a new kind of commitment is emerging that draws on a greater sense of realism about what is required to advance justice and build democratic power.

[6] Article by Ralph Nader, consumer crusader. *New Republic.* 166:10-11. F. 19, '72. Reprinted by permission of The New Republic, © 1972, Harrison-Blaine of New Jersey, Inc.

Two separate drives making headway around the country's colleges and universities show this new realism. The first is the voter registration campaign directed at the newly enfranchised eighteen- to twenty-year-olds. More will be known about the significance of this youth vote after the elections. But we know now that the stage has been set for a shift in political attitudes and responses toward the young by all levels of government. How far that shift will go depends in part, of course, on the number of youth who vote and their reasons for voting. But if the choice between candidates is to be broader than tweedledee or tweedledum, and if government between elections is to operate justly and efficiently, then the second drive centering around citizen action assumes signal importance.

In a dozen states from Washington to Vermont students are signing petitions for the creation of student public interest research groups. PIRGs, as they are called for short, are already under way in Oregon and Minnesota. Composed of lawyers, scientists and citizen organizers, these two PIRGs were established . . . [in 1971] after a majority of college students in those two states voted to raise their student fees by $3 per student a year. The money is used to hire full-time researchers and advocates who represent student social concerns in the community, and projects that enlist the energy and talents of students throughout the states.

A representative student board directs these PIRGs as independent institutions, with no connection to any of the schools. Nor do these student research groups get into partisan politics. They focus on community and state problems that need citizens' attention.

The Minnesota student public interest research group, for example, is operating during its first year on a budget of about $200,000. There are four attorneys, two scientists and other young people working full time on environmental, consumer, property tax, housing and municipal government problems. The group is developing problems for students to research and act upon, often together with older citizens, throughout Minnesota. It is becoming a catalyst for many lively students who have found a way to combine their studies and extracurricular interest with training in recognized community problems.

Students as Citizens

As the PIRG idea catches on in other states, more students will discover that there doesn't have to be an artificial distinction between students as students and students as citizens. Indeed, there is a mutually enriching relationship between the two roles. For too many years, millions of college students have dissipated their energies on courses and subjects that bored them because of their remoteness from the realities of the times or their lack of pertinence to the great public needs that knowledge should recognize. Boredom or lack of motivation continues to plague campuses across the country in a massive epidemic of wasted talents. What students are beginning to experience is that they get a more thorough education in their field of study if they can work on investigating and solving problems that challenge both their minds and their sense of values.

This is the appeal of the PIRG idea. It provides a continuing opportunity for students to connect their growing knowledge to public problems and solutions in the society. Science and engineering students can work on pollution prevention projects that challenge their technical knowledge and their sense of what science and engineering should be doing for human betterment. Political science and economics students will be able to test textbook principles in the context of everyday consumer or governmental problems and develop a deeper understanding of factual and theoretical research that relates to people.

If there is one thing formal education should give all students, it is an opportunity to become proficient citizens. Citzenship can reflect many viewpoints by many people. But its common ground is time and energy spent by people to better their society with the skills and values they have. Compared with earlier generations, it takes an extraordinarily long time for young people in America to grow up today. Preparation for so-called adulthood is taking longer and longer and the impatience of many young people reflects this inordinate stretchout in training. It is useful for students to acquire the skills of citizenship at the same time they acquire the formal tools of learning.

V. YOUTH AND THE FUTURE ECONOMY

EDITOR'S INTRODUCTION

Economic forecasts for the seventies do not suggest that the American economy will change drastically to conform to some of the trends of the youthful counterculture now so evident. That is the general conclusion of the first article in this section by Peter F. Drucker, a well-known management consultant. Even so, the challenge to the work ethic made by many youthful protesters of recent years has not entirely been disregarded by blue-collar workers and those in manual trades; the discontent of the latter groups is reported in the next selection by Herbert J. Gans, a professor of sociology at Columbia University.

The last two articles discuss other facets of youth's problems in the market world. In "The Blueing of America," a reply to the theories put forward by Charles A. Reich in his book *The Greening of America,* two sociologists, Peter L. Berger and Brigitte Berger, point out that even if many youthful protesters eschew the traditional job careers, there are other upwardly mobile young people quite prepared to fill the gap. For those who do "drop out" of the business world and join communes, whether built around alternative work or not, new problems may arise. These are discussed by Louis M. Andrews, graduate student at Stanford Institute for Behavioral Counseling.

THE YOUTH CULTURE AND THE ECONOMY [1]

A great many people, especially the better educated, take it for granted that today's "youth culture" is the wave of the

[1] "The Surprising Seventies," by Peter F. Drucker, management consultant and forecaster, and author of many books on social and economic questions. *Harper's Magazine.* 243:35-9. Jl. '71. Copyright © 1971, by Minneapolis Star and Tribune Co., Inc. Reprinted from the July, 1971 issue of *Harper's Magazine* by permission of the author.

future. They assume that as the present generation of college students become the young adults of tomorrow, their new life-styles will come to dominate American society and our economy. Practically all of the popular forecasters have been telling us that this will mean a dwindling concern with affluence and the production of material goods.

Maybe so. But the only facts that we know for sure about the future make these predictions look quite unreliable. To me it seems far more probable that during the seventies this country will return to a preoccupation with the traditional economic worries. Indeed, during the next decade economic performance—with jobs, savings, and profits at the center—may well become more important than it was in the sixties. Productivity rather than creativity is likely to be the key word. Charles Reich's Consciousness III [see Editor's Introduction to Section I, above—Ed.], in my view, is a description of what happened in the recent past, rather than a forecast of what will happen in the future. No doubt the next ten years will be turbulent; but their central issues and concerns may be familiar ones.

For the only thing we can know with certainty about America's near future—the next ten or twenty years—are a few facts about its population. We can foresee its size, its structure, and its dynamics, because everyone who will enter college or the work force between now and the late eighties already is alive. We know, for example, that this year [1971] marks a true watershed. It is the last year, for as long as we can see ahead, in which teen-agers—that is, seventeen- and eighteen-year-olds—will form the center of gravity of our population. Consequently, tomorrow's population dynamics are sure to be radically different from those of the past ten years, the decade of the Youth Revolution.

Everyone knows that the United States had a baby boom after World War II, but few people realize how violent and unprecedented it was. Within a few short years, mainly between 1948 and 1953, the number of babies born in this country rose by almost 50 percent. This is by far the biggest increase in births ever recorded here or, up until then, in any other country. It destroyed the axiom on which population forecasts had always been based: the assumption that birth-rates change only at a snail's pace, except in times of major catastrophe, such as war, pestilence, or famine. (This tradi-tional rule still seems to hold good for the underdeveloped countries. They have had their population explosion too; but it differs fundamentally from our baby boom. In the underdeveloped countries, birthrates have remained fairly stable. But in recent years, a much larger proportion of all babies have survived the first few years of life, primarily because of better public health services. Window screens, for example, now protect many of them from the fly- and mosquito-borne diseases, such as dysentery and malaria. A similar sharp drop in infant mortality, rather than a higher birthrate, also largely explains the rapid growth in the Ameri-can Negro population since World War II.)

We still have no explanation for this extraordinary baby boom. It may never happen again. But it did happen—not only in the United States, but also in the Soviet Union and in all of the other industrially developed states but one. Great Britain was the sole exception.

An Eruption of Teen-Agers

If the baby boom was unprecedented, so was the baby bust ten years later. The boom crested in 1953. For the next six years the number of births still increased, but at a much slower rate. By 1955 one- and two-year-olds made up a smaller proportion of the total population than they had in the pre-ceding years, and by 1960 the total number of births had started to drop sharply. It kept on dropping for seven years. Like the preceding rise, this was the sharpest fall recorded in population history. Almost 4.3 million babies were born in 1960, but only 3.5 million in 1967—a drop of 20 percent. Today the birthrate is still bumping along at about the same low level and shows little sign of going up.

Because of the violent fluctuations, seventeen-year-olds became in 1964 the largest single age group in the country. For the next seven years—that is, until 1971—the seventeen-year-old group has been larger every year than it was the year before. Throughout that period, then, age seventeen has been the center of population gravity in this country.

Now, seventeen is a crucial age. It is the age at which the youngster generally moves out from the family. Until this time, he has taken much of his behavior, and many of his attitudes and opinions—indeed, his way of life—from the family. At seventeen, however, he is likely to make his first career decisions and to take his opinions, attitudes, and concerns increasingly from his peer group, rather than from his family. Seventeen, in other words, has for centuries been the age of the youth rebellion.

In 1960 the center of population gravity in this country was in the thirty-five—forty age group—older than it had ever been before. Suddenly, within five years, the center shifted all the way down to age seventeen—younger than it had been in our history since the early nineteenth century. The psychological impact of this shift proved unusually strong because so many of these seventeen-year-olds—almost half of the young men—did not join the work force but instead stayed on in school, outside of adult society and without adult responsibilities.

The youth revolution was therefore predictable ten or twelve years ago. It was in fact predicted by whoever took the trouble to look at population figures. No one could have predicted then what form it would take; but even without Vietnam or racial confrontation, something pretty big was surely bound to result from such a violent shift in age structure and population dynamics.

A Population Growing Up

We are now about to undergo another population shift, since the seventeen-year-olds will no longer be the largest single group in the population. Perhaps more importantly,

this is the last year [1971] in which this group will be larger
than the seventeen-year-old group of the year before. From
now on, the center of population gravity will shift steadily
upward, and by 1975 the dominant age year will be twenty-
one or twenty-two. From 1977 to 1985, the total number of
seventeen-year-olds in the population will drop sharply.

In urban and developed economies such as ours, the four
years that separate age seventeen from age twenty-one are the
true generation gap. No period in a man's life—except perhaps the jump from full-time work at age sixty-four and
eleven months to complete retirement at sixty-five—involves
greater social or psychological changes. Seventeen-year-olds
are traditionally (and for good reasons) rebellious, in search
of a new identity, addicted to causes, and intoxicated with
ideas. But young adults from twenty-one to thirty-five—
especially the young adult women—tend to be the most conventional group in the population, and the one most concerned with concrete and immediate problems. This is the
time of life when the first baby arrives, when one has to get
the mortgage on one's first house and start paying interest
on it. This is the age in which concern with job, advancement, career, income, furniture, and doctors' bills moves into
the fore. And this is the age group which, for the next fifteen
years, is increasingly going to dominate American society and
to constitute its center of gravity.

This group is even more likely than comparable age
groups in the past to concern itself with the prosaic details of
grubby materialism. For the shift between the economic
reality they knew when they dominated our population as
seventeen-year-olds, and the economic reality they will experience when, still dominant in terms of population, they
become young marrieds, is going to be unusually jarring.
In the past, most seventeen-year-olds went to work, began to
earn a living and to think about money, jobs, prices, and
budgets. The affluent seventeen-year-old of the past ten years
—especially the very large proportion that went to college
(half of the males, and almost two fifths of the females)—

have never known anything but what the economists call "discretionary income." They may not have had a great deal of money in their jeans, but however much it was they could spend it any way they wanted without worrying about the consequences. It made little difference whether they blew it on the whims of the moment or put it into a savings account. The necessities—shoes, the dentist, food, and, in most cases, tuition—were still being provided by their parents. Now, within a few short years, they will suddenly have to take care of these things themselves. Even if a young woman marries a young man with a good income—an accountant, for instance, a college professor, or a meteorologist in the Weather Bureau —she will suddenly feel herself deprived. Suddenly she will have no discretionary income at all. The demands on her purse will inevitably be much greater than her resources because her expectations have risen much faster than her income will. She now expects health care, decent schools, housing, a clean environment, and a hundred other things her grandmother never dreamed of and even her mother did not take for granted when she first started out in married life.

She and her husband, therefore, will probably demonstrate a heightened concern with economics. Ralph Nader, rather than the Weathermen, is likely to foreshadow the popular mood. And no matter how radical Ralph Nader may sound, his is a highly conventional view of the "system." Indeed, his are the values of our oldest tradition: populism. Nader believes in economic performance above all; he makes it the central touchstone of a good society.

Many sociologists and psychologists in the past few years have pointed out that the significant gap in society today may be not that between generations—that is, between middleclass, affluent parents and their college-age children—but that between the kids in college and the young hardhats who have gone to work after high school. Usually it is the kids in college, the kids of the youth revolution, who are touted as the harbingers of tomorrow, with the hardhats representing yesterday. But it may well be the other way around. It is just conceivable that the nineteen-year-old hardhat—precisely because he is already exposed to the realities of economic life which are soon to shock college graduates—prefigures the values, the attitudes, and the concerns to which today's rebellious youth will switch tomorrow.

Jobs Will Become More Important

The shock the individual college graduate will feel on entering the job market may be severe. The shock to the job market itself may be even stronger. During each year of the next decade, we will have to find jobs for 40 percent more people than in each of the past ten years. The babies of the baby boom are only now entering the work force in large numbers, because so many of them delayed going to work by entering college. There has been a great deal of talk about the "young, educated employee," but he is only now beginning to come out of the colleges, and the full impact his group will make is still three or four years away.

The first implication of this is, of course, that jobs are likely to be of increasing concern to the young during the next ten years. The shift from "abundant jobs for college graduates" in 1969 to a "scarcity of jobs for college graduates" in 1971 is not, as most commentators believe, merely a result of the 1970-1971 minirecession. It is a result of the overabundance of college graduates, which will continue until the end of the decade even if the economy starts expanding again at a fast clip.

At the same time that many more young, college-trained people are out looking for jobs, the largest single source of jobs available to them in the sixties—that is, teaching jobs—will almost completely dry up.

During the past two decades the number of children in school expanded at an unprecedented rate, and, as every anguished taxpayer well knows, new schools had to be built to accommodate them. The reason, obviously, was that the babies born during the postwar boom were then reaching school age. Yet the teachers in the schools during the fifties and early sixties were mostly elderly; the last period of massive hiring had been in the twenties, an era when high schools grew as fast as colleges have recently. Between 1955 and 1970, therefore, an unusually large number of teachers reached retirement age, became disabled, or died. As a result, some five million college-educated young people found teaching jobs available during this period.

During the next ten years, however, no more than two million teaching jobs will open up; some forecasts put the figure as low as one million. One reason is that the school-age populations will be smaller, as a result of the decline in birthrates that began a decade ago. Another reason is that teachers today are the youngest group of workers in the country, so fewer vacancies will occur because of death and retirement.

This decreasing demand for teachers will be partly offset by an increasing demand for computer programmers, medical technologists, and employees of local governments. These jobs, like teaching, traditionally have attracted women with technical training. But an education in the liberal arts, which is what many college women choose, does not qualify them for such positions.

Some college-educated girls will probably not even enter the work force but make straight for marriage, home, and a family. If they do, however, this will only increase the economic pressure on them and their husbands, and intensify their concern with income, prices, and jobs. A good many young women will decide to work and, as they look for jobs in fields other than teaching, they will begin to compete with young men; it is hardly coincidence that there has been a sharp increase these past two years in the number of women applicants in law and accounting, for instance. (There are fewer women in management or the professions today than there were twenty years ago—a staple of Women's Libbers' complaints—but the explanation may lie as much in the tremendous demand for teachers since the fifties as in male chauvinism.) The woman who looks for work in business or government because there is no place for her in the public school is, of course, increasing the pressure for jobs.

The Coming Demand for Capital

If we hope to succeed in creating a vast number of new jobs for the young people coming into the labor market during the years just ahead, the country will have to find a great deal of new capital somewhere. For every additional job requires a capital investment. This is particularly true of the jobs we will need the most—jobs for highly educated people who are supposed to work with knowledge rather than with their hands. The greater the skill or knowledge demanded by a job, the greater the capital investment needed to make it possible.

A computer operator can't work without a computer. A doctor can't function efficiently without a substantial investment by somebody in a nearby hospital, equipped with everything from X-rays to artificial heart-lung machines—not to mention the costly equipment in his own office and in the laboratories on which he depends. A writer (or editor) needs not only his own typewriter, but an investment somewhere in printing presses and the facilities for nationwide distribution of books and magazines. An atomic physicist may need at least part-time access to a nuclear accelerator costing billions. A professor needs not only a classroom, but a good library, perhaps a laboratory, and probably housing for his students. A business executive's job depends on a going business, his own or a corporation's, and anyone who has ever tried to start even a small enterprise knows how much capital that eats up. So on the average a "knowledge job" in the American economy today—whether in business, education, or government —requires a prior investment of something like $20,000. (Even the hippies who go off to live the simple, close-to-nature life on a commune discover, alas, that they need some capital to buy land, spades, seeds, fencing, and liniment for their aching backs. And if they ever try to become truly efficient farmers, they will need a great deal of expensive equipment;

for modern agriculture has become a knowledge industry requiring both specialized training and a high degree of mechanization.)

The rate of capital formation, therefore, will have to go up very sharply if this country is to escape massive unemployment. Capital formation is, of course, simply the economists' term for the savings and profits which become available to create new jobs.

We cannot hope to get this new capital by drawing on fat in the economy—by "reducing excess profits," as youthful rhetoric sometimes bids us to do. Whatever their persuasion or politics, all economists agree that we have not been building up capital reserves in recent years. In fact, we have barely been maintaining our existing capital resources.

For inflation always eats up capital. Last year [1970] American wage earners laid away 7.5 percent of their incomes in savings, one of the highest savings rates on record in this country. Yet this was barely enough to offset what was lost through inflation on the savings they had set aside earlier. Few businesses in this country would have shown any profit at all during the past few years if they had adjusted their earnings figures to take into account the effect of inflation on their fixed assets (The Securities Exchange Commission requires them to do this with their foreign subsidiaries, but not on their domestic operations.)

What Government Can't Do

These are ominous facts, because new capital can come from only two sources: savings and profit. The Government can act in a number of ways to encourage—or discourage—savings and profit; but nothing it can do will create capital directly. Deficit spending, no matter how large, cannot create a "full employment economy" when capital is in short supply. (John Maynard Keynes demonstrated that deficit spending by the government *can* create jobs under certain special circumstances—that is, when capital already in existence is not being invested in job-creating enterprises. The reason this is so is too complicated, and too familiar to economists and most businessmen, to be reviewed here. But even the most devoted Keynesians do not argue that these circumstances exist today, or are likely to in the foreseeable future.)

The problem ahead of us is one we have never faced before. Only once in the past—in the shift to a total war economy in 1942-1943—have we encountered such a sudden jump in the need for capital. And then we were able to shift a massive amount of existing capital from peacetime facilities into war production by Government decree. Today that possibility does not exist, although an end to the war in Indochina should free some capital resources for a return to better uses, such as building homes and cleaning up our environment. Even so, it is impossible to predict whether we can meet the demand for new capital formation, or even how. The situation suggests possibilities for the most sustained boom in American history. It may also produce one of the most severe unemployment crises.

In either case, economics is not likely to fade out of the public consciousness. The graduates from today's youth culture are likely to find themselves far more worried about jobs and money than they now suspect.

The Puzzle of Productivity

Productivity will also be a major challenge and a major concern of the next ten years. Productivity, we have all heard a good many times by now, is the key to managing the inflation which plagues all developed countries today. To have price stability, wages must not rise faster than productivity. But all attempts to gear wages to productivity—guidelines, Mr. Nixon's "jawboning" in the construction industry, and the productivity bargaining which the British are advocating —have concerned themselves primarily with manual workers in manufacturing, transportation, mining, and construction. But manual workers are, increasingly, a minority. The majority of the young are acquiring advanced educations and are unlikely to go into manual work. The bulk of tomorrow's employment will be in service trades, knowledge jobs—in health care, teaching, government, management, research, and the like. And no one knows much about the productivity of knowledge work, let alone how to improve it.

About the only thing we can be sure of is that it has not been going up very fast. The salesgirl in today's department store does not sell more than the salesgirl of thirty or forty years ago did, if the change in the purchasing power of money is taken into account. Hospitals forty years ago had three employees for every ten patients and a very low investment per patient. Today they have up to thirty employees for every ten patients and their investment is high. Yet judged by the most primitive yardstick—the percentage of patients who leave the hospital alive—there has been little increase in productivity. Surely few of us would hold that today's schools are more productive than schools were forty years ago, no matter how one defines or measures the productivity of education. The same is true of government and research. Large businesses, these past twenty years, have added layer upon layer of management and all kinds of specialized staffs, from market research to personnel and from cost analysis to long-range planning. Whether there has been any corresponding increase in productivity and performance of management is, however, by no means proved.

We learned, some seventy years ago, how to define, how to measure, and how to raise the productivity of manual work. But we have yet to learn what productivity really means in any other kind of work. Yet the sales clerk and the college teacher, the nurse and the marketing manager, the policeman and the accountant all expect their incomes to rise as fast as that of the manual worker. In fact, the knowledge workers among them expect their incomes to rise faster and be higher in absolute terms than those of the manual worker.

The "cost-squeeze" of today, on governments, universities, and business, is the first warning—it is really a productivity squeeze. The only way out of it is for the nonmanual employee, whether he is a knowledge worker or a policeman, to become more productive. In his own interest, he will find he has to push for this. It is the only way, in the long run, for him to enjoy a comfortable, let alone a rising, standard of living. As the economy, therefore, employs more and more non-manual and, especially, more knowledge workers, we should increasingly expect concern with productivity to become central. And whatever else productivity may be—and it is a very elusive concept— it is clearly a conventional, an old-fashioned, and, above all, an economic value.

I do not assert that population dynamics will determine the psychology, politics, or even economics of the years to come. I would consider that absurd. No one factor, I am convinced, is decisive. But it seems equally absurd to omit population as an important factor in determining the characteristics of any era, especially of a time marked by swings as extreme as those we are going through now. The new big issues that emerged these past twenty years—race and civil rights, the urban crisis, the environment—will not go away. For this reason alone, the seventies will surely not be at all like the fifties or the thirties. But a study of population dynamics indicates that they will not be like the sixties either.

Whether they will be conservative in their mood or liberal, reactionary or revolutionary, no one can yet foresee. But in the issues that matter to them, in their values, and, above all, in their needs, the seventies may be a very traditional—indeed, a quite old-fashioned—decade.

CHALLENGING THE WORK ETHIC [2]

When students at Berkeley and other elite campuses first began to demonstrate against the university—and against the Establishment—many observers explained their behavior as the consequences of being affluent and elite. Indeed, the myth of Middle America and its Silent Majority that emerged in response to student unrest postulates a basic dif-

[2] From "The Protest of Young Factory Workers," by Herbert J. Gans, professor of sociology, Columbia University, formerly at MIT. *New Generation.* 54:10-13. Fall. '70. Reprinted by permission.

ference between the "masses" and the "classes," suggesting
that the former are satisfied with American society and only
the snobs are unhappy. . . .

This simple dichotomy is just not true; some blue-collar
workers are at least as critical of the factory as students of the
multiversity. While they have not often resorted to media-
covered demonstrations and confrontations, they have probably been more effective in disrupting the assembly line than
students, the university, through high rates of absenteeism
and turnover, wildcat strikes, deliberately shoddy workman-
ship and occasional acts of sabotage.

From the limited journalistic and sociological research
so far available, it would appear that a yet unknown number of blue-collar workers, particularly on the assembly line,
complain, like the students, that their work is inauthentic
and their workplace, dehumanizing. They do not use these
terms, of course, but they find the work boring; they have no
control over the job; they must obey arbitrary decisions by
their foremen and they cannot take time off for personal
business or even a phone call. In short, they are veritable
prisoners of the assembly line and the people who run it.

Any explanation of the current blue-collar protest must
begin with the fact that the feelings behind it are by no
means new; indeed, discontent with working conditions is as
old as the Industrial Revolution itself. Until fairly recently,
the discontent was voiced publicly mainly by middle-class
social critics, novelists, and film-makers (remember Charlie
Chaplin's classic critique of the assembly line, *Modern
Times*), for the workers themselves could not easily protest
about working conditions. Job insecurity was still rampant,
and besides, their first priority was to achieve a living—and
rising—wage. Still there is no doubt that the writers and film-
makers expressed many of the workers' feelings. For example, Ely Chinoy's sociological study, *Automobile Workers
and the American Dream*, published in 1955, concluded that
the assembly-line workers only endured the work to earn

enough money for achieving their American dream: to buy a gas station or garage. When I studied a Boston working-class neighborhood in the late 1950s, I heard many of the same complaints that workers are making today, but the West Enders, for whom even garage ownership was unachievable, had resigned themselves to the working conditions they could not change, and sought their satisfactions in family and peer-group life.

Today, age-old feelings are being translated into action, mainly by some young workers, and especially the better educated among them. They are not saving up to buy a garage but are going to night school to become eligible for a white-collar job, and since they do not expect to spend the rest of their lives in the factory, they can express their discontent or quit when the work becomes unbearable.

A New Protest From Workers

Moreover, these young workers do not accept the traditional working-class belief that the major purpose of the job is to finance the nonwork parts of life. Whether or not they practice middle-class life-styles, many have embraced the expectation, common in the middle class, that the job itself should provide some satisfaction, and this is hard to find on the assembly line. But even for the men who are not looking forward to better jobs, the line no longer provides the same rewards it offered their fathers. When most blue-collar work was unskilled, the line was at least a gold-plated sweatshop, as Walter Reuther put it. Today even the money is not that good anymore; there is less prestige than in skilled work, and opportunities for promotion are rare. Why else would blacks have been allowed on the line, and in such large numbers? (Today, over 60 percent of Detroit's assembly-line workers are black.)

Still, the status of the assembly line has been declining for some time now; other reasons must explain why the protest has only surfaced in the last couple of years. First, young-er men are an ever more important part of the work force;

40 percent of the current UAW [United Automobile, Aerospace and Agricultural Implement Workers of America] members are under thirty. Second, some are increasingly unhappy with the union, which is more responsive to older workers—and *they* are naturally more interested in pensions than working conditions. Also, as B. J. Widick [educator, labor union official, teacher, author] wrote recently in *The Nation,* "The old-timers think of the UAW as an organization that protects them from company abuse. Young workers think of the UAW as an outfit that had better get them what they think they deserve, and now. The young are not burdened with memories of the miseries of the past or the struggles of two decades ago." A third factor is the current recession. During more affluent years, dissatisfied assembly-line workers could find better jobs outside the factory; now, these jobs are scarcer and the men feel trapped....

The Blue-Collar Protesters

Fourth, the blue-collar protest has erupted now because dissatisfied workers, like other protesters, have learned from the civil rights and peace movements that demonstrations and confrontations are frequently more successful in bringing about change than traditional grievance procedures. To be sure, it has taken the workers some years to learn this, partly because such methods have only just become respectable in the politically conservative world of the working class, partly because the number of protesters had to reach a critical mass before they could act with impunity. But now that these conditions have been met, it is likely that the protest will spread.

Nevertheless, the prime reason for the protest comes from beyond the factory, for the discontented workers are expressing a nation-wide upgrading of expectations about how life should be lived which is taking place in many levels and sectors of American society. Although what is happening is often described as a politicocultural revolution or a youthful rebellion, the diverse new expectations also have in common a demand for more equality in America's principal institutions, and I prefer to label the change as the "equality revolution." As a result, one finds similar dissatisfactions and demands in many places: for example, among blacks who want equality with whites, and women, with men; among journalists who question the absolute power of editors, and enlisted men, that of officers; among professional athletes who resent being owners' chattels, clients who doubt the monopoly on wisdom of professionals, consumers who oppose the practices of manufacturers and merchants, adolescents who want the sexual privileges heretofore reserved for adults, and students who seek more power in their schools.

As in the factory, the feelings underlying the discontent are old; what is new is the belief that the time has come to act on them, and all across the societal board. Young people are saying that age should be a lesser justification of authority than it has been; lower income groups, that income and status should not be the sole sources of rights and privileges; the less skilled, that expertise is not limited to experts; and citizens, that not all decisions should be made by politicians and bureaucrats. Seen in the light of the larger equality revolution, then, the blue-collar discontent is a demand for more of the satisfactions and rights of white-collar and even professional workers.

What Will Management Do?

Colleges can close down temporarily or before the end of the semester when they are disrupted, but the assembly line must continue to run. This probably explains why management has not called in the police, but is quietly attempting to make reforms. It is also relevant to note that the Nixon Administration has not called for repression of the blue-collar disrupters, but then they have not questioned Administration foreign or domestic policies, or even raised doubts about the corporate economy in which they work.

Further automation of the line is taking place to root out some of the dullest and dirtiest jobs, and some experiments are going on in "job enrichment," to increase diversity and reduce repetitiveness in the workers' activities, and to allocate specific tasks to teams to cut down the isolation of the individual line worker. Some working conditions are also being improved, and presumably, the workers will eventually get an annual salary instead of an hourly wage and some time off to run personal errands. Still, it is difficult to loosen the bonds that tie the worker to the line, for if it is to keep running, he cannot have the same freedom to go to the bathroom as his white-collar colleague.

It is clear that in the short run, management will do all it can to save the assembly line, for despite automation, it remains essential to the production process. It is not clear, however, whether the current reforms will satisfy the discontented young workers and it is quite possible that unless the recession becomes permanent and workers are forced for economic reasons to surrender their aspirations and expectations for more equality, larger-scale changes will be necessary. It seems likely that in the long run, the assembly line and other dirty jobs elsewhere in the process will be automated as completely as is technically possible, and that the human portion of the work will be made interesting, if not necessarily more meaningful. How basic these changes will be depends in part on the workers themselves. For example, if in the future a critical mass of people became interested in worker control of industry, or just of the manufacturing process, a number of industries would have to decentralize radically and establish smaller factories or perhaps even highly automated workshops.

Although it seems safe to predict that in the years to come the workers will have more influence on company decisions, the direct democracy of the classic concept of worker control does not seem to be in the offing. So far, at least, few employees of any kind, including professionals, seem much interested in a direct role in running their shops and offices. A more realistic prediction is representative democracy on the job, with shop stewards or other workers being assigned by their colleagues to represent them in the manufacturing and corporate decision-making process.

These scenarios for the future assume, however, that management will be unable to replace the unhappy workers with less demanding substitutes. It is possible that industry can find them among presently unemployed or underemployed men, black and white, or that it will import a new set of European or African immigrants. Still, many of them would stay on the line only until they could do better, or else they too would begin to protest. As long as blue-collar work continues to fall further and further behind white-collar work in both status and income, it cannot attract new workers who will make it their life's work. The trend could be reversed if wages were raised high enough to overcome low status but this would require reversal of the long-standing American tradition that the higher a job's status, the higher the pay. A more realistic solution would be for industry to make low-status work a first job for everyone with rapid and rewarding promotions for all, and if this is not feasible, then perhaps society should consider adopting the idea of the industrial army, proposed by Edward Bellamy in *Looking Backward* in 1888, in which every citizen serves a couple of years in the worst jobs before moving up. At the least, such service should be an alternative to the draft for those unwilling to participate in America's wars.

A New Economic Scene?

All of these solutions will raise the cost of production, and this is as important a problem as the future of the production process itself. Here, American companies really have only three alternatives: to lower production costs, for example by doing more manufacturing in Europe and other low-wage areas; to pass higher costs on to the consumer through higher prices; or to reduce profits. The first alternative is undesirable as long as unemployment is high here, although it may become feasible and even necessary when no Americans can be found to do the dirtiest blue-collar jobs. (At that point, however, the international economy might benefit if America became a tertiary or service economy for the whole world, letting other economies do the world's manufacturing.) The second alternative is equally undesirable, for higher prices have regressive consequences for low and moderate income customers. The third solution seems politically unfeasible at present, but has much to recommend it. The higher costs of more egalitarian working conditions will have to be paid by someone. When a company like General Motors can earn well above 20 percent on investment for the past two decades, corporate profit is the best source of financing the changes in the social organization of the economy that are now beginning to be demanded.

THE BLUEING OF AMERICA [3]

A sizable segment of the American intelligentsia has been on a kick of revolution talk for the last few years. Only very recently this talk was carried on in a predominantly Left mood, generating fantasies of political revolution colored red or black. The mood appears to have shifted somewhat. Now the talk has shifted to cultural revolution. Gentle grass is pushing up through the cement. It is "the kids," hair and all, who will be our salvation. But what the two types of revolution talk have in common is a sovereign disregard for the realities of technological society in general, and for the realities of class and power in America. . . .

The cultural revolution is not taking place in a social vacuum, but has a specific location in a society that is organized in terms of classes. The cadres of the revolution, not exclusively but predominantly, are the college-educated children of the upper-middle class. Ethnically, they tend to be Wasps and Jews. Religiously, the former tend to belong to the mainline Protestant denominations, rather than to the

[3] From article by Peter L. Berger, professor of sociology at Rutgers University, and Brigitte Berger, associate professor of sociology at Long Island University. *New Republic.* 164:20-3. Ap. 3, '71. Reprinted by permission of The New Republic, © 1971, Harrison-Blaine of New Jersey, Inc.

more fundamentalist or sectarian groups. The natural focus of the revolution is the campus (more precisely, the type of campus attended by this population), and such satellite communities as have been springing up on its fringes. In other words, the revolution is taking place, or minimally has its center, in a subculture of upper-middle-class youth.

The revolution has not created this subculture. Youth, as we know it today, is a product of technological and economic forces intimately tied to the dynamics of modern industrialism, as is the educational system within which the bulk of contemporary youth is concentrated for ever longer periods of life. What is true in the current interpretations is that some quite dramatic transformations of consciousness have been taking place in this sociocultural ambience. These changes are too recent, and too much affected by distortive mass-media coverage, to allow for definitive description. It is difficult to say which manifestations are only transitory and which are intrinsic features likely to persist over time. Drugs are a case in point. So is the remarkable upsurge of interest in religion and the occult.

Revolution and the Protestant Ethic

However, one statement can be made with fair assurance: the cultural revolution has defined itself in diametric opposition to some of the basic values of bourgeois society, those values that since Max Weber have commonly been referred to as the "Protestant ethic"—discipline, achievement and faith in the onward-and-upward thrust of technological society. These same values are now perceived as "repression" and "hypocrisy," and the very promises of technological society are rejected as illusionary or downright immoral. A hedonistic ethic is proclaimed in opposition to the "Protestant" one, designed to "liberate" the individual from the bourgeois inhibitions in all areas of life, from sexuality through esthetic experience to the manner in which careers are planned. Achievement is perceived as futility and "alienation," its ethos as "uptight" and, in the final analysis, inimi-

cal to life. Implied in all this is a radical aversion to capitalism and the class society that it has engendered, thus render-
ing the subculture open to leftist ideology of one kind or
another.

Its radicalism, though, is much more far-reaching than
that of ordinary, politically defined leftism. It is not simply
in opposition to the particular form of technological society
embodied in bourgeois capitalism but to the very idea of
technological society. The rhetoric is Rousseauean rather
than Jacobin, the imagery of salvation is intensely bucolic,
the troops of the revolution are not the toiling masses of the
Marxist prophecy but naked children of nature dancing to
the tune of primitive drums. . . .

The matrix of the green revolution has been a class-
specific youth culture. By definition, this constitutes a bio-
graphical way station. Long-haired or not, *everyone,* alas,
gets older. This indubitable biological fact has been used
by exasperated over-thirty observers to support their hope
that the new youth culture may be but a noisier version of
the old American pattern of sowing wild oats. Very probably
this is true for many young rebels, especially those who indulge in the external paraphernalia and gestures of the
youth culture without fully entering into its new consciousness. But there is evidence that for an as yet unknown number, the way station is becoming a place of permanent settle-
ment. For an apparently growing number there is a movement from *youth culture to counterculture.* These are the
ones who drop out permanently.

For yet others, passage through the youth culture leaves,
at any rate, certain permanent effects, not only in their private
lives but in their occupational careers. As with the Puritanism that gave birth to the bourgeois culture of America, this
movement too has its fully accredited saints and those who
only venture upon a *halfway covenant.* The former, in grim
righteousness, become sandal makers in Isla Vista. The latter
at least repudiate the more obviously devilish careers within
"the system"—namely, those in scientific technology, business

and government that lead to positions of status and privilege in the society. They do not drop out, but at least they shift their majors—in the main, to the humanities and the social sciences, as we have recently seen in academic statistics.

The overall effects of all this will, obviously, depend on the magnitude of these changes. To gauge the effects, however, one will have to relate them to the class and occupational structures of the society. For those who become permanent residents of the counterculture, and most probably for their children, the effect is one of downward social mobility. This need not be the case for the halfway greeners (at least as long as the society is ready to subsidize, in one way or another, poets, T-group leaders [in group relations training] and humanistic sociologists). But they too will have been deflected from those occupational careers (in business, government, technology and science) that continue to lead to the higher positions in a modern society.

What we must keep in mind is that whatever cultural changes may be going on in this or that group, the personnel requirements of a technological society not only continue but actually expand. The notion that as a result of automation fewer and fewer people will be required to keep the technological society going, thus allowing the others to do their own thing and nevertheless enjoy the blessings of electricity, is in contradiction to all the known facts. Automation has resulted in changes in the occupational structure, displacing various categories of lower-skilled labor, but it has in no way reduced the number of people required to keep the society going. On the contrary, it has increased the requirements for scientific, technological and (last but not least) bureaucratic personnel. (The recent decline in science and engineering jobs is due to recession, and does not affect the long-term needs of the society.) The positions disdained by the aforementioned upper-middle-class individuals will therefore have to be filled by someone else. The upshot is simple: *There will be new "room at the top."*

The Emerging New Elites

Who is most likely to benefit from the sociological wind-fall? It will be the newly college-educated children of the lower-middle and working classes. To say this, we need not assume that they remain untouched by their contact with the youth culture during their school years. Their sexual mores, their esthetic tastes, even their political opinions might become permanently altered as compared with those of their parents. We do assume, though, that they will, now as before, reject the antiachievement ethos of the cultural revolution. They may take positions in intercourse that are frowned upon by Thomas Aquinas, they may continue to listen to hard rock on their hi-fi's and they may have fewer racial prejudices. But all these cultural acquisitions are, as it were, functionally irrelevant to making it in the technocracy. Very few of them will become sandal makers or farmers on communes in Vermont. We suspect that not too many more will become humanistic sociologists.

Precisely those classes that remain most untouched by what is considered to be the revolutionary tide in contemporary America face *new prospects of upward social mobility*. Thus, the "revolution" (hardly the word) is not at all where it seems to be, which should not surprise anyone. The very word *avant-garde* suggests that one ought to look behind it for what is to follow—and there is no point asking the *avant-gardistes*, whose eyes are steadfastly looking forward. Not even the Jacobins paid attention to the grubby tradesmen waiting to climb up over their shoulders. A technological society, given a climate of reasonable tolerance (mainly a function of affluence), can afford a sizable number of sandal makers. Its "knowledge industry" (to use Fritz Machlup's term) has a large "software" division, which can employ considerable quantities of English majors. And, of course, the educational system provides a major source of employment for nontechnocratic personnel. To this may be added the expanding fields of entertainment and therapy, in all their forms. All the same, quite different people are needed to occupy the society's command posts and to keep its engines running. These people will have to retain the essentials of the old "Protestant ethic"—discipline, achievement orientation, and also a measure of freedom from gnawing self-doubt. If such people are no longer available in one population reservoir, another reservoir will have to be tapped.

There is no reason to think that "the system" will be unable to make the necessary accommodations. If Yale should become hopelessly greened, Wall Street will get used to recruits from Fordham or Wichita State. Italians will have no trouble running the RAND Corporation, Baptists the space program. Political personnel will change in the wake of social mobility. It is quite possible that the White House may soon have its first Polish occupant (or, for that matter, its first Greek). Far from weakening the class system, these changes will greatly strengthen it, moving new talent upward and preventing rigidity at the top (though, probably having little effect at the *very* top). Nor will either the mechanics or the rewards of social mobility change in any significant degree. A name on the door will still rate a Bigelow on the floor; only there will be fewer WASP and fewer Jewish names. Whatever other troubles "the system" may face, from pollution to Russian ICBMs, it will not have to worry about its being brought to a standstill by the cultural revolution.

It is, of course, possible to conceive of such economic or political shocks to "the system" that technological society, as we have known it in America, might collapse, or at least seriously deteriorate. Ecological catastrophe on a broad scale, massive malfunction of the capitalist economy, or an escalation of terrorism and counterterror would be cases in point. Despite the currently fashionable prophecies of doom for American society, we regard these eventualities as very unlikely. If any of them should take place after all, it goes without saying that the class system would stop operating in its present form. But whatever else would then be happening in America, it would *not* be the green revolution. In the even remoter eventuality of a Socialist society in this country, we would know where to look for our greeners—in "rehabilitation camps," along the lines of Castro's Isle of Pines.

Toward the Blueing of America

We have been assuming that the children of the lower-middle and working classes remain relatively unbitten by the "greening" bug—at least sufficiently unbitten so as not to interfere with their aspirations of mobility. If they too should drop out, there would be literally no one left to mind the technological store. But it is not very easy to envisage this. America falling back to the status of an underdeveloped society? Grass growing over the computers? A totalitarian society, in which the few remaining "uptight" people run the technocracy, while the rest just groove? Or could it be Mongolian ponies grazing on the White House lawn? Even if the great bulk of Americans were to become "beautiful people," however, the rest of the world is most unlikely to follow suit. So far in history, the uglies have regularly won out over the "beautiful people." They probably would again this time.

The evidence does not point in this direction. The data we have on the dynamics of class in a number of European countries would suggest that the American case may not be all that unique. Both England and Western Germany have been undergoing changes in their class structures very similar to those projected by us, with new reservoirs of lower-middle-class and working-class populations supplying the personnel requirements of a technological society no longer served adequately by the old elites.

What we have described as a plausible scenario is not terribly dramatic, at least compared with the revolutionary visions that intellectuals so often thrive on. Nor are we dealing with a process unique in history. Vilfredo Pareto [economist and sociologist] called this type of process the "circulation of elites." Pareto emphasized (rightly, we think) that such circulation is essential if a society is going to survive.

In a Paretian perspective, much of the green revolution would have to be seen in terms of decadence (which, let us remark in passing, is not necessarily a value judgment—some very impressive flowerings of human creativity have been decadent in the same sociological sense).

But even Marx may, in a paradoxical manner, be proven right in the end. It may be the blue-collar masses that are, at last, coming into their own. "Power to the people!"—nothing less than that. The "class struggle" may be approaching a new phase, with the children of the working class victorious. These days we can see their banner all over the place. It is the American flag. In that perspective, the peace emblem is the old bourgeoisie, declining in the face of a more robust adversary. Robustness here refers, above all, to consciousness —not only to a continuing achievement ethos, but to a self-confidence not unduly worried by unending self-examination and by a basically intact faith in the possibilities of engineering reality. Again, it would not be the first time in history that a declining class leaned toward pacifism, as to the "beautiful things" of esthetic experience. Seen by that class, of course, the blue-collar masses moving in suffer from considerable esthetic deficiencies.

"Revolutionary" America? Perhaps, in a way. We may be on the eve of its blueing.

COMMUNES AND THE WORK CRISIS [4]

Until recently, work has enjoyed a good reputation. For most Americans who grew up during the Depression, work and life were synonymous. Finding a job, any job, was the prime directive. Liberals and radicals criticized the capitalist economy, but their aim was to "humanize" work, to make it "fulfilling,"not to eliminate it.

Now, however, work has fallen into disrepute, especially among young adults. Whereas it was once a solution to life's

[4] From article by Louis M. Andrews, a free-lance writer and coauthor of *Requiem for Democracy? Nation.* 211:460-3. N. 9, '70. Reprinted by permission.

problems—were they as straightforward and fundamental as survival or as elusive as the need for self-expression—work is now in itself a problem. The question, "Plastics?," from the film *The Graduate* symbolizes an entire generation's disenchantment with the job options offered by the most diversified society in the world. The famous identity crisis, which is intimately bound up with occupational goals, is becoming a major problem for school guidance counselors. (Almost 65 percent of students who consult school psychologists and guidance counselors present themselves as vocationally confused.) A recent study of Stanford and Berkeley undergraduates found that vocational choice is seen by students as a threat instead of an opportunity.

Increasingly, the reaction of the young to the Establishment work scene is to drop out. For some this means revolutionary political activism, for others it means "taking a few years off" to find themselves, and for still others it means an irrevocable break with "straight" society. Many bright college graduates become taxi drivers, waiters and supermarket checkers, in order to "keep themselves together" with a minimum of effort. Others go off to join one of the three hundred known (and myriad unknown) hippie communes which have sprouted up across rural America during the past five years. . . . For obvious reasons, no one knows exactly how many are dropping out, but sociologists agree that the number is accelerating geometrically, with estimates ranging as high as 20,000 per year. More significant, however, is the fact that the dropouts are often among the most intelligent and best educated young people. Communes have been founded by renegades from Yale, Princeton, Stanford, Dartmouth and Berkeley. [See "Communes: The Alternative Life-Style," in Section II, above.—Ed.]

This rebellion against the work ethic has potential dangers which even the dropout recognizes. A completely work-free society is impossible to attain. Even if we could mechanize or eliminate all the menial, superficial and redundant jobs, society would still require doctors, programmers, teachers, technicians, firemen, maintenance men, supervisors and other skilled professionals. (I leave out lawyers and police on the premise that such a society would be free of conflict—a dubious assumption.) Unfortunately, the more leisure-oriented our society becomes, the more unevenly the work load is distributed. The burden of servicing an advanced technology falls upon its most intelligent and technically competent members—those very bright young people who are most ready to drop out! In short, the rebellion against the work ethic, if it continues, could lead to a bizarre economic situation: we may find ourselves dependent upon a complex technology that nobody can or will run. Dr. Stanley F. Yolles, former director of the National Institute of Mental Health, sees "serious dangers that large proportions of current and future generations will reach adulthood embittered towards the larger society, unequipped to take on parental, vocational and other citizen roles."

But even if society can successfully convince—that is, bribe—intelligent young people to assume the burdens of technology management, as most economists believe it can, work alienation still presents a major social problem. Dissatisfaction with work is a growing source of emotional illness. Psychiatrist Salvatore Maddi finds that people who see themselves as mere players of social roles and who have an acute awareness of superficiality, two symptoms of work dissatisfaction, are highly susceptible to what he calls "existential neurosis"; that is, feelings of chronic meaninglessness, aimlessness and apathy, culminating in severe depression.

Why has work fallen into disrepute among the young? There are legitimate reasons which by now have become clichés: work seems meaningless in a redundant economy that creates needless wants through advertising; work seems meaningless in a society that ignores real problems of poverty and pollution; the nine-to-five routine saps spontaneity and precludes the evolution of individual life-styles, etc. But none of these reasons justifies the complete rejection of work. A doctor, lawyer, teacher, even a businessman, can always find work that is meaningful and flexible, *if he wants to find it*. To understand the work crisis, we must explore several illusions that have become axioms to many young Americans.

The first illusion is that work should be a continuous experience of intellectual and emotional delight. Synonyms: self-actualizing and self-fulfilling. Television has undoubtedly played a major role in cultivating this particular illusion. Marcus Welby, M.D., performs at least one medical miracle each week, while over at NBC "The Bold Ones" are resolving crucial social issues at the same rate. And those TV characters who opt for a meaningful family life never have job problems. Did Jim Anderson ("Father Knows Best") ever stay up late working on his clients' insurance policies? Ever see Donna Reed's doctor husband lift as much as a tongue depressor? And who could figure out what Ozzie Nelson did for a living?

Educators also bear responsibility for supporting this particular illusion. They spend so much time preparing students for future work that they forget to explain what the word *work* represents. Our neolithic ancestors were hardly concerned with "the quality of life." For them work—hunting, fishing, farming—was existence. Civilization offers three work advantages: it can reduce the work load and, by dividing labor, it can offer individuals a choice among more or less satisfying jobs. But even the most rewarding work has its drawbacks. Doctors hate to read medical journals, psychologists dislike treating alcoholics, writers resent deadlines, and so on. Work does not promise Nirvana. That's why people are paid for their labor.

The illusion that work must be an orgasm leads to the corollary illusion that people should be drawn to work by some calling, irrepressible commitment or mystical force. True, a few people know what they want to do at the age of ten, and follow this inspiration for the rest of their lives. Most of us, however, have to be introduced to a subject before we become interested in it. How many people who are happy in their present jobs have ever said, "I never thought I'd end up doing this!"?

The Rise of Neo-Puritanism

The work ethic is further depreciated by two seemingly divergent pseudophilosophies gaining popularity among the nation's young. The first is a neo-Puritanism which holds that each man must justify his existence by forsaking personal gain and doing something socially constructive. This frequently means ghetto teaching, working in a free clinic, or community organizing. As Edward Banfield [educator and author] cogently observes in *The Unheavenly City* [Little, 1970], self-justification has become a growth industry. Dedication to solving social ills is an admirable quality, but neo-Puritanism has had the effect of demeaning any form of work which is done for money, which includes about 99 percent of all existing jobs. As a result, many college graduates are ashamed to say they are working *just* for a living.

In opposition to neo-Puritanism among the young is a neo-Freudianism, which also depreciates work but for different reasons. Popularized by Norman Brown *(Life Against Death)*, Herbert Marcuse *(Eros and Civilization)*, neo-Freudianism strives for the resurrection of what Freud called the Pleasure Principle. According to Brown, civilization represses the Pleasure Principle by instilling a sense of guilt which we literally work out in our respective jobs. The more guilty and repressed we are, the harder we work. The solution, writes Theodore Roszak, is the evolution of a counterculture that will turn our mundane work existence into a joyous festival, a spontaneous "celebration of life."

Neo-Freudianism has obvious merits. The fact that psychosomatic illnesses are so prevalent among society's most "successful" members demonstrates a partial validity to Freud's theory of cultural repression. However, neo-Freudianism is grossly misinterpreted, especially by social malcontents who equate liberation with anarchy. Freud himself recognized that a certain degree of repression is necessary in order to buy freedom from a primitive existence. Further-more, many modern psychologists disagree sharply with the premise of neo-Freudianism, arguing that discipline and acquisition of skills are highly satisfying activities. One psychologist has argued that the drive for competence, like the sex drive, is an innate motivation.

The young are not to be blamed for their susceptibility to illusion. They have nothing else to trust. The young are, in a sense, the most victimized generation in history. "Manipulated for goals they cannot believe in," writes Paul Goodman, "the young are alienated." They have been exploited by status-conscious parents ("It's for your own good, my dear"), by businessmen eager to sap the youth market for dad's last penny, and by ambitious politicians, Left and Right. Even the most independent jobs demand a degree of trust that many members of the new paranoid generation are unwilling to give.

How is the work crisis to be resolved? In theory, the solution is simple; a little realism would do the trick. The young must recognize that work is necessary for survival and, further, that any form of work necessarily involves discipline and sacrifice. At the same time, adult champions of the work ethic must learn what they already feel—that the good life is more than an impressive financial statement. Unfortunately, people would rather create illusions to justify their past actions than confront reality. Many dropouts support what youth psychologist Kenneth Keniston has called "the fallacy of romantic regression"—that is, an idealized vision of primitive living which never has and never will exist.

Similarly, "successful" businessmen and professionals extol ulcer-producing work and competition as Christ-like virtues. These fantasies are supported and enriched by media that specialize in what their audiences want to hear. Underground papers such as the Berkeley *Barb,* the Los Angeles *Free Press,* and the New York *Rat* weekly herald the decline of the decadent Establishment, while the respectable press gives us front-page stories about hippie teen-agers (especially girls from wealthy families) who come to a bad end as a result of drugs and shiftless commune living.

A few businesses have tried to solve the work crisis with token gestures. Many law firms, for example, encourage young attorneys to spend part of their workday doing poverty law. People who work in television, advertising and other communications industries are allowed liberal dress, liberal hours and frequent leaves of absence for educational purposes. But tokenism wears thin. If the aspiring lawyer wants to stay with the firm, he works overtime to finish the firm's work. And the copywriter is still responsible for servicing the soap account.

Work Communes: A Solution?

A more successful approach to the work crisis is the rapidly growing phenomenon of the "work commune." Unlike the hippie commune which is organized around a simple lifestyle, the work commune is organized around a professional skill or interest. Members strive for a secure income while, at the same time, advancing each person's independence and work satisfaction.

One such commune is the Farallones Institute, an architecture commune, founded in Berkeley by two University of California graduate students. Members develop their own environmental design projects and then seek financial assistance to carry them off. The commune's first paycheck came from a Government grant. (Work communes have few qualms about taking Government money.) Assistance now comes from the Berkeley High School system, which is interested in the commune's ideas about new educational environments. In neighboring Sausalito is another architecture commune which calls itself the Ant Farm. Founded by two former architecture students, Chip Lord from Tulane and Doug Michaels from Yale, the Ant Farm currently specializes in building plastic "inflatables," balloon-type environments which are used at rock festivals and on children's playgrounds. The Berkeley area also includes numerous legal communes. Some specialize in reform projects; others simply seek a relaxed legal practice.

Work communes are not limited to professional skills. The Portola Institute of Menlo Park, California, is a thriving commune of full-time dilettantes. Billed as "a nonprofit cooperative to encourage, organize, and conduct innovative educational projects," it is actually a group of creative people ranging in education from Ph.D. to high school dropout, whose common bond is the desire to play for a living. Current projects of the Portola Institute include maintaining a playroom for creative high school students, developing a teacher-training laboratory, exploring music theory, and publishing the *Whole Earth Catalog,* which provides the reader with information about books and tools and "enables him to shape his environment, internal and external." ...

California, especially the San Francisco Bay Area, has the largest concentration of work communes, but the phenomenon is spreading. The Communications Company, in Columbus, Ohio, publishes a handbook on alternative life-styles. The Meeting, in Minneapolis, Minnesota, is an experimental school. New York City's East Village houses numerous film communes and group-run psychedelic shops. The growing number of free universities and underground newspapers are also part of the work-commune movement.

Work communes provide a promising model for a realistic balance between society's need for productive work in order to sustain itself, and the individual's need for autonomy. ...

However, not all dropouts are enthusiastic about the work-commune movement. Phil Trounstein, a Stanford radical, refers to the Portola Institute as a "Fascist organization" in disguise. "No matter how they dress or act, they still exploit people with their products." A lot of hippies are also critical, but their reasons are more personal than political. "It's still work and routine," remarked one Berkeley nomad.

The fact that rebels from the traditional work ethic disagree among themselves is probably more significant than any particular viewpoint. The work crisis will not be resolved by black-white distinctions between glorified Puritanism and un-bridled hedonism. The young must feel free to experiment with new life-styles to find their own solutions to the problem of work.

VI. YOUTH'S FUTURE ROLE

EDITOR'S INTRODUCTION

The topic of this section has, of course, been touched on repeatedly throughout the compilation. Is the youth rebellion waning? Will student revolt on college campuses continue? Will youth continue to protest domestic and foreign policies relating to poverty, war, and other social ills? Will alienated youth truly withdraw into a culture of unreason? And is the force of the new counterculture so great as to preclude reconciliation with the established culture? These questions are more broadly discussed in this last section.

A general report on the waning of the youth rebellion is given first by Douglas E. Kneeland in a special report to the New York *Times*. The president of Columbia University, William J. McGill, next suggests that tensions on college campuses, although different from those of the sixties, may well continue. Then follows an article by Gresham M. Sykes, director of the Administration of Justice Program at the University of Denver's College of Law, commenting on the calm which prevailed throughout the fall of 1970 and the following months and pointing out that all the sources of unrest are still in existence and need to be dealt with.

Kenneth Keniston, author of the last selection in Section I, here gives his assessment of the recent agonizing evaluation which members of the youthful counterculture have undertaken and indicates that the potential for violence lies not only in established American society but within the youth movement itself.

In the last selection, Philip E. Slater, former chairman of the department of sociology at Brandeis University, tackles the problem of whether the two cultures he feels now exist in America can be reconciled. He argues for a reversal of our old pattern of technological radicalism and social conservatism and suggests instead the need to construct new utopian communities which could replace a failing old culture. His article is excerpted from his book *The Pursuit of Loneliness: American Culture at the Breaking Point.*

THE WANING YOUTH REBELLION [1]

The great youth trip, that heady, sometimes breathtaking, sometimes frightening, roller-coaster ride that careened through the late years of the 1960s and plunged headlong into this decade, is slowing down and may be almost over.

Two or three years ago, a member of the administration of Stanford University . . . recalled . . . , he was entertaining a group of students at his home when he asked: "Who are your heroes? Whom do you really admire?"

After a few awkward moments in which nobody spoke, a young man replied. "Us," he said. No one disputed him. And he may have spoken for a generation of high school and college students, of young people in general.

This fall [1971] it is still almost impossible to find individuals who are heroes to the young. But the self-worship of the young cult, the easy assumption that youth has all the answers, is dying, too.

At Dartmouth College in Hanover, New Hampshire, Peter Willies, a senior from Weston, Connecticut, declared recently that he distrusts . . . [his] generation as much as any other.

And at the University of Wisconsin in Madison, Gerald Peary, a bearded, twenty-six-year-old graduate student who had been a political activist, took an even harsher view. "The youth revolution has turned sour," he complained. "There's no indication that this generation will be any less piggy than the rest. I'm a skeptic."

[1] From "Youth Rebellion of Sixties Waning," by Douglas E. Kneeland, reporter. New York *Times.* p 1+. O. 24, '71. © 1971 by The New York Times Company. Reprinted by permission.

Quality of Life

That is a hard judgment, one not many people, particularly of the younger generation, would be willing to make. More would be likely to agree with Robert W. Fuller, president of Oberlin College, who gave a more positive interpretation to what seems to be essentially the same phenomenon. Noting that youth today seem to feel "ineffectual" about bringing about "institutional change" in the country, he added:

"The students I've seen have been talking about more personal issues. There is a desire for greater quality of life in the private sphere as opposed to the reformist zeal and the personal price you have to pay for change."

Whatever the interpretation, the young, whether in college or high school or working, are undergoing some major changes in their attitudes and approaches to life. This was the conclusion drawn from visits to and reports by correspondents of the New York *Times* from a score of campuses and ten large cities from Maine to California.

With the war in Vietnam becoming less visible, with the draft lottery accepted as more equitable, with the eighteen-year-old vote a reality, with a lagging economy threatening the affluent society and, perhaps, with just plain passage of time, some distinctly new patterns are emerging among young people.

They are more serious, but having more fun. They are studying more but relaxing more. Their concern for the problems of the world continues, but their search for solutions has generally narrowed to what they can do as individuals, usually on a local level.

Their radicalism, where it exists—and it exists in many places—has become a more personal matter and not something to be constantly paraded in the streets.

Though the rhetoric superficially resembles the typical radical charges of past years [said a Boston University student describing activists at the crowded Commonwealth Avenue campus], the action they seek differs considerably.

Where student leaders would have called for a march for peace, now it's for teach-ins and lobbying; where they would have moved to take over a building and harass its occupants, now the problems are hashed out over a cup of coffee; where unnegotiable demands flew across the streets through megaphones, now requests for forums between students and more responsive administrators come in the form of telephone calls and letters.

Among other things, the young's dread of working in or with the Establishment seems to have lessened, but most want to do something self-satisfying and constructive.

All in all, their sense of apocalypse has diminished. They have become—to cite some descriptions that are frequently encountered—more patient, more tolerant, more cynical, more skeptical, more apathetic, more subdued, more prone to take the longer view, more mature.

No one is burning inside for immediate upheaval, or even drastic change [a Harvard senior said], figuring perhaps that there isn't much to be done anyway—that the apocalypse is not just around the corner after all, that anarchy may not be the answer, that the wheels of government and society aren't going to change much regardless of what students do or say.

Among noncollege youths, most of whom tend to be somewhat more conservative, but still upset by the war in Vietnam and occasionally by other problems, the words may be different, but the feelings can be similar to those expressed by the Harvard man.

Mellowing Process

"I don't give a damn," said a nineteen-year-old Ohio State dropout who works in an office in Coral Gables, Florida. "The war, the bombing, the waste and all that—it's so insane that it isn't worth getting mad about."

The uneasy calm that descended on the nation's campuses . . . [in 1970] after the major upheavals that followed the Cambodia incursion and the shootings at Kent State seems to have mellowed into something much less than euphoria but much more than alienation. In fact, alienation, a key word in any campus discussion . . . [then], seldom arose this fall. . . .

[In 1970] as the colleges went silent, the word was out to "watch the high schools, that's where the real action is." This fall, if Boston, Pittsburgh, Washington, Charlotte, Miami, Chicago, St. Louis, San Francisco, Los Angeles and San Diego are any indication, high school students are following the quiet paths of their older brothers and sisters.

"There definitely is a lot less militancy among students," said Ted Tishman, editor of the student paper at Taylor Allderdice High School in Pittsburgh, echoing words heard across the nation. At a school that had had racial fights and antiwar demonstrations in the past, he added:

"Nobody's bugging anybody else. There has been little tension and no discussion of antiwar activity. They seem to be turning inward. There has been a big attendance at football games."

Attitudes of Black Youths

Harder to put a finger on in the overall picture is the attitude of black youths. Over the last few years, most of them have tended to shun the militant radical movements and the hippie class that could afford to play at politics and poverty.

On campuses, for instance, most blacks have concentrated their efforts on matters that they considered of paramount interest to themselves. With the battle for black studies won at many institutions they seem to be concerning themselves primarily with working with college administrations for the admission of more minority students.

Like their white counterparts, black student leaders appear to be more interested in working quietly and forcefully through the system rather than taking their grievances into the streets.

Although the trend is not widespread, there also seem to be some signs of cracks in the wall of separatism between blacks and whites. Blacks and whites are fraternizing more on some campuses. At Harvard for instance, a white student noted that where three years ago all the blacks sat together in a dining hall in a sort of self-enforced segregation, they now mingle freely with their white friends without risking the contempt of other blacks.

Reasons for Change

Many things, most observers agree, are responsible for the changes that are appearing among youth across the nation.

There is an acceptance among the young that the war in Vietnam is being ended. It is happening more slowly and less conclusively than they would like, but most are convinced that they have exhausted, without avail, their efforts to persuade the Nixon Administration to speed up the process.

The draft lottery has eased the anxiety of many young men and at least given others a certain choice to make when their number comes up.

The lagging economy has made scarce jobs more attractive to some and has put pressure on others to work harder in high school and college to meet stiff competition for jobs or for advanced education. Many more youths also seem to be working part time or seeking such work while they are going to school to meet higher costs, achieve more independence or ease the demands on families that are feeling the economic squeeze.

The eighteen-year-old vote has had an effect that is difficult to measure. In many college communities, for instance, hundreds and in some cases, thousands of youngsters have registered. Most insist that they intend to vote and there are some indications that many are using that as a rationalization for not taking a more activist role on current issues. However, most also seem pessimistic that their votes will bring about much change.

Even at the University of California in Berkeley, where youthful workers helped . . . [in April 1971] to produce a radical-moderate deadlock on the City Council, there is disillusionment.

"So we elected three radical councilmen," said Barbara Kane, a senior in sociology. "What difference did it make? It's the same City Council."

Another factor that has contributed to the changing attitudes of the young has been the yielding over the last few years by many colleges and high schools to most demands for revisions in rules and curriculum.

Many Changes Cited

Dress codes have been dropped and course requirements changed in high schools across the country. Countless other demands, as varied as the imagination of local student leaders, have been met. At Palo Alto High School, for instance, the administration has even agreed to stop ringing bells between classes, since some students found them annoying.

At many, if not most, colleges, dormitory rules have all but evaporated. At quite a few, birth control information and contraceptives are distributed at the college dispensary. Required courses have been curtailed. Great numbers of new courses requested by students have been offered.

At the University of Michigan, for example, courses may be taken for credit in the history of the blues, comics and their place in American literature, science fiction, and the history of the student movement in the United States, which may be symptomatic of something.

All the battles may not have been won in all places, but it is hard to find many schools now where reforms seem to be of overwhelming importance to the students.

At our rap sessions, students are encouraged to express their views and criticism of the educational system and society [said Dr. Jean Hausler, a high-school teacher and counselor in Miami]. We don't try to appear all-knowing. Perhaps for the first time we are listening to their complaints and adjusting our thinking accordingly. I am beginning to be optimistic about our relations now. I wasn't last year.

As important as all the other reasons, perhaps, is an apparently growing conviction among many young people that they have survived years of crises, conflicts and turmoil, of war, assassinations, riots and demonstrations and that now is a time for settling down, for pursuing individual interests, even pleasures.

Return to the Fifties?

There is a temptation to view the new attitudes as a return to the fifties, when another generation felt the need for respite from years of war and personal displacement. Some people do.

"It seems like a return to the 1950s," said Josh Peckler of Massapequa, Long Island, a sophomore at Brandeis. "There's more booze, more nice clothes, the music's becoming less radical and softer—Carole King and James Taylor—and people seem to be getting into their middle-class shells and worrying about their future."

He said that more people seemed to be talking about grades, medical school, law school "and less about what's really happening, less about politics, less about universities and less about themselves."

While many people would disagree that there has been a return to the mood of the fifties, he touched on a number of the external aspects of change that are apparent in most sections of the country.

As the use of marijuana has spread through more segments of the population, it no longer serves to divide the "hip" from the "straight." Perhaps for that reason, beer and liquor are no longer put down among the young as the "drugs" of an alien culture. And wine has soared in popularity, sometimes in partnership with marijuana, but more and more for itself. . . .

Despite the increased acceptance of alcohol among the young, the use of marijuana does not seem to have dropped noticeably. However, in most places the use of hard drugs and hallucinogens is reported to have peaked and probably to have declined.

Another visual mark of change has been in clothing styles. As radical groups have all but disappeared from most colleges and high schools and the street people have virtually vanished from many of their old haunts, the street-fighting uniforms, the Army-surplus look, the blue jeans and work shirts, and the costumes of "freaks," the tie-dyed, thrift-shop and frontier-scout styles, have become rarer and rarer.

With some exceptions, notably at colleges and high schools in the South and in other rural areas that frequently lag behind the national pacesetters, students are dressing up more—not high-style, but neater, cleaner and brighter.

THE NEW TENSIONS ON CAMPUS [2]

This year . . . [1971] the campus climate seems so outwardly calm as to make one wonder whether the last several years might not have been just a nightmare. That calm is deceptive. It was clear to me last year that universities could not be as badly off as most people seemed to suppose; it is equally clear this year that we are much more troubled than most people seem to realize.

Almost all thoughtful observers now recognize that what we have been witnessing on campus since the Berkeley uprising in 1964 is the leading edge of a massive pattern of social change that has gone on to envelop not just Western society but indeed all the technologically advanced countries. This year, our students are no longer displaying the diffuse anger at the world around them which marked earlier stages of disorder. Instead, the campus is witnessing the growth of a new and powerful variety of narrowly defined "liberation movements" which provide a new system of tensions. They will affect us immediately, and we may safely suggest that they will probably affect society at large within two or three years' time.

The angry arousal of our Columbia student body, which peaked in May 1970, was particularly dangerous because it made our campus, like others, continuously explosive. A well-organized radical group could simply wait for an effective

[2] From article by William J. McGill, president of Columbia University, New York City. *Life*. 71:55. O. 8, '71. Reprinted by permission.

cause, or attempt more deliberately to promote one. Then ensued a series of rallies and mass meetings, culminating all too often in outbursts of hysterical violence. The process, called "radicalization," was a little morality play constructed in roughly equal measure of student alienation, radical leadership, administrative ineptitude, lack of communication and a multitude of associated pressures that combined to make students feel oppressed and angry.

But the radicalization of the Columbia campus was always a kind of game, and suddenly last year it seemed to be over. The radicals persisted with their formerly foolproof methods, but there were few listeners and even fewer joiners. The loss of effectiveness was partly due to cleverer handling of disputes on campus, partly also to increasingly sophisticated students. The main change, however, was the abrupt inward turning of many students who, tired of being manipulated by campus radicals, moved away from large-scale political causes and toward the diffident despair of the counterculture.

The new pattern involves the rapid growth of sensitive alienated groups, each pressing for a special identity and using techniques of confrontation in order to achieve a sense of personal freedom. The idea is not to seek acceptance or assimilation but to close ranks with your own kind in order to feel free. A multitude of such groups is now visible on campus. They are in mutual competition and in joint contention with administrators who, it is claimed, are insensitive to them. I believe that our universities are furnishing an important model for a developing pluralism in society at large.

Toward a New Pluralism

The process began several years ago in confrontations with black students over the intellectual and fiscal resources that universities were willing to devote to black studies. Other groups harboring similar, although perhaps less intense, feelings of alienation and lack of identity watched the effort conducted by organized black students very closely. These groups

are now moving to define their own status. They have copied
the combination of confrontation and moral pressure used
by the blacks in achieving their objectives, and developed
objectives of their own: day-care activities, women's rights,
civil rights for homosexuals and ethnic studies.

Besides the organized women's rights groups which are
attempting to correct centuries of intellectual discrimination,
there are several groups of militant young radical women
who are using confrontation methods in order to force the
university to provide space for day-care activities. If you have
not endured a sit-in by dozens of angry ladies arranged
resolutely on the floor of your office while their crying and
damp children conduct play time on your office furniture,
you have not lived! Such problems, of course, are not unique
to Columbia. Perhaps we have more variety and intensity,
but campuses all over the country are feeling the push of
the new pluralism. And, of course, other parts of society are
feeling it too. Federal authorities did not offer the rest of us
an example of decisive action in their dealings with militant
Indians on Alcatraz.

One of the most interesting features of the new campus
pluralism is the involvement of Federal and state agencies.
The Federal involvement usually takes the form of compliance enforcement of the equal-rights provisions of an
Executive order. The interpretation of such provisions is not
a matter in which we have any voice. Aggrieved groups on
campus complain about us. Federal agencies respond by investigating and threatening to cut off funds. The ordinary
initiatives of a university's administration are largely eliminated from the power equation.

If society at large does seek to use universities in this way;
if, for example, we are to move quickly to truly equal opportunity for women under Federal pressure while the rest of
society watches, then I think it would be advisable to protect
the integrity of the experiment by suitable exercise of due
process. To take one example, in late June . . . [1971] Columbia received a letter addressed to "President Andrew Cardier"

stating that we were out of compliance with the terms of the Federal Executive order enforcing equal rights in Federal contract activities. We were instructed to get into compliance within thirty days or face a cut-off of Federal grant funds. There was no prior warning. There was no notice of hearing or right to appeal; no clear indication in fact of the manner in which we had failed in compliance. All this required discovery.

Such methods seem to me a bit heavy handed. One would think that an agency threatening to cut off all our Federal funds would at least make an effort to get the president's name straight. (I succeeded Andrew Cordier in 1970.) Even with the best intentions we cannot accomplish overnight what our social order has failed to achieve throughout all its history.

Thus, as the liberation movements develop, we must seek to play our leadership role in building a new society sensitive to the aspirations of previously excluded groups. We are prepared to do this by using all the university's resources to discover the forms of institutional pluralism compatible with stable institutional functioning. One of the greatest achievements of American law has been construction of the rules of orderly conflict between management and labor, embodied in our now classical concepts of labor law. We need a closely related legal framework for working with social change and with the conflicts engendered by the variety of liberation movements now developing on campus. We do not now have such formal procedures. Thus for a while we may safely expect much pressure for liberation and repeated tense confrontations. If somewhere someone slips in the heat of such action, we may again see occasional outbursts of real violence.

We in the universities are grappling with some of our society's toughest problems. Our problems this year are also likely to be someone else's problems next year. We conduct our affairs before the internal critical eyes of thousands of young idealistic students who are repelled by any form of

discrimination and who side with any kind of underdog. Passing that scrutiny is not easy. Earning that respect means a
great deal to us.

YOUTH AND TOMORROW'S PROBLEMS [3]

The eerie calm that settled over the campuses in the fall
of 1970 and apparently still dominates so many colleges
and universities around the country has puzzled most aca-
demics. It is one of those inexplicable shifts in mood that
make social history a series of abrupt quantum jumps rather
than a slow, continuous process.

Some writers see it as a happy cooling down of the American scene. "The kids," they say, "have turned serious; they've
learned to work within the Establishment"; and for the
writers of *Time* the sentimentality of *Love Story* becomes
a beguiling indication of a widespread return to the verities.
Others say that the students have tuned out completely and
are happily waiting for the spread of Consciousness III [See
Editor's Introduction, Section I, above.—Ed.] to set the
world aright.

I certainly cannot tell just what has caused this moment
of calm; but I think it would be a great mistake to suppose
that 1971 marks the beginning of the end of unrest in American society. Instead, there is good reason to believe that 1971
is no more than a lull in the storm and that the decade of the
seventies may very well make the sixties look like a picnic.

The fact is that the major social issues that shook this
country in the sixties have not been resolved at all and show
every sign of getting worse. The war may or may not be wind-
ing down in Vietnam, but the terrifying truth is that it doesn't
make very much difference. The important point is that the
United States is well on the path to learning how to make
money out of war and the machines of war. Back in the
thirties, we used to think that books like *Cry Havoc* [by Bev-

[3] From "Today's Campus: The Eerie Calm," by Gresham M. Sykes, director
of the Administration of Justice Program at the College of Law, University of
Denver, author of *The Society of Captives* and *Crime and Society*. *Nation*. 212:
490-1. Ap. 19, '71. Reprinted by permission.

erley Nichols] were somewhat exaggerated, and the indictment of munitions makers too simple in their search for personal villains. The idea of international cabals to promote
war may have been naive, and trying now to single out political figures who actually want war may be a wild distortion,
but the spectacle of a society that allows or encourages its
economy to become deeply enmeshed in military production
is another matter. It took World War II to pull the United
States really free of the Depression and we today seem to be
moving into an era where a great many people are convinced
that military spending is necessary for economic health. If
that is true—if an ABM system is thought to be good for the
Gross National Product, whether it works or not; if we keep
engaging in "incursions" when we have finished with Laos
and Cambodia—we will be ready for a new version of *Catch
22*, wherein Americans will argue that the only way to be
productive is to gear the economy to destruction.

Coming Social-Economic Crises

The area of race relations seems in scarcely better shape.
The riots have diminished, and the violent rhetoric of black
militants has slacked off considerably, but who can say that
we have taken more than a faltering half-step toward "solving" the race problem? The central city gets blacker and
poorer, school integration lumbers from one petty statistic of
supposed progress to another, and the Congress stalls and
stalls whenever it is confronted with a welfare plan that might
ease the plight of the black community. I cannot believe
that the anger of the Negro is somehow spent, that we can
close the book on the racial disturbances of the last ten years
and sigh with relief that the "pushy" demands of minority
groups have ended.

Finally, the great issue that dominated so much social
and political thought in the early sixties—the threat of widespread unemployment among young people who were entering the labor market just when the jobs usually available to
them were disappearing—seems to be on the verge of re-

awakening with a roar. It is true that we missed that crisis, to some extent, but now the problem has reappeared in a more complex guise. We are perhaps approaching a time when the educational system and the occupational structure will be seriously out of step in this country.

In the first place, unemployment rates are beginning to shoot up for the younger age groups in the labor force—and particularly for Negro youths in the ghetto, where unemployment rates are horrendous. This apparently is more than a matter of the current recession and is not likely to go away. It is due in part to inadequate education and a lack of vocational skills that trap large masses of young people at the bottom of the socioeconomic ladder where they drift into a mood of violent alienation. Continually dazzled by a vision of the affluent society dangled before them by the mass media, they must finally face the squalor of their own lives.

To make matters worse, as Ivan Berg points out in his recent *Education and Jobs: The Great Training Robbery,* we have elevated educational prerequisites for jobs out of all proportion to the realistic requirements, so that even when people at the bottom of the heap do manage to get some degree of schooling, they still find much of the occupational structure closed to them. And the problem is also hitting the college student, who suddenly finds that the diploma held out in front of him for so long is neither a ticket of entry into the world of work nor a true symbol of an education received.

In the second place, jobs and education are progressively diverging because schooling turns large numbers of students away from the whole concept of work, even when their education is relevant to jobs and careers. It is not just that a "counterculture" absorbs the interests and commitments of a new generation, nor simply that the politics of protest is in ascendancy. What seems to be happening, rather, is that an increasing number of students take what goes on in the school as a model of what will happen in the adult workaday world; and they then say, "If that's what it's like, we don't want it." The tyranny of grading that is often badly done or based on whims, so that it breeds anxiety rather than a sense of being objectively evaluated; the standardized mush that is compressed into textbooks and passed off as scholarship; the prison routines, particularly in the secondary schools that make obvious that the educational system places a higher priority on order than on learning; the inability of students to gain more than a token vote in the administration of a system where they may spend as much as a quarter of their lives—all these help to create a resentment that is likely to spawn a rejection of the world to which the school is supposed to lead. It is quite possible that some of the student dissatisfaction is not justified and that the students dismiss too lightly the discipline of deferred gratification. The resentment is nonetheless there and must somehow be confronted.

Professor Peter Berger [professor of sociology at Rutgers] has recently suggested . . . that all this may lead to a "blueing of America"—that if upper-middle-class students want out of the system, plenty of lower-middle-class and working-class students will be happy to oblige by shouldering them aside to get at the levers of power. [See "The Blueing of America," in Section V, above.—Ed.] Maybe so. But it's more important, I think, to take this attitude as evidence that the unrest of the sixties has not collapsed into sweet contentment or even apathy. [See "The New Tensions on Campus" and "Youth and Tomorrow's Problems," above.—Ed.]

A society devoting a large share of its productive capacity to the engines of war, and caught up in bitter discrimination and in an educational system that neither liberates the mind nor provides occupational skills—that sums up the major American dilemmas of the sixties that are still with us, ready to generate new social upheavals. We will surely encounter them again in this decade.

THE AGONY OF THE COUNTER-CULTURE [4]

Anyone who spent much time on an American campus last year [1970-1971] knows that it was a bad year for Consciousness III. [See Editor's Introduction, in Section I, above.—Ed.] At the very moment when its virtues were being celebrated by Charles Reich, the alleged possessors of Consciousness III fell into self-doubt, nostalgia and despair. The expressive exuberance and romantic optimism of 1970 were replaced by an "eerie tranquillity." The same students who were working toward major changes in national priority turned inward—to meditation, to studying the *I Ching*, to communes, to macrobiotic diets, to reliving the TV programs of their childhoods, or even to doing their homework.

One explanation sometimes heard in Washington is that the calm at college results from the firmness and adroitness of the Nixon Government. I suspect that I express more than my own views when I doubt that these policies explain the tranquillity. Unresponsiveness to the expressed wishes of the American people—three quarters of whom now seek an end to the war by the end of 1971—hardly seems to be a solution. Widespread wiretapping, underground agents on campus, harassment of dissenters and illegal confinement of demonstrators hardly seems consistent for an Administration pledged to preserve law and order. Certainly it is not a way of increasing confidence in the political process. In talking to students, I do not find a new burst of faith in Mr. Nixon.

A second explanation comes closer to the truth. In May of 1970, following the invasion of Cambodia and the killings at Kent State and Jackson State, at least a million and a half students were mobilized in largely peaceful demonstrations

[4] From article by Kenneth Keniston, research psychologist at the Yale Medical School and author of the *Young Radicals* and *The Uncommitted*. This article is adapted from a commencement address at the University of Notre Dame. *Yale Alumni Magazine.* 35:10-13. O. '71. Reprinted with permission from the October 1971 issue of *Yale Alumni Magazine;* copyright by Yale Alumni Publications, Inc.

of concern and grief. Almost half of America's 2,500 campuses were affected. There was a massive outpouring of revulsion against the war.

But that outpouring led to no visible shift in national policy. Despite the withdrawal of American land forces, aerial bombardment of Southeast Asia has actually increased, as have the civilian and military casualties of all groups except Americans. The pleas of the President's Commission on Campus Unrest that the President should act as a reconciling force in American life went largely unheeded. As a result, students became even more discouraged about the political process.

Beyond that lies still another element: a sense of embarrassment or even shame. Many students in the spring of 1970 nourished the secret fantasy that their efforts might produce a "total change" in American politics, a revolutionary reordering of our society. But when autumn came, a more sober reappraisal was inevitable. Students who had thought the Black Panther Party a "revolutionary vanguard" realized that the Panthers neither expressed the aspirations of most American blacks, nor were they above deceit, exploitation and racism. Radical students painfully realized that most young people are motivated mainly by a desire to take part in the American system, not to change it. The result was a sense of embarrassment at their own naiveté—a shame that they had allowed themselves to entertain such revolutionary dreams.

The Potential for Violence

But underlying all these feelings is what I call the agony of the counterculture—an awareness that the potential for violence lies not only within the rest of American society, but within the student movement itself.

First, however, let me make my position clear. In emphasizing the flaws of the student movement, I do not wish to draw attention from the real evils of American society. If we tally deaths, cracked skulls or even minor injuries, the members of the counterculture have suffered far more violence than they have perpetrated. I make these comments in the hope that if you who are part of the youth culture and we who sympathize with it can gain insight into its inner weaknesses, that culture may be strengthened. For if we can understand what is wrong in ourselves, we can be better adversaries of the wrongs of society.

The agony of the student movement ultimately revolves around the issue of violence, which I believe to be the central issue of American life today. As a nation we possess history's most terrible weapons of world destruction. Domestically we are one of the most violent nations of the world. And in a distant war in a far-off land, we have been implicated in the deaths of two million men, women and children, of whom less than 2 percent are Americans.

From the start of the student movement in the early 1960s, violence has been its unwanted companion. The civil rights movement was committed to nonviolence, but it constantly brought upon itself the violence of those who opposed it. Throughout the 1960s there were killings of campus activists: students shot at Orangeburg, at Isla Vista, at the People's Park in Berkeley, in Lawrence (Kansas), at Kent State, at Jackson State. Members of the student movement have come to expect routine harassment, brutality and even death from their adversaries, including the very forces pledged to maintain law and order. Yet if there is one goal that has been central to the movement, it has been the abolition of violence—whether it be the violence inflicted upon blacks by American racism, or the violence that our nation has inflicted on the people of a third-rate military power in Southeast Asia.

This commitment to nonviolence corresponded with the particular psychology of its white members, most of whom are children of fairly prosperous, educated, decent and idealistic middle-class parents. If we study the childhood experiences of such students, we find that physical violence was almost completely absent. Death was eliminated from the public landscape, isolated in distant hospitals and antiseptic funeral homes. If we ask most college students how often they were involved in major physical fights, the answer is generally once or twice, if ever. Parents rarely expressed anger physically: verbal attacks took the place of physical assault.

In other words, we have taught our children to express their rage in indirect and verbal ways. Middle-class Americans take out their anger on themselves by becoming depressed, or they express it verbally with cutting remarks or in the form of obscenity. But hitting and hurting other people has been almost taboo.

This upbringing has made it easy for members of the student movement to see rage and destructiveness as existing only "out there"—only in their adversaries, only in American racism, only in American foreign policy. An obscenity shouted at a policeman did not seem violent, but the policeman's billy club in response is seen as a shocking aggression.

Now, however, the student's denial of their own rage and destructiveness has been undercut. Two events in particular —the murder of an innocent onlooker at the rock festival at Altamont, and the killing of an innocent student in the terrorist bombing of the mathematics building at the University of Wisconsin—have had great symbolic importance. They proved that *within* the youth movement there were emerging groups who were prepared to use violence in a systematic way to attain their ends. And this forced members of the student movement to reexamine their self-justifying assumption that rage and destructiveness only belonged to their adversaries.

Suddenly the inner significance of earlier events became clearer. Recall, for example, the position adopted by the Weathermen in their "days of rage" in Chicago, when they marched virtually unarmed against a much larger force of armed police. Recall, too, the explosion in the townhouse in Greenwich Village which ended by killing three Weathermen who were making bombs. Or recall the speed with which a number of the peace-loving flower children became embroiled in the sordid exploitativeness of the hard drug culture.

At the time, these events could be written off as exceptions which demonstrated that the student movement, like any social movement, had its share of "crazies." But in retrospect the ugly truth has emerged: that the counterculture had become infected by the very violence it opposed. The obscenity shouted at a policeman was all along a form of violence. So, too, was the classifying of opponents as subhuman—as pigs. And the argument that the youth movement's distaste for violence was only a "bourgeois hang-up" that had to be overcome by terrorism was no less a symptom of America's pathological violence than the police riots at Chicago in 1968.

So the murders at Altamont and Madison symbolized the end of an era. When the violent rhetoric that pervaded the student movement culminated in murder, the members of that movement had to face their own complicity. They realized that if they allowed themselves to be led by their most rigid and destructive factions, dogmatism and death lay at the end of the road.

An Analogy From Psychology

I am a psychologist, and I see an analogy between the agony of the counterculture and the agony of the psychiatric patient. In the course of any prolonged psychotherapy, the patient eventually comes to the point where he must confront his own complicity in his misery, his own involvement in the motives which he criticizes in others.

One task of any therapist is to help promote this agony, to enable his patients to perceive their own dark side. And if the process is successful, the result is a stage of inner agony, often a period of withdrawal, gloom and depression; the evils that were seen as largely outside of the patient are now acknowledged as existing inside him as well.

But an agony is also a struggle, a crisis and a potential turning point. In psychotherapy the recognition of one's own dark motives can lead to either of two outcomes. One can lead to the abandonment of treatment, to flight, to escape and to regression. The patient who is unable to look at himself in a clear mirror flees from his truthful image in order to preserve his illusions and, with them, his neurosis.

But there is also a more hopeful outcome, which takes courage and psychological strength. It involves accepting the awareness of one's own destructiveness and covetousness. As the acknowledgment of inner evil is extended, and only then, a more creative and integrative process may begin. The patient comes to acknowledge that he shares in the complicity of others and to realize that he is his fellows' brother. It becomes progressively harder for him to divide mankind neatly into good and evil, for he recognizes that both coexist. And he becomes more effective, for he is less prone to an unconscious complicity with the forces he seeks to overcome. From this agony of self-confrontation, then, can come a more mature and integrated person.

A social movement is very different from an individual patient. Yet the analogy between the agony of the counter-culture and the agony of the patient suggests two outcomes. One possibility is a dark one, yet it is not altogether unlikely; in fact, it could well mark the counterculture's imminent death. The youth movement which gave so much to America in the 1960s—which exposed the persistent wrongs of American society, which began to define new life-styles and values and institutions for the rest of us—could continue to splinter, go underground, be suppressed and eventually disappear. Members of the movement would become profoundly alienated from society and convinced of their inability to change it. Or, unable to confront the potential for evil that lies within the student movement, they might continue the disastrous externalization that leads to dogmatism, to the denial of the humanity of one's adversaries, or to a withdrawal into private pleasures. Human idealism is immensely fragile: it can easily be corroded into the destructive cynicism of the ex-idealist. This would be the worst thing that could befall our country. We would lose the idealism of the young, morality would become soured, and those who were once hopeful would be overwhelmed by a sense of impotence.

The second scenario is a more hopeful one, and it is also within the realm of possibility. Just as the individual patient may confront his own dark side and thereby gain in compassion and maturity, so the recognition of violence within the student movement could ultimately strengthen and renew it. The result could be a generation more inoculated against secret self-righteousness, dogmatism and collusion with violence, a counterculture that could recognize the huge difficulties in resolving the problem without losing its determination to resolve them.

Toward a Movement of Affirmation

It is clearly not appropriate for a middle-aged psychologist to tell students how they should conduct their lives. Yet I would be derelict if I did not at least share my own convictions and hopes. Your culture has been so far too much of a *counter*culture, too much an outcry against our culture's failure to fulfill its promises. It is time for the student movement to become a national movement of affirmation. To transform this movement will require not merely the enthusiasm of Consciousness III, but the professionalism of Consciousness II [see Editor's Introduction, Section I, above—Ed.]. It will require not only the celebration of life and the expansion of consciousness, but the respect for hard work, persistence and the dedication that characterized the old culture. It will require an alliance not merely of the young, the privileged and educated, but of those who are not young, or privileged, or educated.

We are in a period of national crisis because our society is out of control. The technology that we created to serve us has come to dominate us and now threatens to destroy us. The institutions that we founded to express the popular will have come to manipulate public opinion and exploit public anxieties. Nobody has a prescription for reversing these trends.

But to do so will not be the work of one apocalyptic moment, one revolutionary spasm, one outcry of opposition and despair. It will be the work of a lifetime, of a generation of men and women dedicated to making the best visions and ideals of the youth culture real throughout society—who are willing to continue in that struggle long after they themselves cease to be students.

WHITHER THE TWO CULTURES? [5]

In the new there is always an admixture of the old, and this is true of the protean counterculture now burgeoning in the United States. This makes it very difficult ... to tell what is a true counterculture and what is simply a recruiting outpost for the old culture. But the mere fact that the old culture tries to gobble up something new does not invalidate the potential revolutionary impact of this novelty. At some point a devourer always overreaches himself, like the witch or giant in folk tales who tries to drink up the sea and bursts, or like the vacuum monster in *Yellow Submarine* who ultimately devours himself and disappears. This seems to me the most probable future for the old culture in America.

When I talk of two separate cultures in America I do not mean rich and poor, or black and white (or science and humanism), but rather the opposition between the old scarcity-oriented technological culture that still predominates and the somewhat amorphous counterculture that is growing up to challenge it. At times this distinction may seem synonymous with old-versus-young, or radical-versus-conservative, but the overlap is only approximate. There are many young people who are dedicated to the old culture and a few old people attracted to the new; while as to politics, nothing could be more old-culture than a traditional Marxist.

I speak of two cultures, first because each is in fact a total system with an internal logic and consistency: each is built upon a set of assumptions which hangs together and is viable

[5] From *The Pursuit of Loneliness: American Culture at the Breaking Point*, by Philip E. Slater, former chairman of the department of sociology, Brandeis University. Beacon Press. '70. p 96-7, 100, 126-30, 132-3, 147-50. Copyright © 1970 by Philip E. Slater. Reprinted by permission of Beacon Press.

under some conditions. Second, I wish to emphasize a fact which has escaped the liberal-centrist group that plays so dominant a role in America: that they are no longer being wooed so fervently by those to the left and right of them. The seduction of the center is a phenomenon that occurs only in societies fundamentally united. This has in the past been true of the United States and most parliamentary democracies, but it is true no longer.

I speak of two cultures because we no longer have one. Mixing the two that exist does not add up to the American way of life. They cannot be mixed. From two opposing systems—each tightly defined—can only come a collision and a confusion. No meaningful compromise can be found if the culture as a whole is not articulated in a coherent way. American centrists—liberal university presidents are the best example—are still operating under the illusion that all Americans are playing by the same rules, an assumption which puts the centrists into the advantageous position of mediators. But this is not the case. Indeed, the moderates are increasingly despised by both radicals and conservatives as hypocritical, amoral, and opportunistic people who will take no stand and are only interested in their own careers. . . .

Differences of the Two Cultures

There are an almost infinite number of polarities by means of which one can differentiate between the two cultures. The old culture, when forced to choose, tends to give preference to property rights over personal rights, technological requirements over human needs, competition over cooperation, violence over sexuality, concentration over distribution, the producer over the consumer, means over ends, secrecy over openness, social forms over personal expression, striving over gratification, Oedipal love over communal love, and so on. The new counterculture tends to reverse all of these priorities.

Now it is important to recognize that these differences cannot be resolved by some sort of compromise or "golden mean" position. Every cultural system is a dynamic whole, resting on processes that must be accelerated to be self-sustaining. Change must therefore affect the motivational roots of a society or it is not change at all....

We need now to consider seriously what the role of those over thirty is to be during the transition to and emergence of the new culture. Many will of course simply oppose it, with varying degrees of violence. A few will greet it with a sense of liberation, finding in it an answer they have long sought, but will experience a sense of awkwardness in trying to relate themselves to what has been so noisily appropriated by the young. Many more will be tormented with ambivalence, repelled by the new culture but disillusioned by the old.

It is to this latter group that what follows is addressed, for I do not believe that a successful transition can be made without their participation. If the issue is left to generational confrontation, with new-culture adherents attempting simply to push their elders out of the way and into the grave, the results will probably be catastrophic. The old culture will not simply fall of its own weight. It is not rotten but wildly malfunctioning, not weak and failing but strong and demented, not a sick old horse but a healthy runaway. It no longer performs its fundamental task of satisfying the needs of its adherents, but it still performs the task of feeding and perpetuating itself. Nor do the young have the knowledge and skill successfully to dismantle it. If the matter is left to the collision of generational change it seems to me inevitable that a radical-right revolution will occur as a last-ditch effort to stave off change.

Only those who have participated fully in the old culture can prevent this. Only they can dismantle the old culture without calamity. Furthermore, no revolution produces total change—much of the old machinery is retained more or less intact. Those intimate with the machinery are in the best position to facilitate the retooling and redirection.

But why should they? Why should they tear down what they have built? What place is there for them in the new culture?

The new culture is contemptuous of age and rejects most of the values by which moderates have ordered their lives. Yet it must be remembered that the contempt for age and tradition, the worship of modernity, is not intrinsically a new-culture trait but a foundation stone of a technology-dominated culture. It is the old culture that systematically invalidates learning and experience, that worships innovation and turns its back on the past, on familial and community ties. The new culture is preoccupied with tradition, with community, with relationships—with many things that would reinstate the validity of accumulated wisdom.

Social change is replete with paradox, and one of the most striking is the fact that the old culture worships novelty, while the new would resuscitate a more tradition-oriented way of life. The rhetoric of short-run goals, in which the young shout down the present and shout up the future, masks the fact that in the long run there is more room for the aged in the new culture than in the old. This is something about which new-culture adherents, however, are also confused, and old-culture participants will have much to do to stake out a rightful place for age in the new culture. If they fail the new culture will be corrupted into a reactionary parody of itself.

My main argument for rejecting the old culture is that it has been unable to keep any of the promises that have sustained it for so long, and as it struggles more and more violently to maintain itself, it is less and less able to hide its fundamental antipathy to human life and human satisfaction. It spends hundreds of billions of dollars to find ways of killing more efficiently but almost nothing to enhance the joys of living. Against those who sought to humanize their physical environment in Berkeley the forces of "law and order" used a poison gas outlawed by the Geneva Conventions. The old culture is unable to stop killing people—deliberately in the case of those who oppose it, with bureaucratic indifference in the case of those who obey its dictates or consume its products trustingly. However familiar and comfortable it may seem, the old culture is threatening to kill us, like a trusted relative gone berserk so gradually that we are able to pretend to ourselves he has not changed.

But what can we cling to—what stability is there in our chaotic environment if we abandon the premises on which the old culture is based? To this I would answer that it is precisely these premises that have generated our chaotic environment. I recognize the desperate longing in America for stability, for some fixed reference point when all else is swirling about in endless flux. But to cling to old-culture premises is the act of a hopeless addict, who, when his increasingly expensive habit has destroyed everything else in his life, embraces his destroyer more fervently than ever. The radical change I am suggesting here is only the reinstatement of stability itself. It may appear highly unappealing, like all cold-turkey cures, but nothing else will stop the spiraling disruption to which our old-culture premises have brought us.

New Priorities Needed

I am arguing, in other words, for a reversal of our old pattern of technological radicalism and social conservatism. Like most old-culture premises this is built upon a self-deception: we pretend that through it we actually achieve social stability—that technological change can be confined within its own sphere. Yet obviously this is not so. Technological instability creates social instability as well, and we lose both ways. Radical social change *has* occurred within the old culture, but unplanned and unheralded. The changes advocated by the new culture are changes that at least some people desire. The changes that have occurred under the old culture were desired by no one. They were not even foreseen. They just happened, and people tried to build a social structure around them; but it has always been a little like building sand castles in heavy surf and we have become a dangerously irritable people in the attempt. We have given technology carte blanche, much in the way Congress has always, in the past, given automatic approval to defense budgets, resulting in the most gigantic graft in history.

How long is it since anyone has said: "This is a pernicious invention, which will bring more misery than happiness to mankind?" Such comments occur only in horror and science-fiction films, and even there, in the face of the most calamitous outcomes that jaded and overtaxed brains can devise, the audience often feels a twinge of discomfort over the burning laboratory or the lost secret. Yet who would dare to defend even a small fraction of the technological innovations of the past century in terms of human satisfaction? The problem is that technology, industrialism, and capitalism have always been evaluated in their own terms. But it is absurd to evaluate capitalism in terms of the wealth it produces, or technology in terms of the inventions it generates, just as it would be absurd for a subway system to evaluate its service in terms of the number of tokens it manufactured.

We need to find ways of appraising these systems in terms of criteria that are truly independent of the systems themselves. We need to develop a human-value index—a criterion that assesses the ultimate worth of an invention or a system or a product in terms of its total impact on human life, in terms of ends rather than means. We would then evaluate the achievements of medicine not in terms of man-hours of prolonged (and often comatose) life, or the volume of drugs sold, but in terms of the overall increase (or decrease) in human beings feeling healthy. We would evaluate city planning and housing programs not in terms of the number of bodies incarcerated in a given location, or the number of millions given to contractors, but in terms of the extent to which people take joy in their surroundings. We would evaluate the worth of an industrial firm not in terms of the money made or the number of widgets manufactured or sold, or how distended the organization has become, but in terms of how much pleasure or satisfaction has been given to people. It is not without significance that we tend to appraise a nation today in terms of its gross national product—a phrase whose connotations speak for themselves.

The problem is particularly acute in the case of technology. Freud suggested forty years ago that the much-touted benefits of technology were "cheap pleasures," equivalent to the enjoyment obtained by "sticking one's bare leg outside the bedclothes on a cold winter's night and then drawing it in again." "If there were no railway to make light of distances," he pointed out, "my child would never have left home and I should not need the telephone to hear his voice." Each technological "advance" is heralded as one that will solve problems created by its predecessors. None of them have done so, however, but have merely created new ones. Heroin was first introduced into this country as a heaven-sent cure for morphine addicts, and this is the model followed by technological "progress." We have been continually misled into supporting a larger and larger technological habit. . . .

The old-culture American needs to reconsider his commitment to technological "progress." If he fails to kick the habit he may retain his culture and lose his life. One often hears old-culture adherents saying, "What will you put in its place?" ("If you don't want me to kill you, give me something else to do"). But what does a surgeon put in the place of a malignant tumor? What does a policeman put in the place of a traffic jam? What does the Food and Drug Administration put in the place of the poisoned food it confiscates? What does a society put in the place of war when peace is declared? The question assumes, first, that what exists is safe and tolerable, and second, that social systems are mere inert mechanisms with no life of their own.

The Risks of Radical Change

Some of this resistance comes from the old culture's dependence upon the substitutes and palliatives that its own pathology necessitates. "Without all these props, wires, crutches, and pills," its adherents ask, "how can I function? Without the 'extensions of man' I am not even a person. If you take away my gas mask, how can I breathe this polluted air? How will I get to the hospital without the automobile that has made me unfit to walk?" These questions are serious, since one cannot in fact live comfortably in our society without these props until radical changes have been made—until the diseases that necessitate these palliatives have been cured. Transitions are always fraught with risk and discomfort and insecurity. . . . No matter how difficult it seems to engage in radical change when all is changing anyway, the risk must be taken.

Our servility toward technology, however, is no more dangerous than our exaggerated moral commitment to the "virtues" of striving and individual achievement. The mechanized disaster that surrounds us is in no small part a result of our having deluded ourselves that a motley scramble of people trying to get the better of one another is socially useful instead of something to be avoided at all costs. It has taken us a long time to realize that seeking to surpass others might be pathological, and trying to enjoy and cooperate with others healthy, rather than the other way around.

The need to triumph over each other and the tendency to prostrate ourselves before technology are in fact closely related. We turn continually to technology to save us from having to cooperate with each other. Technology meanwhile, serves to preserve and maintain the competitive pattern and render it ever more frantic, thus making cooperation at once more urgent and more difficult. . . .

I can best summarize my various predictive comments by saying that old-culture moderates or liberals will be given the choice, during the next decade or so, between participating in some way in the new culture and living under a Fascist regime. The middle is dropping out of things and choices must be made. If the old culture is rejected, the new must be ushered in as gracefully as possible. If the old culture is not rejected then its adherents must be prepared to accept a bloodbath such as has not been seen in the United States since the Civil War, for genocidal weapons will be on one side and unarmed masses on the other.

The University: Key to the Future

The best key to the kind of future we can expect is the university—the first victim of the clash between the two cultures. The university is a remarkably vulnerable institution, since it lies directly in the path of the rapidly swelling ranks of the new culture yet bears a poorly concealed parasitic relation to the old. It is thus caught in a vise—it cannot ignore the new culture as the rest of society attempts to do, yet it cannot accommodate to it without losing old-culture support and going bankrupt. No solutions will be found to this dilemma until some of the institutions on which the university depends begin to yield and change, and many universities will go under before this happens. If the universities—notoriously rigid and archaic institutions—can find ways to absorb the new culture this augurs well for the society as a whole. If, on the other hand, the campus becomes a police state, as many are suggesting, it seems likely that the nation as a whole will follow the same path.

The most serious internal danger to the new culture is the insidious transmission of individualism from the old culture, in part through confusion with the new culture's otherwise healthy emphasis on emotional expression. Ambivalence about the issue of individualism-versus-social-commitment is deep and unresolved. On the one hand there is increasing experimentation with communes and communal arrangements, and a serious awareness of the Nuremberg Trials and their proclamation of man's personal responsibility to all men. On the other hand there is great fascination with the concept of anarchy—with the attempt to eliminate coercion and commitment in any form from human life.

But to generalize the need to free oneself from the emotional barrenness and depersonalized control mechanisms of the old culture to freedom from *all* social conditions is simply to return the new culture to the old one. Anarchy is merely a radical extension of the old culture. It is also a way of retaining the pristine American fantasy of being special—a condition which American society promises, and withholds, more than any society in history. The unstated rider to "do your own thing" is that everybody will watch—that a special superiority will be granted and acknowledged by others. But in a satisfying society this specialness is not needed, and for a satisfying society to exist the recognition that people can and must make demands upon one another must also exist. Any community worthy of the name (one in which the relationships between people are regulated by people, instead of by machines) would seem "totalitarian" to today's youth, not in the sense of having an authoritarian leadership structure, but in the sense of permitting group intrusion into what is for most Americans the private sphere.

This will be the most difficult problem new-culture adherents will face, for we are long accustomed to an illusory freedom based on subtle compulsion by technology and bureaucratic mechanisms. But there is no way for large numbers of people to coexist without governing and being governed by each other, unless they establish machines to do it; at which point they risk losing sight and understanding of the interconnectedness itself—a process well advanced in our culture today. . . .

The goal of many early Americans was to find or to create or to participate in a utopian community, but they became distracted by the dream of personal aggrandizement and found themselves farther and farther from this goal. When we think today of the kind of social compliance that exists in such communities (as well as in the primitive communities we romanticize so much) we shrink in horror. We tell each other chilling stories of individuals in imagined societies of the future being forced to give up their dreams for the good of the group, of not being allowed to stand out. But this, in some degree, is just the price we must pay for a tolerable life in a tolerable community. We need to understand this price, to consider it, to reflect on its consequences and the consequences of not paying it. . . .

Past efforts to build utopian communities failed because they were founded on scarcity assumptions. But scarcity is now shown to be an unnecessary condition, and the distractions that it generated can now be avoided. We need not raise the youth of new utopias to feel that life's primary gratifications are in such short supply. Hence the only obstacle to utopia is the persistence of the competitive motivational patterns that past scarcity assumptions have spawned. Nothing stands in our way except our invidious dreams of personal glory. Our horror of group coercion reflects our reluctance to relinquish these dreams, although they have brought us nothing but misery, discontent, hatred, and chaos. If we can overcome this horror, however, and mute this vanity, we may again be able to take up our original utopian task.

BIBLIOGRAPHY

An asterisk (*) preceding a reference indicates that the article or a part of it has been reprinted in this book.

BOOKS, PAMPHLETS, AND DOCUMENTS

Altbach, P. G. and Laufer, R. S. eds. The new pilgrims: youth in transition. McKay. '72.

*American Council on Education. A declaration on campus unrest; a statement formulated by a group of educational administrators, trustees, and foundation officers who met April 4-5, 1969. The Council. 1 Dupont Circle. Washington, D.C. 20036.

American Council on Education. Selected bibliography on institutional governance and campus unrest. The Council. 1 Dupont Circle. Washington, D.C. 20036. '70.

American Council on Education. Special Committee on Campus Tensions. Campus tensions: analysis and recommendations; report. The Council. 1 Dupont Circle. Washington, D.C. 20036. '70.

Aya, Roderick and Miller, Norman, eds. The new American revolution; with an epilogue by Christopher Lasch. Free Press. '71.

Babcox, Peter and others, eds. The conspiracy, [by] Abbie Hoffman and others. Dell. '69.

Becker, H. S. ed. Campus power struggle. Aldine. '70.

Blassingame, J. W. ed. New perspectives on black studies. University of Illinois Press. '71.

Brenner, J. H. and others. Drugs and youth: medical, psychiatric, and legal facts. Liveright. '70.

Brustein, Robert. Revolution as theatre; notes on the new radical style. Liveright. '71.

Brzezinski, Z. K. Between two ages: America's role in the technetronic era. Viking. '70.

Burkhart, J. A. and Kendrick, F. J. eds. The new politics: mood or movement? Prentice-Hall. '71.

Carmichael, S. S. and Hamilton, C. V. Black power: the politics of liberation in America. Random House. '68.

Commager, H. S. The commonwealth of learning. Harper. '68.

Conant, R. W. The prospects for revolution: a study of riots, civil disobedience and insurrection in contemporary America. Harper's Magazine Press. '71.

Cranston, M. W. ed. The New Left. Lib. Press. '71. [for sale by World Pub.]

Crick, Bernard and Robson, W. A. eds. Protest & discontent. Penguin Books. '70.

Dellinger, Dave. Revolutionary nonviolence; essays. Anchor. '71.

Douglas, W. O. Points of rebellion. Random House. '70.

Feuer, L. S. The conflict of generations: the character and significance of student movements. Heinemann. '69.

Foley, J. A. and Foley, R. K. The college scene: students tell it like it is. McGraw. '71.

Friedenberg, E. Z. ed. The anti-American generation. Aldine-Atherton. '71.

Gagnon, J. H. and Simon, William, eds. The sexual scene. Aldine. '70.

Glazer, Nathan. Remembering the answers: essays on the American student revolt. Basic Books. '70.

Goodman, Mitchell, ed. The movement toward a new America: the beginnings of a long revolution. Knopf. '70.

Goodman, Paul. Growing up absurd: problems of youth in the organized system. Random House. '60.

Goodman, Paul. New reformation; notes of a neolithic conservative. Vintage. '71.

Grinspoon, Lester. Marihuana reconsidered. Harvard University Press. '71.

Gross, Beatrice and Gross, Ronald, eds. Radical school reform. Simon & Schuster. '70.

Handlin, Oscar and Handlin, M. F. Facing life: youth and the family in American history. Little. '71.
    Review. New York Times Book Review. p 4+. Ap. 2, '72. Martin Duberman.

Hoffman, Abbie. Woodstock nation; a talk-rock album. Random House. '69.

*Hook, Sidney. Academic freedom and academic anarchy. Cowles. '70.

Houriet, Robert. Getting back together. Coward, McCann & Geoghegan. '71.

Howe, Irving, ed. Beyond the New Left. McCall. '70.

Hutchins, R. M. The learning society. Praeger. '68.

Illich, Ivan. De-schooling society. Harper. '71.

Kaplan, Abraham, ed. Individuality and the new society. (The sanctity of life, v2) University of Washington Press. '70.

Katz, Joseph and others. No time for youth: growth & constraint in college students. Jossey-Bass. '68.

Keniston, Kenneth. The uncommitted: alienated youth in American society. Harcourt. '65.

Keniston, Kenneth. Young radicals; notes on committed youth. Harcourt. '68.

*Keniston, Kenneth. Youth and dissent: the rise of a new opposition. Harcourt. '71.
    Excerpts: Social Policy. 2:6-19. Jl./Ag. '71
    Review. New York Times Book Review. p 4+. Ap. 2, '72. Martin Duberman.

Klein, Alexander, ed. Dissent, power, and confrontation; theatre for ideas/discussions no. 1. McGraw. '71.

Kostelanetz, Richard, ed. Beyond Left & Right: radical thought for our times. Morrow. '68.

Liebert, Robert. Radical and militant youth: a psychoanalytic inquiry. Praeger. '71.

Lipset, S. M. and Schaflander, G. M. Passion and politics: student activism in America. Little. '71.

Lipset, S. M. and Wolin, S. S. eds. The Berkeley student revolt: facts and interpretations. Doubleday. '65.

Lowi, T. J. The politics of disorder. Basic Books. '71.

Marcuse, Herbert. Counterrevolution and revolt. Beacon. '72.

Michael, D. M. ed. The future society. Aldine. '70.

Miles, M. W. The radical probe: the logic of student rebellion. Atheneum. '71.

Moffett, Anthony. The participation put on. Delacorte. '71.

Nichols, D. C. ed. Perspectives on campus tensions. American Council on Education. 1 Dupont Circle. Washington, D.C. 20036. '70.

Nisbet, R. A. The degradation of the academic dogma: the university in America, 1945-1970. (The John Dewey Society. Lecture Ser. no. 12) Basic Books. '71.

Nobile, Philip. The Con III controversy: the critics look at the greening of America. Pocket Books. '71.

O'Neill, W. L. ed. American society since 1945. (N.Y. Times book) Quadrangle. '69.

Orr, J. B. and Nichelson, F. P. The radical suburb: soundings in changing American character. Westminster. '70.

Reich, C. A. The greening of America: how the youth revolution is trying to make America livable. Random House. '70.
    Excerpts. New Yorker. 46:42-6+. S. 26, '70.

*Revel, Jean-François. Without Marx or Jesus: the new American revolution has begun. Doubleday. '71.
    Excerpts. Saturday Review. 54:14-31. Jl. 24, '71.

Rossman, Michael. The wedding within the war. Doubleday. '71.
    Review. The New York Times Book Review. p 4+. Ap. 2, '72. Martin Duberman.

Roszak, Theodore, ed. The dissenting academy. Random House. '68.

Roszak, Theodore. The making of a counter culture: reflections on the technocratic society and its youthful opposition. Doubleday. '69.

Skolnick, J. H. and Currie, Elliott, eds. Crisis in American institutions. Little. '70.

*Slater, P. E. The pursuit of loneliness: American culture at the breaking point. Beacon. '70.

Stickney, John. Streets, actions, alternatives, raps. Putnam. '71.

Taylor, Harold. How to change colleges; notes on radical reform. Holt. '71.
    Review. New Republic. 164:23-4. Ap. 24, '71. What, no pornography course at Yale? Louis Coxe.

United States. President's Commission on Campus Unrest. Campus unrest: the report; William W. Scranton, chairman. Supt. of Docs. Washington, D.C. 20402. '70.
    Excerpts. Chronicle of Higher Education. 5:1-24. O. '70. The Scranton report; text of the findings of the President's Commission on Campus Unrest (1970).

Wheeler, Harvey. The politics of revolution. Glendessary Press. '71.

White House Conference on Youth. Report [of the first conference, Estes Park, Colorado, 1971]. Supt. of Docs. Washington, D.C. 20402.

Wolin, S. S. and Schaar, J. H. Berkeley rebellion & beyond: essays on politics & education in the technological society. Random House. '70.

*Yankelovich, Daniel, Inc. Press release issued December 18, 1970; report on research for John D. Rockefeller 3rd and the Task Force on Youth. Daniel Yankelovich, Inc. 575 Madison Ave. New York 10022. '70.

Yankelovich, Daniel, Inc. Youth and the establishment: a report on research for John D. Rockefeller 3rd and the Task Force on Youth. JDR 3rd Fund, Inc. 3 Rockefeller Plaza. New York 10020. '71.

PERIODICALS

*AFL-CIO American Federationist. 78:12-17. N. '71. The youth vote: how many, which way? M. G. Zon.

Annals of the American Academy of Political and Social Science. 382:83-94. Mr. '69. The student revolt against liberalism. Jonathan Eisen and David Steinberg.

Annals of the American Academy of Political and Social Science. 395:1-194. My. '71. Students protest. P. G. Altbach and R. S. Laufer, eds.

*Atlantic. 223:37-41. Je. '69. Black studies: trouble ahead. E. D. Genovese.

Change. 1:10-47. S.-O. '69. The American academy 1970. Judson Jerome.

Change. 3:44-6. My.-Je. '71. Notes on the new youth. David Bazelon.

*Christian Science Monitor. p 9. Ja. 14, '70. The voluntary university; excerpts from address at Michigan State University. Kingman Brewster, Jr.

Christian Science Monitor. p 1+. Ja. 20, '72. Fresh religious interest on campus. K. D. Nordin.

*Christian Science Monitor. p 1+. F. 11, '72. U.S. youth refocuses activism. Guy Halverson.

*Chronicle of Higher Education. 3:8. Mr. 13, '72. Who are/were those kids and why do/did they do those awful/wonderful things? M. G. Scully.

Commentary. 47:33-41. Je. '69. Reflections on youth movements. Walter Laqueur.

Commentary. 50:25-9. Ag. '70. The non-generation gap. S. M. Lipset and Earl Raab.

*Commonweal. 94:188-90. Ap. 30, '71. Winds from the East. Jacob Needleman.

Commonweal. 95:519-23. Mr. 3, '72. A state of quiet calamity. D. L. Warren.

Daedalus. 97:1-317. Winter '68. Students and politics.

Daedalus. 99:1-221. Winter '70. The embattled university.

Daedalus. 99:531-712. Summer '70. Rights and responsibilities: the university's dilemma.

Educational Record. 52:301-13. Fall. '71. Campus unrest, 1970-71: was it really all that quiet? A. E. Bayer and A. W. Astin.

*Harper's Magazine. 243:35-9. Jl. '71. The surprising seventies. P. F. Drucker.

Harper's Magazine. 243:40-2+. Jl. '71. The rush for instant salvation. Sara Davidson.

Harper's Magazine. 244:62-4. Mr. '72. The imponderable young. R. S. Beecher.

Horizon. 13:104-5. Autumn '71. The impossibility of dropping out. Anthony Hartley.

*Life. 71:55. O. 8, '71. The new tensions on campus. W. J. McGill.

Modern Age. 15:259-67. Summer '71. Youth unrest and our cultural crisis. E. M. Adams.

Nation. 208:755-8. Je. 16, '69. Black studies: the real issue. John Hatch.

*Nation. 211:460-3. N. 9, '70. Communes and the work crisis. L. M. Andrews.

*Nation. 212:490-1. Ap. 19, '71. Today's campus: the eerie calm. G. M. Sykes.

Nation. 212:524-7. Ap. 26, '71. Wear and tear in the communes. Albert Solnit.

National Observer. p 24. Ja. 11, '71. Even the Romans had the hippies. Nathan Adler.

National Observer. p 1+. F. 26, '72. "American pie." D. S. Greene.

National Review. 23:635-50. Je. 15, '71. Opinion on the campus. P. P. Ardery.

*New Generation. 54:10-13. Fall '70. The protest of young factory workers. H. J. Gans.

New Republic. 163:15-17. S. 26, '70. An honest, intelligible radical politics. Robert Brustein.

*New Republic. 164:20-3. Ap. 3, '71. The blueing of America. P. L. Berger and Brigitte Berger.

*New Republic. 166:10-11. F. 19, '72. Student activists. Ralph Nader.

New York Review of Books. 12:6+. Ja. 30, '69. Revolution in America? Barrington Moore, Jr.

*New York Review of Books. 14:3-10. My. 7, '70. Where we are now. J. H. Schaar and S. S. Wolin.

New York Times. p 12. N. 6, '70. Charles Reich—a negative view. Herbert Marcuse.

New York Times. p 1+. Mr. 1, '71. The Panthers: dead or regrouping. Earl Caldwell.

New York Times. p 29. Je. 17, '71. Poll finds drugs No. 3 issue in U.S.

New York Times. p 45. S. 4, '71. Federal study says TV can make youths more violent. Boyce Rensberger.

New York Times. p 39. O. 22, '71. As students age. . . . S. M. Lipset and E. C. Ladd, Jr.

*New York Times. p 1+. O. 24, '71. Youth rebellion of sixties waning. D. E. Kneeland.

New York Times. p 1+. D. 20, '71. Nation's collegians turning to courses keyed to job goals. Robert Reinhold.

New York Times. p 1+. D. 26, '71. The Jesus movement spreading on campus. D. E. Kneeland.

*New York Times Magazine. p 32-3+. S. 14, '69. The new reformation. Paul Goodman.

New York Times Magazine. p 36-7+. N. 7, '71. Status of the movement: the energy levels are low. Joseph Lelyveld.

New York Times Magazine. p 9+. Ja. 16, '72; 22. F. 6, '72. What code of values can we teach our children now? W. V. Shannon.

New York Times Magazine. p 14-17+. Ja. 30, '72. Metamorphosis of the campus radical. John Leggett.

*Newsday. p 7W-9W+. Je. 1, '68. Why student rebellion? H. S. Commager.

Newsweek. 78:28-30+. O. 25, '71. How will youth vote?

Public Interest. No. 25:99-113. Fall '71. College generations—from the 1930's to the 1960's. S. M. Lipset and E. C. Ladd, Jr.

Saturday Review. 48:64-6+. D. 18, '65. Causes of the student revolution. Joseph Katz and Nevitt Sanford.

*Saturday Review. 54:16-21. Ap. 24, '71. Communes: the alternative life-style. H. A. Otto.

Saturday Review. 55:32-7. Ap. 1, '72. The new naturalism. Daniel Yankelovich.

Science. 173:1006-8. S. 10, '71. The Berkeley scene, 1971: patching up the ivory tower. R. J. Bazell.

Sexual Behavior. 2:4-10. Ja '72. The generation gap in sexual beliefs. R. H. Walsh.

Social Policy. 2:58-61. S./O. '71. Crack in the hardhat: the children of the working class. Leonard Quart.

Social Problems. 17:340-57. Winter '70. Social and cultural meanings of student revolt: some informal comparative observations. Richard Flacks.

Society. 9:6-8. F. '72. Vista, pepsi and poverty. David Gottlieb.

Society. 9:18-27. F. '72. Post-1984 America. Lee Rainwater.

Society. 9:50-6. F. '72. Mainlining Jesus; the new trip. R. L. Adams and R. J. Fox.

*Studies in Comparative Communism. 1:40-54. Jl./O. '68. Neo-Communism and the students' revolts. Maurice Cranston.

*Teachers College Record. 72:495-504. My. '71. Civil rights of public school students. R. M. Blankenburg.

Time. 97:10-19. F. 22, '71. The cooling of America: symposium.

*Time. 97:56-63. Je. 21, '71. The new rebel cry: Jesus is coming!

Trans-Action. December 1967 issue: Hippies—their past and their future.

U.S. News & World Report. 71:26-31. Ag. 9, '71. End of the youth revolt?

U.S. News & World Report. 71:40-3. O. 25, '71. Turn from campus violence, the reasons.

University. No. 51:1-4+. Winter '72. The youth revolution is over: how it changed us. Willard Dalrymple.

*University Bookman. 12:3-13. Autumn '71. Right on—up with higher education! D. M. Dozer.

Wall Street Journal. p 1+. Ap. 7, '71. The new educators: radical professors exert growing power on college campuses. William Wong.

Wall Street Journal. p 1+. Ap. 27, '71. Riches in rags: companies find profits in the "antimaterialism" of the youth culture; factory-frayed blue jeans, invisible makeup products preserve a "natural" look. Barry Newman.

*Wall Street Journal. p 10. Je. 28, '71. Some popular myths on youth. Landrum Bolling.

Washington Post. p B 1+. Jl. 4, '71. The revolution in American values. Haynes Johnson.

Washington Post. p B 1+. F. 13, '72. The transformation of the Panthers. R. K. Baker.

Win. 7:16. D. 1, '71. Statement, New American Movement.

Worldview. 14:13-15. S. '71. What student revolution? R. J. Stupak.

*Yale Alumni Magazine. 35:10-13. O. '71. The agony of the counter-culture. Kenneth Keniston.

Yale Review. 61:69-75. O. '71. The death of the American ethic. O. S. Kramer.